China: the race to market

FT Prentice Hall
FINANCIAL TIMES

In an increasingly competitive world, we believe it's quality of thinking that will give you the edge – an idea that opens new doors, a technique that solves a problem, or an insight that simply makes sense of it all. The more you know, the smarter and faster you can go.

That's why we work with the best minds in business and finance to bring cutting-edge thinking and best learning practice to a global market.

Under a range of leading imprints, including *Financial Times Prentice Hall*, we create world-class print publications and electronic products bringing our readers knowledge, skills and understanding which can be applied whether studying or at work.

To find out more about our publications, or tell us about the books you'd like to find, you can visit us at
www.pearsoned.co.uk

PEARSON
Education

China:
the race to market

What China's transformation means for business,
markets and the new world order

Jonathan Story

FT Prentice Hall
FINANCIAL TIMES

An imprint of **Pearson Education**

London • New York • Toronto • Sydney • Tokyo • Singapore
Hong Kong • Cape Town • Madrid • Paris • Amsterdam • Munich • Milan

PEARSON EDUCATION LIMITED

Head Office:
Edinburgh Gate
Harlow CM20 2JE
Tel: +44 (0)1279 623623
Fax: +44 (0)1279 431059

Website: www.pearsoned.co.uk

First published in Great Britain in 2003

ISBN: 0 273 66321 6

British Library Cataloguing in Publication Data
A CIP catalogue record for this book can be obtained from the British Library

This publication is designed to provide accurate and authoritative information in regard to the
subject matter covered. It is sold with the understanding that neither the author nor the
publisher is engaged in rendering legal, investing, or any other professional service. If legal
advice or other expert assistance is required, the service of a competent professional person
should be sought.

The publisher and contributors make no representation, express or implied, with regard to the
accuracy of the information contained in this book and cannot accept any responsibility or
liability for any errors or omissions that it may contain.

10 9 8 7 6 5 4 3

Designed by Sue Lamble
Typeset by Pantek Arts Ltd, Maidstone, Kent.
Printed and bound in Great Britain by Biddles Ltd, *www.biddles.co.uk*

The Publishers' policy is to use paper manufactured from sustainable forests.

Contents

Politicians and political scientists have little understanding of business and business executives and business school professors have little understanding of international politics. This in part accounts for the current mess and the heightening risk of a systemic breakdown. As Jonathan Story powerfully put forward in *The Frontiers of Fortune* politics, markets and business are closely interconnected, even if often in surprising and unexpected ways. The connections and the unexpected apply with great emphasis to China. In this new book, Story undertakes a masterful analysis of Chinese dynamics and from there, an appeal for a holistic business strategy encompassing both the market numbers and the socio-politcal intangible forces. Story must be listened to.

Jean-Pierre Lehmann. D. Phil,
Professor of International Political Economy, IMD
Founding Director, the Evian Group

Story's approach to contemporary China makes a lot of sense for those of us who live it from within. His advice on business strategy is based on an historical analysis of the broader forces shaping China's future. An invaluable insight for Western business people, as well as for a general audience. Unlike many Western authors writing on contemporary China, Story's book makes a lot of sense to the learned people inside China.

Professor Lu Feng
Tsinghua University

About the author

Jonathan Story is Shell Fellow in Economic Transformation, and Professor of International Political Economy at INSEAD. Over the past years, he has served as a consultant to governments, international corporations, banks and service companies on European and world politics and markets. Before joining INSEAD, he worked in Brussels and Washington, where he obtained his PhD from the Johns Hopkins School of Advanced International Studies (SAIS). He has written widely in professional reviews, and his previous book, *The Frontiers of Fortune*, was published in 1999 with Financial Times/Prentice Hall. He also co-authored with Ingo Walter of New York University *The Political Economy of Financial Integration in Europe: the battle of the systems*, published in 1998 by Manchester University Press in Europe and by MIT Press in the USA. He writes regular analyses for the international press on international political and economic developments.

List of tables

List of figures

Abbreviations

ACFTU	All China Federation of Trade Unions
ADB	Asian Development Bank
AFTA	Asian Free Trade Area
AMC	Asset management Corporation
AMCHAM	American Chamber of Commerce
AMF	Asian Monetary Fund
APEC	Asia-Pacific Economic Cooperation
ASEAN	Association of South East Asian Nations
CCP	Chinese Communist Party
CEIBS	China European Business School
CITIC	China International Trust & Investment corporation
CNPC	China National Petroleum Corporation
CSRC	China Securities and Regulatory Commission
DPP	Democratic Progressive Party
EU	European Union
EVSL	Early voluntary sectoral liberalization
FDI	Foreign direct investment
FFE	Foreign-funded Enterprises
GATT	General Agreement on Tariffs and Trade
GDP	Gross domestic product
GITIC	Guandong International Trust & Investment Corporation
GNP	Gross national product
HDI	Human Development Index
IMF	International Monetary Fund
INSEAD	European Institute of Business Administration
MEI	Ministry of Electronics and Informatics

MFN	Most favored nation
MPT	Ministry of Post and Telecommunications
NATO	North Atlantic Treaty Organization
NMD	National missile defense
NYSE	New York Stock Exchange
NPC	National People's Congress
PAP	People's Action Party
PBoC	People's Bank of China
PLA	People's Liberation Army
PNTR	Permanent normal trading relations
PPP	Purchasing power parity
PRC	People's Republic of China
SEC	Securities and Exchange Commission
SEZ	Special Economic Zone
SME	Socialist market economy
SOE	State-owned enterprise
SPC	State planning commission
TMD	Theater missile defense
TVE	Town and village enterprise
UN	United Nations
WTO	World Trade Organization

Preface

How can we make corporate strategy for a country as complex and multi-faceted as China? many businesspeople ask. An answer to this question requires us to look at a much broader canvas than we conventionally do when we consider business strategy. Conventional business strategy divides conveniently into three parts, like Caesar's description of Gaul: what's going on inside the corporation, what's happening in terms of competition in the firm's markets, and by deduction what both inquiries hold for the firm's future.

Why is this conventional approach inadequate in the case of China? Indeed, we may ask why such an approach is inadequate – to say the least – anywhere in the world. We can provide an initial answer by asking the question of business that the Prussian theoretician, Clausewitz, asked of war: what, asked the student of Napoleonic war, is the essence of war? "Frictions" was his answer – all the unexpected events that make the experience of battle one of chaos unleashed. So what is the essence of business? My reply is that the essence of business activities, very different to warfare, is to have to deal with a future about which we know little, because that is where risk and reward lie. I have spelt out some of the implications for this in the companion volume of this book, *The Frontiers of Fortune* (Pitman, 1999). Briefly, corporate strategy as conventionally delimited is much too narrow a focus. To be sure, the future of the firm is going to be shaped by firm-level decisions and circumstances, but it will also be shaped and penetrated by developments in the broader congeries of markets into which its own activities are tied, and by the all-pervasiveness of politics. As I have argued in *The Frontiers of Fortune*, business, markets and politics dance forever together. It follows that the activity of corporate strategy in the world as it is must make the world the stuff out of which policy is made. To make my point clearer, this book's subject is about China's transformation: that is the stuff of corporate strategy with regard to China.

Businesspeople ask of China the following questions: (1) What direction is China's development taking? (2) Will China emerge as a world power, and if so when? (3) What do we need to know in order to do business with/invest in China?

This book is my answer. China has an opportunity to become a great power on the cheap, not by war but through peaceful development at home, and the pursuit of a foreign policy inspired by an ambition to exercise a moderating influence on world affairs. Over time, as China realizes its potential, the structure of world politics is transformed. What happens during this evolution is told differently according to whether you believe the realist story about the way the world works, or whether you are more optimistic, and believe in the beneficial workings of international trade and exchange. The realist story suggests that the USA prevents China's emergence in the future as a challenger to the position of world leader. The more optimistic story about how the world works suggests that China will be folded into the World Trade Organization (WTO) and helped towards democratization. Prosperous democracies, the contention is, do not go to war against each other.

What happens in the future depends very much on what choices the Chinese leadership makes between alternative prescriptions for policy. Which prescriptions are selected depends on the preferences of those who decide what is significant and what is not. This is difficult enough in a business, where information is always partial, interpretation thereof is always individual and implementation always controversial. It is all the more so for a country the size, age and complexity of China. The only guide we have to what prescriptions are likely to be selected in the future is to develop an understanding of those that have been chosen in recent decades, why they were preferred, what alternatives were discarded, and how policies have evolved.

Inserting discretion into China's story may seem obvious. After all, it was Mao Zedong who decided to launch the country on the Cultural Revolution, and Deng Xiaoping, his diminutive lieutenant and successor, who decided to substitute economic development for class war. But it is rather less obvious for a Communist Party like China's. Here is a party that came to power with the conviction that it knew which side of history it was on, claimed therefore to have a special insight into the drift of human affairs, and went about destroying what it conceived of as "capitalist" society. It then set about building socialism, and lost its way. In the process, tens of millions of people lost their lives, and the lives of countless others were ruined or reduced to misery.

My contention is that the Chinese Communist Party – one that can lay claim with some justification to be among the most radical of all – has become a sinicized version of the British Tory Party. This is meant as a compliment. The Tories are the oldest political party in the world and have a stock of experience on which to draw. Their origins are in the Celtic fringes of the British islands, where they learnt well the arts of survival.

The traditional Tory approach to human affairs is a deep skepticism: ameliorism, the doctrine that we all bring our pebble and add it to the beach of progress, is laughed out of court as the happy assumption of enlightened brothers and sisters who believe in improvement and progress. It is, of course, true that human knowledge accumulates in the physical sciences. There are bad and better methods of governance. But there is strictly no change whatsoever in the moral domain. To consider with Rousseau that all that people have to lose is their chains for their innate goodness to emerge is a tragic delusion.

It is one that the Chinese people, and with it the Chinese Communists, have paid very dearly to learn. But it is my contention that they have learnt their lesson well. Not for them the heady conviction that their doctrine provides them with a guide to action. Not for them the certainty that they are Marxist, and therefore right. At most, the Chinese Communists know that they have a lease on power in China from the Chinese people, and that it is they who will ultimately decide what to do about who wields authority there. So they keep the future at bay by determined tinkering with inherited problems.

Just as I was concluding the final chapters to this book, this point was brought home to me with force. The French presidential elections of 2002 were in full swing. It was the run-up to the first round, and we were treated to an extraordinary spectacle on television of various brands of socialism.

There was champagne socialism, bubbling away at how well the Jospin government had reconciled justice and efficiency. There was republican socialism, which gave the thumbs down to Brussels and all its works. There was watered-down French Communism on display, a couple of Trotskyites who proposed nationalizing everything that moved, in addition to a clutch of socially concerned écolos. *Bref*, it was entertainment of a kind.

Zheng Ruolin (2002), correspondent of the Shanghai newspaper, *Wenhibao*, could hardly contain his amazement. "When I write for my newspaper in Shanghai", he wrote in the radical-chic newspaper, *Libération*, "that more than 10% of the population of France still votes for the Communist and far left parties, I can hardly believe it myself. And yet it's a reality. For a journalist from one of the last countries which continues to pretend to be Communist, this fact is as surprising as it is moving." He went on to say that he respected the various Communist politicians for seeking to defend the interests of poor people, who would otherwise not be so well defended. At least they believe in what they do and say, which is more than can be said for "certain Communist countries". But he ended up professing to prefer Chirac to the left.

Chirac is elected, and the Chinese Communists are not. They won power over fifty years ago, when over 75% of the present 1.3 billion Chinese were not alive. Chirac won eventually in 2002 with over 80% of the French vote. He'll be in office for five years, during which time he will no doubt experience *l'usure du pouvoir*, a decline in his stock of political capital. Putting the two examples side by side illustrates, perhaps too vividly, the challenge facing the Chinese Communists. That challenge is to answer effectively the question that is being asked of them: by what right do you rule? The answer that I consider them to be making is that they know they have no right that can stand up to examination.

If we wish to understand, and then act on that understanding, of whither China may be heading, we should examine the logic that is informing the actions of the Chinese Communists. We should observe their collective body language. This is saying: be careful; we'll deal with that one when it comes up; nothing is out of the question; we'll consider it.

But the Chinese Communists are Tories in another sense: they are used to power and privilege, and they are clearly reluctant to abandon it. Sharing it, maybe, but not abandoning it. That would mean surrendering the mandate of heaven, which is theirs, they consider, by conquest. It would precipitate China in all probability into civil war and worse. The fear is that foreigners would then carve up China, as they have done in the past. In short, China's Communists are a collective Louis XV, who is said to have stated, "*Aprés moi, le déluge.*"

My contention is that the power of this statement resides in the belief that the Chinese people confer on it. They, too, do not want experiments. They have had enough of big leaps to accelerate the advent of Utopia. They prefer a post-heroic world where the buzz words are "gradualism", "step by step", and "perhaps" instead of "certainly". To put it bluntly, the Chinese Communist Party now explores the future tentatively, looking backwards for precedent rather than forwards for imaginary vistas. Like George W. Bush's dad, they are not very good at the "vision thing".

Perhaps this is not so foolish, given the complexity of China's ongoing transformation. We can gauge how complex this process is by stylizing somewhat and chopping it up into four distinct, but related and synchronous, features. These we can present as follows.

China is experiencing a transition from a command economy to a market economy. Soon after introducing Soviet-style Plans in the 1950s, Mao Zedong, China's Communist emperor, realized that Soviet methods were ill-suited to China's peasantry. Instead, he mobilized mass enthusiasm in the service of his revolution. Disaster ensued. Mao died in September 1976. Two years later, Deng embarked on his reform policies. No transition to a market economy without Communist Party command, says official policy.

China is undergoing a transition from a rural to an urban society. When China took first, tentative steps to economic reform, it was a desperately poor country, unable to feed its growing population. As family farming revived, and most of Mao's collective farms were disbanded, China returned to food self-sufficiency. Surplus rural population was absorbed by the rapid growth of village and township enterprises. The result is large income gains, a surge in household savings, and unprecedented pollution.

China is in transition from autarky to interdependence. The extraordinary economic success stories of Taiwan, Hong Kong, South Korea and Singapore have fascinated China's leaders. They have all deployed the resources of authoritarian states to promote dynamic market economies. They have all been drawn into the vortex of the Asia-Pacific system dominated by the USA and Japan. Since the mid-1960s, their per capita incomes have grown sevenfold. China's large population, the regime calculates, can only benefit by exploiting the opportunities on offer.

China is in transition from membership of the international Communist system to participation in a global polity. Since 1972, when President Nixon and Chairman Mao agreed to the Shanghai Communiqué, China's main relationship has been with the USA. Collapse of the USSR in 1991 deprived the Chinese Communist leadership of their fraternal rival, accentuated their drive to create a "socialist market economy" under one-party rule, and has left China the alternative of either joining the global polity or shouting disapproval from the sidelines.

These four facets of China's transition – from command to market, from a rural to an urban society, from autarky to interdependence, from membership in the Communist system to participation in the global polity – are occurring simultaneously with the transformation of world affairs. I have presented my argument on what is called "globalization" in *The Frontiers of Fortune*. For the sake of brevity, some of its key features may be summarized as follows:

The world's transformation is composed of four related, but distinct, phenomena. The first of these records the collapse of the Communist system, the primacy of the USA, and the trend to fragmentation of political authority, as the number of states multiplies and the variety of regulatory bodies proliferates. The second element is the relentless retreat of any alternative forms of government to "market democracy", as various forms of despotism collapse, populations become better informed, market scope widens, and institutional competition takes its toll. The third element is the recreation of the world market under the aegis of the Western powers, and by the USA in particular, to reach a level of integration unknown since the first decade of the twentieth century. The fourth element is the growth of the industrial or service corporation, initially based in a home country, and with subsidiaries or market outlets in host countries, towards becoming a transnational group with subsidiaries and markets located around the globe, and with a widely dispersed shareholder community, and a non-national recruitment policy.

As will become apparent in this book, the world and China's transformation are related intimately to each other, for obvious reasons. Take the most obvious, the collapse of the Communist system, and China as a relic thereof. This very fact alone makes it less than likely that China will survive as it is presently constituted into the next couple of decades. Where China is heading is a familiar question: some say it is heading with its regime to the dustbin of history, while others argue that it is heading for the sunny uplands of "market democracy". I say it all depends on the discretion exercised by public officials. But I add that if you read the body language of China's public officials, although they'll deny it, they are leading China in the direction, and with the general outcomes, illustrated in this book.

In other words, the question we ask about China is also the question we ask about the world. Where are we heading? The question yields two, contradictory, answers.

The first runs thus: The post-cold-war world is in many respects more integrated than at any period of history. There is no viable political alternative to constitutional democracy and market economy. We are all going to be "common marketized" (Fukuyama, 1989), so the world will get more homogeneous and dull. But the good news is that we are all converging on great wealth, the elaboration of global norms of governance, and the emergence of a truly global civilization. That is where the forces driving humanity forward are propelling us. China is no exception.

What the world needs is a new architecture for global governance. More open world markets have to be organized from above, through government cooperation and through international organization. The WTO is a case in point. Its global elitism is necessary to mitigate interstate rivalries and the abuse of political or corporate power by the strong. Ultimately, a global public interest is best served by international organizations, governments and non-governmental organizations working together for the good of "the international community" (Kaul et al., 1999).

This progressive vision is of a radiant future for mankind. The world will be increasingly wealthy and inclusive as global civil society develops a public law that overrides state sovereignties. Problems of adaptation to the new technologies, the uses to which they may be put, and imbalances in world labor or financial markets will be facilitated by the power of the driving forces impelling the world towards unity. The assumption is that wealth creation will act as a great dissolvent on the tensions inherent to mankind's progress to a higher civilization.

The second answer runs along different lines: the post-cold-war world may well be more integrated than ever, but we know that the historical world in which the human drama is played out is one of inherited inequalities, different capabilities, and very diverse motivations. China is particularly exposed. Globalization in this light is not a dissolvent to old conflicts but a stimulus to old and new tensions. Humankind is not engaged in a great trek to a single destination, because peoples and individuals have very different purposes in life. They have their own histories and memories, and therefore they have very different visions of the future. Nothing is traced out in advance. Human discretion prevails in that the choices that people make as individuals or collectivities are informed by the particular purposes they pursue. In such a highly political world, the same factors that are seen by many as contributing to convergence become sources of divergence. Common norms hold a variety of intents; institutional differences wax rather than wane over time; and as the world becomes a smaller place, frictions between peoples from different civilizations will rise (Huntington, 1993).

These three factors of divergence point to a future of revolutionary upheavals and international conflicts. International institutions will be blown away in the fury. Overall, this world of history introduces discretion in human affairs, diversity and divergence, rather than linearity, integration and convergence. States have particular policy processes and varied capabilities to adapt, and they secrete many types of capitalism. Globalization, maintain the antiglobalization brigade, is the new capitalist diktat; it engenders civilizational clashes and provides the technical means for the weak to retaliate against the strong. There is no dissolvent to the tensions afflicting the world. Quite the contrary: globalization is a stimulus.

The paradox is that both propositions provide a partial description of what is going on: a diversity of states in a non-homogeneous world, penetrated and shaped by global markets, operating powerfully to create a more homogeneous world civilization, alongside aspirations to create a system of global governance out of the world's existing institutional framework as the counterpart to a world of relentless competition between peoples, states, corporations and currencies. It is this double condition of hope in a radiant future and fear flowing from very divergent capabilities to adapt that is characteristic of global affairs. This double condition blows strongly through the affairs of China. China's present and future challenge is as follows: the real China revolution, which Mao side-stepped by closing the country off from outside contact, lies ahead.

A number of caveats are required. China is not what political scientists call a unitary actor, meaning the existence of a close correspondence between government, policy and people. China is a highly complex, informally decentralized entity. Nonetheless, I use the shorthand, "China", as a way into the subject, and unravel new layers of complexity, onion-like, as the chapters roll by. Similarly, we have to understand the forces making China's future as a preamble to consider what we can learn about business strategy there. Those forces, too, make their appearance as the chapters procede. They include demographics, technologies, shifts in ideas about the role of government, the spread of markets, politics, and the major changes that have occurred, and will continue to occur, in international affairs.

The structure of this book is simple: the first chapter presents four interpretations of China's transformation, with a view to introducing the subject. Then I start on the big picture, assessing China's fundamental foreign policy in the context of the present structure of world affairs. This is followed by an analysis of China's incorporation into the global economy. The subsequent two chapters examine economic and political policy reforms and contrasts. This sets the scene for a chapter on China's entry to the WTO. By this time, we can broach the complex reforms of China's business system. This in turn allows us to assess some key lessons for multinational corporations operating in China. The final chapter is presented in the form of a conclusion scenario. In this chapter, there is both an indication of the type of forces at work pushing China towards market democracy and a warning of the precipices on either side of the Chinese Communists' Long March away from their ideological roots.

References

Francis Fukuyama, 1989, "The end of history", *National Interest*, 16(89), pp. 3–18.

Samuel P. Huntington, 1993, "The clash of civilizations", *Foreign Affairs*, 72(3), pp. 22–49.

Inge Kaul, Isabelle Gruberg and Marc A. Stern (eds), 1999, *Global Public Goods: International Cooperation in the 21st Century*, New York, Oxford: Oxford University Press.

Zheng Ruolin, 2002, "Immunable extreme gauche: un Chinois stupéfait par les scores de Laguiller et Hue", *Libération*, March 12.

Acknowledgements

I would like to thank INSEAD Research Committee for supporting my case studies written over the past decade on China. Funds were generously provided for work on this book from my Shell Fellowship. I am particularly grateful for the hospitality shown me by Mrs Chen Weilan, Vice President, National School of Administration, Beijing, and the participants in the workshops I conducted for the China Training Centre for Senior Personnel Management Officials. Professor Paolo Urio of the Sino-Swiss Management Training Programme was instrumental in setting up the workshops. I have also had the good fortune of teaching many times at the China European International Business School (CEIBS), based at Shanghai. This has enabled me to get to know businesspeople from all over China. I have also been active in courses organized at the Fontainebleau campus under the aegis of the Euro-Asia Centre, and dealing with China and Asian business conditions. Many people have been kind enough to allow me to interview them in the course of writing this book, including Xie Ping, Director General of the Research Bureau at the People's Bank of China; Ms Yuan Wang, Deputy Division Chief, People's Bank of China; Vice-President Su Ge, Senior Research Fellow at the China Institute of International Studies; Wang Yuanhong, Senior Economist at the State Development Planning Commission; and Min Tang, Chief Economist at the ADB Resident Mission in Beijing. Many helpful comments on the manuscript, and various parts of it, have been provided by Professor Eric Hyer from Brigham Young University, Utah; Professor Li Chunfang from the Chinese Academy of Social Sciences, Beijing; Dr Liu Manquiang from the Chinese Academy of Social Sciences; Professor Lu Feng of Qinghua University; Professor Wang Yong from the School of International Studies, Beida; Jean-Pierre Cabestan,

Director of the French Centre for Research on Contemporary China, Hong Kong, and Chief Editor, *China Perspectives*. My colleagues Ethan Kapstein, Gordon Redding and Wilfried Vanhonacker have been most helpful in their comments and advice as have John Stopford from the London Business School and Shaun Breslin from Warwick University's Centre for the Study of Globalisation and Regionalisation. Among businesspeople, I would especially like to thank Art Kobler, President of AT&T, China, Jean-Luc Chereau, President of Carrefour, China, Adam Williams, Chairman of the British Chamber of Commerce, Michael Wang of the China-British Business Council, and Edward Radcliffe, then of BateyBurn, who helped very much in opening doors for a case on Chinese telecommunications. Dr Jun Ma, senior economist with the Global Markets Division, Deutsche Bank Hong Kong, provided valuable insights and advice. I must also thank my research assistants, particularly Rafael Bueno Martinez, who worked closely with me throughout the book. My thanks also to Robert Crawford, Bing Xie, Hans Meyerhans, Adam Pearson of The Boston Consulting Group, Emilio Manso-Salinas and Jocelyn Probert, who have written with me cases on China over the past decade or so. Richard Stagg has been most considerate as the timetable for finishing the manuscript has slipped. The reason is that my wife Heidi and I met Mme Laure-Marie Meyer, who communicated her enthusiasm for singing to us. Zarastro, Leporello, Don Carlos and others have been demanding on my time. In conclusion, I would like to dedicate this book to Heidi and to our children, Henry, Christina, Nicholas and Alex.

Fontainebleau, August 2002.

1

China's curse: to live in exciting times

TIME HANGS HEAVILY on Chinese civilization. For nearly 4000 years, depending on when the first dynasty is dated, sixteen – some say nineteen – dynasties ruled for varying lengths of time over the Middle Kingdom until 1911. Marco Polo, the Venetian traveler, wrote in the thirteenth century of China as "the richest country in the world", where science was far more advanced than in Europe – where many Chinese inventions, such as gunpowder, the marine compass and printing, were unknown. Yet the prevalent Chinese interpretation of history remains cyclical, trapped in a pre-industrial monotony of repetition whereby the broad tapestry of human existence is for ever replayed. Typically, traditional Chinese historiography has a new dynasty beginning with capable rulers receiving the mandate of heaven to carry out various reforms and extend the boundaries of Chinese administration. These are followed by a golden age of stability, prosperity and cultural achievement. However, as routine sets in, so do corruption and decay. Finally, the dynasty loses heaven's mandate through internal rebellion or external invasion, only for a new dynasty to be established in war and violence, and for the pattern to repeat itself.

So, we may ask, how far along its cycle is the present Communist dynasty? Is it heading for a new golden age, or is it about to succumb to corruption and decay? The answer depends much on the evidence deployed and the time horizon adopted. The two are associated intimately: the closer the future is, the more turbulent China appears. The farther ahead the future lies, the more serene the judgment becomes (Pei, 1999). This trick of perspective is explained by the many facets of China's present transition. Let us look at these first, before presenting the different prognoses about China's future.

China's transition

When China's paramount leader, Deng Xiaoping, embarked on a policy of reforms in 1978, he was well aware that his formula of marketization combined with continued Communist Party primacy would create trouble. As the Chinese proverb goes, an open window inevitably attracts in flies. Over two decades later, the house of China was abuzz. Growth statistics reported the highest rates in the world, wealth disparities were widening, major social changes were under way, and faith was draining from the Communist dynasty's promise to create a new, more just society. Within the party-state, divisions ran deep about the content, direction and speed of reforms. Official policy adopted pragmatism, as portrayed in the slogan, *"mo zhe shi ziguo he"*, which translates as "feeling the stones as you cross the river". But there was no evading discussion about China's ultimate destination. This became evident during the democracy movement of the late 1980s, culminating in the student demonstrations in Tiananmen Square in May–June 1989—the first known major push within China to reform the regime. The students wanted an end to corruption, more intraparty democracy, and a curb on the abuse of power by officials. Many leaders, notably Zhao Ziyang – former premier and leader of the Communist Party (CCP) – as well as party intellectuals sympathized with the students, and understood that a market economy and political reform went together. As Wu Jiaxing, a young researcher at the Investigation and Research Division of the Communist Party's Central Office, wrote, Deng's policies were "an express train toward democracy through the building of markets" (Rosen and Zou, 1990). He was arrested in July on account of his association with regime reformers.

Perhaps one of Wu Jiaxing's errors was to have underestimated the importance of values as shaping policy practice, or – in more academic terms—substantive goal rationality. Rationality here has two components, one being value rationality, which is concerned with means, and the other being instrumental rationality, being concerned with ends.[1] The means used by the party-state on Tiananmen Square was brute force, but the rationality governing its deployment was one of preserving China's political order. Here, the regime could draw on values or guiding principles for action that were rooted deeply in China's long history, and that can be presented in the following form:

◆ Confucian ethics tend to legitimate paternalism in the household and patrimonialism in the state, and provide a moral justification for *hierarchy*, stressing reciprocal vertical obligations.

◆ Chinese civilization is predicated on individuals being socialized into a belief in the need for appropriate conduct in the interests of *harmony*, all within a dominant state structure with a mandate to preserve order.

◆ Given the limited trust between individuals, and between individuals and public officials, in China, the architecture of horizontal order is based on identity with *family* as the core social unit.

◆ The party-state is both a beneficiary of these age-old patrimonial values, as a guarantor of a certain order, and a major source of *insecurity*, because of its record as a revolutionary force in seeking to uproot tradition and deny families their property rights.

Drawing on China's deep yearning for order and security in the short term by resort to force against the students in 1989 could win plaudits in a country paralyzed by the fear of a return to past disasters. But Tiananmen Square made clear that satisfying yearning in the longer term presented an awesome challenge. For the closer one looks, the more immediate and overwhelming the problems confronting China appear. So far, they have been

---

[1]For a discussion of Max Weber's concept of rationality applied to China, see Gordon Redding, 2002, "The capitalist system of China and its rationale", Asia Pacific Journal of Management, 19, pp. 221–49. The following paragraph draws on his work.

met with some success, crediting a more serene judgment of China's chances. In the meantime, opinions range from a real and present danger of sudden regime death, to China as an introverted regional power, through to China as a belligerent and assertive rising great power, or China's triumphant osmosis to a successful developmental state. Let us consider these, and subject each of them in turn to a critical look. We'll then conclude on the book's theme of the reasons for China's emergence as a prime pillar of global society.

Sudden regime death syndrome

The Chinese Communist regime is destined for the dustbin of history. The disaster about to overwhelm China is triggered by massive rural emigration, as get-rich-quick practices push aside the Communist regime's prime constituency of the working class and peasantry. Such is the harsh verdict of a best-selling book, *Viewing China Through a Third Eye*, published in 1994, and written by a confidant of one of the regime's "princelings", or sons of prominent regime members (*FBIS Daily Report*, 1995). Signs of collapse lie all around: corruption, the proliferation of sects to fill the vacuum left by the death of Communist ideals, major policy rifts within the Communist "emperor's household", center–province tensions, widening income disparities, rising pollution, weak public finances, a floating population of up to 200 million unemployed, and mounting lawlessness.

China, this line of reasoning continues, is about to revisit the nineteenth century, when the Manchu government suffered crushing defeats at the hands of the British and French expeditionary forces dispatched to open China's closed markets in the first and second Opium Wars of 1838–42 and 1856–60. China was forced to open its ports and to conclude humiliating, inequitable treaties, as well as to pay huge amounts in indemnities. Hong Kong, a barren rock, was ceded to the British Crown in perpetuity, and later Kowloon and the New Territories were leased for ninety-nine years. A succession of civil wars wracked the country, by far the most savage of which was the Taiping Rebellion of 1851–64. About twenty million people died before the dynasty managed to quell its leader, Hong Xiuchuan, a self-declared younger brother of Christ. Further humiliating defeat by Japan in 1895 prompted government officials to try to convince the ruling dynasty of the necessity of self-strengthening and reforms, and particularly of developing a modern ordnance industry. But the imperial court feared it would lose power and influence if economic and political reforms were implemented. The Qing dynasty collapsed in 1911.

The historian Ho Pingti (1959) picks up the story:

> *For a whole decade from 1917 to 1927 there were incessant civil wars in various parts of the country ... From 1928 on the Nationalists were repeatedly at war with the Communists ... These wars were brought to an end in 1936; then war with Japan broke out in July 1937 ... In August 1945 civil war between the Nationalists and Communists was soon renewed.*

Within four years of the defeat of Japan and the end of World War II, the Communists were able to defeat the US-backed, more modern, and four times as numerous Nationalist forces. Chiang Kai-shek, the Nationalist Generalissimo, fled to Taiwan, still claiming to be the legal leader of China. Mao Zedong proclaimed the People's Republic of China (PRC) on October 1, 1949, declaring that at last "the Chinese people have stood up".

Just as in 1839 China was on the verge not of independent industrialization but of more than a century of *da luan* (great chaos), so in 1989 this horrendous past is about to be repeated, declare the sudden-regime-death protagonists.

The first clear indication is the worldwide failure of Communist ideology, most noticeably in its voodoo economics and the battery of bogus statistics that they produced. Consider, for instance, China's growth record compared with that of Japan, the world champion, whose national income rose from 1% of the world's total in 1950 to 18% by the turn of the millennium. Official figures claim that China's rate of industrial output grew even faster than Japan's, at 12.5% per annum. But somehow, these superlative growth figures do not seem to have translated into wealth. China ranks number 140 in the world league tables in terms of per capita income, ahead of Africa and India, while Japan ranks number six.

A second indication of China's predicament is the strength of centrifugal forces, reminiscent of the 1920s when regional warlords carved up the country and held sway in defiance of central authorities. Previous dynastic collapses had been preceded by the decay of the central power's ability to extract resources from the provinces. The Communist dynasty has to rely on the People's Liberation Army (PLA) to impose its authority by force, while suffering from political paralysis, administrative gridlock, and a further weakening of central government authority. This is particularly evident in provinces inhabited by ethnic minorities, whose demands for autonomy or political independence have been stimulated by Western sympathy (Tibet), Uighur irredentism (Xinjiang Province) or the Soviet Union's collapse (Inner Mongolia). Whatever channels provincial leaders take to assert themselves, the outcome is the same: the country is threatened with disintegration in the manner of Yugoslavia and the Soviet Union.

A third sign of impending collapse is that the regime faces a crisis of legitimacy. It has been in power for over fifty years and has never faced an election. Discontent is rife in the Party's core constituencies of workers and peasants, and the Western barbarians are once again at the gates; worse, they are inside the citadel of China's economy and society. No doubt it was gloomy thoughts such as these that prompted the Chinese Communist leadership in December 1992 to sit through a special performance of Durrenmatt's *Romulus the Great*. The barbarians (the Western democracies) are at the gates of Rome (Beijing), and the emperor Romulus (Deng) announces that he intends to save the empire (Communist China) by transforming it. The only hope, he says, is to go into business with the barbarians in order to avoid a catastrophe – collapse and annihilation – worse than the introduction of capitalism.

> The regime has been in power for over fifty years and has never faced an election

The fourth, and conclusive, sign of impending collapse is that China faces Malthusian conditions of rising population, limited arable land, and diminishing returns (Goldstone, 1995). China's arithmetic is simple: at the turn of the millennium, its population of 1.3 billion holds a peasantry of 800 million, who produce only one-third of the country's total output. By 2015, China's population may number 1.5 billion, 800 million of whom will live off the land in some way, with the other 700 million having to live off non-farm occupations. That means that the Chinese economy has to generate hundreds of millions of jobs in the private sector, as well as keep the hundreds of millions of peasants on the land. The party is neither agreed nor united enough to meet the challenge: as the author of *Viewing China Through a Third Eye* forecasts, China's coming disaster will be triggered by a massive and uncontrollable rural emigration. Foreign powers will be tempted, in the words of the Qing's Dowager Empress, Ci Xi, to "compare China with a watermelon, to be cut in small pieces" (cited in Hsu, 2000). Their instrument for doing so will be "the knife of Taiwan".[2]

Why such a gloomy prognosis? After all, the Western press often presents China in a favorable light. The answer lies in the authors' identity. *Viewing China Through a Third Eye* represents a call to action by Chinese Communist princelings who have woken to a world where the party-state is a church without religion. Marxism–Leninism–Maoism is dead. We, the heirs to China's revolutionaries, they are saying, cannot afford to preach the class struggle. Quite the contrary: we must offer China's masses the prosperity, stability and pride they aspire to. That can be achieved only by centralization of power away from the provinces, and the maintenance of existing political structures. Because we cannot foretell what the Chinese would vote in open and free elections, we must offer substitutes. One is the daily plebiscite of consumers in the shops. Another is the language of patriotism. What cannot be permitted is the sale of books favoring political reform or recounting the extraordinary careers of the Communist party-state's princelings.

"The latent crisis in Chinese society is very serious", write the authors of *Viewing China Through a Third Eye*. Look what has happened in the ex-Soviet Union. This great edifice collapsed overnight, and with it went the few comforts granted to the average Soviet citizen. China may take the same route, were it not for the Communist party-state. Stay with us, the authors say, because we are the barrier that stands between you and chaos.

---

[2] Speech of Jiang Zemin, quoted in Sheng Lijung, "Taiwan's new president and cross-strait relations", No. 11 September 2000. Published by Institute of Southeast Asian Studies, Singapore, p. 291.

Here lies a crucial paradox. The authors know that the regime's legitimacy depends on Mao's legacy, and therefore they call for a positive reinterpretation of the Communist emperor's thought and action. But they also appeal to the widespread fear of social chaos in a population that remembers Mao's disastrous Great Leap Forward, when thirty million people died in the manmade famine generated by Mao's effort to accelerate China's industrialization in the years 1959–61. Then came the Cultural Revolution, lasting from 1966 to 1976, when Mao sought to transform China's culture and wrench it from its historical moorings. At least one million people died during its excesses, in addition to the millions of school-going age who lost out on their education. China's present elite, the authors are saying, must learn that they are not likely to be forgiven if they should perpetrate another disaster through bad policy, oversight or muddled thinking. They must stand firmly on an agenda of law and order, and their instrument can only be the PLA. In the last resort, the regime depends on its willingness to use force against dissent.

The authors' fears are also fed by the thrust of market reforms in a society increasingly differentiated along class lines. The reforms threaten urban working populations, 90% of whom in the big cities are employed by the party-state. They are employed either in administrative tasks or in the state enterprises. On both accounts, their future is clearly in jeopardy. The state's lack of fiscal resources means that civil servants receive risible wages, delayed payment or, at worst, no wages at all. Any attempts by Beijing to claw back revenues from provincial and city governments are resisted. State enterprises are in parlous condition and can no longer ensure job security. Their financial health can be restored only by a root-and-branch reform. Such reform means ending the implicit pact between the urban working class and the party-state, whereby job security is provided in exchange for no strikes, no votes. *In other words, what the regime's princelings propose is to slow down the pace of reform, in order to defend a status quo, which is not defensible in practice.*

Hence, their all-encompassing appeal to the urban population to gather around the regime against the threat of an uncontrollable inflow of desperate people from the countryside, in search of jobs at any price. The appeal to urban resentment at the floating, rural masses is all of a piece with the call for moral renewal, for a revival of patriotism, for a restoration of central authority, and for the rescue of Mao's thoughts from Deng's pragmatic purgatory. Mao's power base, originally founded on the peasantry, has shrunk to the urban masses. Like the Nationalists under Chiang Kai-shek, the regime is digging itself in around the urban centers, while seeking to preserve its hold in the countryside as best it can. Marketization is not compatible with the regime: so long live the regime. There is no strategy to save the status quo, say the authors, other than defending it. Sudden regime death syndrome is the ideology of bourgeois conservatism.

An introverted regional power

China's Communist regime may not be destined for the dustbin of history, but it is definitely not a great power and it is unlikely to be so for years to come. By any measure of power resources, China is at best a second-rank middle power (Segal, 1999), and it has a long march ahead of it to regain the position held in a very different world nearly two centuries ago. Indeed, relative decline has gone on unchecked over the whole period, accelerating through the nineteenth century, furthered by the wars and revolution of the first part of the twentieth century, and continuing unabated over the next fifty years of the Communist dynasty. Clearly, the first fifty years of the Communist dynasty have not been a great success. The least to be said is that such results are not worth the sacrifices demanded, and that the Chinese people have had to pay (see Table 1.1).

Marxism–Leninism is a failed anachronism. It remains the glue that holds the regime together, and it is the main reason for the widening gap between party-state, with its monopoly claim on resources, and the ever greater pluralism evident in Chinese society. Yet the regime has not progressed

Table 1.1 ◆ China as a percentage of world totals

	1820	1900	1950	2000
Population	35	25.6	21.7	21
Income	28	13.2	6.2	3.35
Western Europe's per capita income	41	16.2	6.6	3.1

Source: IMF and Angus Maddison, 1998, Chinese Economic Performance in the Long Term, Paris, OECD.

far beyond the Four Cardinal Principles enunciated by Deng at the start of his reforms. These state that the regime must continue to follow "the socialist road", maintain "the dictatorship of the proletariat", champion Communist Party leadership, and stay loyal to Marxism–Leninism and Mao Zedong thought. Not surprisingly, the Chinese Communist leadership was aghast at the Polish comrades' initial willingness to accede in 1980–81 to the demands of Poland's non-official opposition, Solidarity, for union autonomy and political reform; at Soviet Party-Secretary Gorbachev's political reforms in the late 1980s; and then at Gorbachev's refusal to use military force to crush opposition in the Caucasus, the Baltics and the satellite states in 1988–9. Deng, stated the leaderships' main lesson from the former Soviet Union: "The CCP status as the ruling party must never be challenged. China cannot adopt a multiparty system." (Lam, 1995).

China is likely to remain a "conservative power" for the foreseeable future (Ross, 1997). It does not have the capabilities to project military force much beyond its boundaries, and it is thoroughly dependent on the advanced industrial democracies for everything that counts in managing the process of its multiple transitions to a successful outcome. There is no advantage for the Western powers, in particular the USA, to exaggerate China's potential. China's priority is economic development, and for that it has to become a fully-fledged member of the (Western-dominated) international community, abiding by its procedures, living up to its standards, and cooperating in its development. That also means that the heart of China's relations with the international community will be domestic to China: whether China lives up to the powers' criteria for human rights in China, or whether it implements the Western powers' interpretation of its commitments as a full member of the World Trade Organization (WTO), will be of greater consequence to its future than any revisionist ambitions that some people inside and outside of the regime may hold to assert China's claim to great power rank and status. The real changes thus have to occur in China's political culture: the world where China could consider itself as the Middle Kingdom to which the barbarians paid allegiance has gone for ever. China is one large but impoverished part of the world polity and economy. In short, it is not the Western powers that have to accommodate China's whims, so much as the Communist dynasty that has to implement Western preferences through its own transformation. A successful Chinese foreign policy begins at home.

The argument about China as a second-rank, mid-range power is directed at Western powers: stand up to Chinese pretensions, it says, because they are built on a delusion of China's claim to be different. There is no doubt that China is a great power in the realm of population and area. But the fortunes of the Middle Kingdom have not been turned around, despite the exertions of the past century. Indeed, if China's share of global income in 2000 is compared with that one hundred years before, then either the terrible sufferings of the Chinese people have been in vain or China's weakened condition provides fuel for those who anticipate the regime's sudden death.

Let us assume that we consider the sufferings to have been in vain. Why, Chinese people with such ideas might think, should we suffer anew? Better to jettison the heroic endeavor of Nationalists and Communists to modernize China while retaining roots in China's cultural past and embracing the prosperous materialism that the Western powers are offering us. Politics may be a location for heroic action, but we know from experience how deadly such an assumption can be. Mao's heroic wrestlings with the realities of China's backwardness only inflicted tragedy. A non-heroic politics of improving living conditions for millions of people is a far more desirable objective. We may lose many attributes of being Chinese in the process, but that is nothing to be concerned about. It is precisely the problems of our Chinese inheritance, the memories of our past glories and of a world view that placed China at the center, that have been holding us back. Once we can divest ourselves of these illusions, China will be able to grow prosperous and at ease with itself in an interdependent world.

China's major problem, this position holds, lies in its political culture. Simply, China's self-perception is grander than the reality. To turn around China's history of the last two centuries, the country has to go through a true cultural revolution. Internally, such a revolution involves China embracing the Western world's formulas for good governance, including the rule of law, the recognition of property rights, the creation of accountable institutions with the capabilities to regulate a market economy, the citizen's right to freedom of religion and therefore to freedom of speech, the establishment of regular, free and multiparty elections, and the writing of a new constitution for a China in the twenty-first century. This domestic dimension of China's necessary transformation is the precondition to China's being able to deal conceptually with the complexities of existence in an interdependent world. In such a world, there are no enemies, only potential clients.

Hence, visions of barbarians at the gate of a Communist Qing dynasty about to collapse or China's posturings on the international scene are all manifestations of the same inability to disentangle fact from fiction: the fact is that China's military, economic and cultural influence is very small, and the fiction is that the world is hostile. Never before have the conditions in a stable and secure Asia been so favorable to China's domestic transformation (Abramowitz, 1997).

China's self-perception is grander than the reality

The real threat to China's own scaremongers, who preach the regime's impending death or strut their pride abroad, is this favorable constellation of a stable environment and a regime with little credibility at home. Indeed, Chinese leaders' own fears of impending collapse and Western propensities to pander to Chinese pretensions mutually reinforce each other. The first exaggerates domestic threats and foreign intentions in order to justify a hardening of the regime to perpetuate the status quo. The second provides apparent evidence to China's public that the regime's huffings and puffings deliver tangible results. Worse, Western failure to stand up to Chinese demands or to press Western interests with sufficient vigor serves only to perpetuate China's outdated views of its true position in the world. As these attitudes are at the source of China's inability to come to terms with the world, they have to be revealed for what they are: dirty little lies that serve to cover the interests of those who wish to cling to power. China's democratization is furthered by firm and fair dealing with a regime, many of whose members fear the success that cooperation with the Western powers is most likely to deliver. The firmer the Western position is towards China, the more likely is the country's favorable evolution. Democratization of China comes from a clear, Western appreciation of China's and the world's true interests. Those are for China to modernize, and to join the democracies. *They are not advanced by efforts to nurture China's historical hubris and the security paranoia in the mind of some Western analysts.*

A belligerent, assertive, rising power

China is heading towards a clash with the USA. While China appears to be adapting to Western preferences, the Party is transforming the state to maintain its hold on power, with the support of an expanding privileged class. Mao's egalitarianism is being ditched in favor of unashamed elitism, crass materialism and great power aspirations. China is like Germany a century ago, seeking its own "place in the sun" (Christensen and Betts, 2000). Underlying this observable trend is the broader shift in world politics in 1990 away from Western dominance of the past 500 years, to the clash of civilizations and cultures between the Western and non-Western civilizations (Huntington, 1993). Civilizations imply basic differences among people regarding language, culture, tradition and religion, and in the past they have generated the most prolonged and violent conflicts. As the world becomes a smaller place, frictions between peoples from different civilizations will rise. Resistance to the dominant Western world will likely take the form of assertion of a Chinese identity, perhaps in alliance with Islam, in order to modernize but not on Western terms. East Asia, Kishore Mahbubani has written, "wants to succeed in its own right, without trying to become a member of a European Club" (Mahbubani, 1995). It does not want to be at the receiving end of "human rights imperialism".

A first reminder that China is its own master came in June 1989 when the PLA suppressed the student movement in blood. Deng could scarcely have made a clearer statement that he was not prepared to follow Gorbachev's lead in allowing an extra-regime opposition to form. The precondition for China's evolution to a wealthy society under a powerful state was that the Communists hold on to power, while transforming it in substance. Once the Maoist backlash to the events of 1989–91 had been played out, Deng seized the initiative in his famous southern tour, where he stated that "it is glorious to get rich". In effect, the deal he was offering the Chinese people was for a de facto opening up of the sphere of private liberties, combined with a clear warning for the population at large to stay out of politics. For the privileged members of the party-state, he opened a huge gray zone where the nomenklatura capitalists of the new China could seek to maximize business opportunities outside of or alongside an incomplete legal system. Buoyant optimism was fed by World Bank figures showing that China's national income in terms of purchasing power in local currency was already number three in the world pecking order. Continued growth at similar rates pointed to China as an emerging superpower, destined to over-take the USA by 2015. By 2025, Asia with China at its heart would represent 55–60% of the world economy, while the West – the USA and the European Union (EU) – would be down to 30%.

A second reminder of the leadership's intent is that China is not just another little dragon, like Taiwan, Singapore or South Korea. As Lee Kuan Yew, Singapore's Senior Minister, has noted, it is the biggest dragon of all. China's model is now that of the developmental states of the Asia-Pacific region. The formula is straight forward enough: modernization transforms economic structures, social classes and state tasks. If the process is to be mastered and breakdown avoided, then a balance must be kept between political development and economic modernization. This requires strong government, guided by an elite who act as masters of the market. As popu-lations move away from traditional occupations, and become more educated, democratic development evolves alongside the extension of the rule of law, and the developmental state gradually withdraws in favor of the decentralized market decisions of citizens.

Such an open-ended program describes the regime's evolutionary move away from Leninist mass organizations towards a "new authoritarianism" (Unger, 1995), as sketched in the reform leader Zhao Ziyang's 1987 report to the thirteenth National People's Congress (NPC). This direction of policy was ratified at the fourteenth NPC in October 1992. Marketization of the party-state – in official speak, moving to the "socialist market econ-omy" – was twinned with an open-door policy favoring inward direct investment, expanded international trade, and promotion of urban areas. The result is a mutual dependence between bureaucratic elites emerging from the party-state and business elites linked to the modern economy. This implies limited political pluralism within the broader bounds of a pro-business regime, continued dominance of a strong executive, and the evolution of a still rudimentary rule by law.

An assertive and aggressive foreign policy is the external face of this domestic authoritarianism. China, the argument runs, is in the grip of a relentless "nationalism of aggrievance and thwarted grandeur" (Bernstein and Munro, 1998). Its aim is to dominate Asia not so much by conquest as by filling out into its historic space as East Asia's prime power, without whose consent nothing will be allowed to happen. This ambition is fired by a widely shared and deep-seated psychological need in China to compensate for past humiliations. Inevitably, such a China is bound to conflict with the USA, whose global balance of power politics, as played out in the Asia-Pacific region, is to prevent any single country from dominating the region. Great Britain returned Hong Kong in 1997 to the motherland, followed by Portugal's return of Macao in 1999. The next step is for China to absorb Taiwan, whose main protector is the USA. According to China's July 1998 White Paper on defense, the USA is the main threat to world peace and stability. Through the North Atlantic Treaty Organization (NATO), or its network of global alliances, the USA continues its cold-war strategy and operates as a self-appointed global police officer. China's task is therefore to "say no" to US hegemonism, build up its power base, and nurture its grievances until the moment is ready to strike (Ch'iang *et al.*, 1996).

> China is in the grip of a relentless "nationalism of aggrievance and thwarted grandeur"

Conflict between a rising China and the USA, this argument holds, is inevitable. The inevitability is rooted in the careful cultivation by the Chinese elite of resentment at past humiliation. Because the regime has no intention of abandoning power, and even less of evolving towards Western-type democratic forms, it asserts its distinctiveness in the world. Before 1989, this was not necessary because China was a member of the international Communist system. The interplay of regime and Chinese nationalism took place within acknowledged bounds. Clearly, Beijing's alliance with the USA to contain the Soviet Union meant that the national dimension of the party-state's external relations was taking precedence over its Communist identity. Since 1989–91, the party-state has wrapped itself in a flag of nationalism, of greater Chinese patriotism, of Asian values, of Confucian paternalism (Hsu, 2000). This enables it to assert its own standards of conduct in favor of order and efficiency and to reject Western preaching in favor of more freedom and justice. By deploying flags that appeal beyond the borders of mainland China, the party-state shows that it is not alone. It can reach back in history into the Confucian past and across geographic space into the Asia-Pacific region. I am different, the regime says, and many others in my neighborhood agree.

It is one thing for the regime to claim that it is different but another to cover that distinctiveness with different flags. So many different flags suggests that China's mansion holds multiple identities:

- The flag of nationalism continues to be disputed between Taipei and Beijing in that both subscribe to the doctrine of "one China, two systems" (*Yi guo, liang zhi*).

- The flag of a greater China embraces the fifty million overseas Chinese throughout the Asia-Pacific region, whose skills, money and business acumen the mainland government seeks to attract.

- The flag of Asian values is shared with the governments of Singapore and Malaysia, both of whom join China in challenging Western human rights imperialism.

- The flag of Confucian paternalism links China's present and future to its tradition of governance by mandarinate, of respect paid by citizens to the emperor, of young to old.

The fact that China has so many identities suggests that the picture of a rising and aggressive China is too simple. A China in need of many symbols to express itself is clearly not of one mind. It is not even necessarily the case that China has many minds. It may well be that China as it were has not yet made up its mind. The regime wants to hang on to power while changing its substance. There are privileges to protect and commitments to live up to. There is no precedent in China of countrywide democracy, and the analogy of India as the world's largest democracy is easily explained away. The traditions and history of India differ, and its record of development, many would argue, is much less impressive than China's. The worst sin to commit, the regime says, would be to throw the dice of open-ended political reform and bet the future of China on chance, in the manner of Gorbachev and the Soviet Union. Holding on to political power, though, is different from clinging to the status quo. Under party guidance, the party-state is in evolution, moving away from its totalitarian past towards authoritarian structures, which themselves have strong democratic elements such as village elections, or vigorous debates in the NPC. China is in transition, moving to an unknown destination.

That is why the coming clash between China and the USA, or between China and its neighbors, is far from inevitable. It is one possibility, but one among many. What is particularly dangerous about this view of China's relationship to the world's sole great power is that it appeals to national conservatives on both sides of the ocean. Both fear the triumph of modern materialism, with its appeal to the senses, its stimulation of the passions, and its view of politics as an occupation for pigs competing for scarce resources. If nations are not to melt slowly into a post-historical morass, then their citizens must be able to identify clearly We from They. They are easier to identify if their purpose is defined as irredeemably hostile, rooted in the case of China in resentment of past insults and unrequited desire for future glory. Such passion is not amenable to appeasement by foreign powers, but it grows as one concession follows another. China's passions, it is alleged, drive it to oust the USA from Asia. It will not be assuaged by material plenty but will use wealth to accrue power. China's thirst for glory – for subservient adulation of its splendor – may not even be satisfied when China becomes the world's hegemone.

Definitely, the value of this perspective is to place the emphasis on China's potential. China has much of it. As, and if, it steers a path through its multiple transitions, its purposes, now hidden, may become clearer. Because they are undetermined, they can be influenced. But because they are so many in the present, China is inscrutable. As Samuel Kim suggests: "Ultimately, the critical question in assessing China as a great power is behavior. What matters most is not so much the growth of Chinese power but how and for what purpose a rising China will actually wield its putative or actual power in the conduct of its international relations" (Kim, 1997). Portraying China as gripped by a passion for glory simplifies the task of diagnosis. It provides the grounds for a new cold war, and it facilitates the drawing of boundaries between We and They. *This vision is the counterpart US national conservatives offer to the princelings' nightmare of the regime's sudden death.*

China and the end of history

The regime has no option in the longer run but to introduce market democracy. So far, it is introducing the market by transforming itself into a successful developmental state. As China's modernization is accelerated, it will be propelled into the front rank of great powers in record time. There is no need for anxiety, as China will provide an ever larger market, has to be incorporated into the global polity, and will democratize. China cannot escape "the end of history", where the future is nothing more than implementing the already known standards of good governance. China will take many years to join the developed nations of the West as a liberal society, but its inevitable future is to be "common marketized", like

> China cannot escape "the end of history"

the rest of the world (Fukuyama, 1989). The age of tragedy, and therefore of heroes and tyrants on the scale of Mao, Stalin and Hitler, is a thing of the past. Large-scale conflicts are passing from the scene to be replaced by a United Nations of global governance, agreement on collective and individual rights and duties, the elaboration of common rules and regulations to govern trade, investment or the environment, and the guarantee of equal access for all to world markets. China's task is to be a full participant in this dull, rich, global village.

China's strategy of economic growth is much more like South Korea's than its discredited former Communist companions: "Contemporary China is not another Soviet Union, nor the totalitarian state that China was in 1966, but rather a gigantic, vintage 1972 South Korea" (Overholt, 1993). Not for China the big bang reforms of the Soviet Union and the Eastern European states; they are too reminiscent of Mao's Big Leap. Rather, the philosophy is one of careful exploration of those stones under the feet as the river is crossed. The aim is to build up a constituency of support for the reform strategy, summarized as *fangquan rangli*, or devolving authority and yielding benefits. The devolving of authority entails both promotion of the market and the building of institutions to accompany its supervision. The key to longer-term success is to build an ever-expanding constituency of support. This is vital because the process of marketization is bound to mobilize opposition, and democratization would only strengthen the trend, making reform next to impossible. The sequence should be economic reforms, more freedoms and then democratization.

Domestic politics in China are likely to remain authoritarian for some time, with some limited degree of pluralism permitted. In the longer run, the regime may evolve in the manner of South Korea or Taiwan, but for the moment and for the foreseeable future, the mainland regime's strategy for China's development rests on making sure that it provides political stability and prosperity. There are a number of reasons for believing that this is what the majority of Chinese people want. Definitely, no one in the regime wants to risk its collapse, especially after having watched on television the dramatic end of the Ceauşescu dictatorship in Romania. In any case, there is a major difference between the Communist party-states of central and Eastern Europe, which were sustained by a foreign power, and the national Communism of China, which conquered power in a civil war. There has always been an easy blend between Communism and nationalism in China that the regime has been able to deploy to boost its legitimacy. But it does mean that the regime can count on extensive passive support of the many who fear a Soviet-style collapse, who are not very keen on democracy, and who do not get enthused over human rights. People may be cynical, but they prefer the devil they know to the ones that they do not know.

China is very unlike Japan, with its closed and insular mentality, fearful of penetration by foreign business and culture. Rather, it is an ancient civilization, a network of families paying tribute to their ancestors, a developing country with much to learn and more than ready to do so. The Chinese do not suffer from exacerbated nationalism, and the Chinese economy is wide open. China is not a rogue state with hegemonic ambitions, but has been an ever more active and responsible member of the international community since taking up its seat as a permanent member of the Security Council in

1971 (Lampton, 1998). Rather than throw its weight around, Chinese foreign policy has shown that its prime purpose is to participate in global rule-writing, rather than in having the rules written for it. It is true that China will seek to complete reunification, now that Hong Kong and Macao have returned to the motherland. Taiwan will therefore remain a flash point in relations with the USA, and there is no certainty that war can be avoided. But China's military clout is weak, and the amount spent on the military is subject to much dispute. The evidence suggests that China will tend to go the extra mile in negotiations to avoid confrontation, just as it has sought to improve relations with its neighbors, despite outstanding problems regarding frontiers. Not least, China is no longer a totalitarian regime, personal freedoms have been expanded considerably, and the regime's powers of censorship have shrunk. Its influence in Washington, London and Brussels is modest. Beijing is not a major foreign-policy threat.

China's main task, the end-of-history thesis suggests, is to move peacefully via "common marketization" to join the democracies. This is the song that China's reformers sing in counterpart to Westerners who propose to promote China's normalization. There is much common ground between the two. Western calls for China's democratization and regime reformers' efforts to modernize China both accept that there is no alternative to being part of this world. China could opt, like the regimes in Myanmar and North Korea, for life in autarky, but that would be only illusion. However cut off from the rest of the world, all states are, by definition, units in the global system of states. Being in it, they can opt to live poor and separate, or they can join the rest of the world. China decided to do so in 1978. That means acceptance of growing economic and political interdependence: acceptance of economic interdependence because China's opening on to world markets makes it more vulnerable to the policies of foreign governments, the decisions of foreign corporations, and the preferences of foreign customers; and acceptance of political interdependence because China finds foreign corporations lobbying its provincial or central governments for this favor or that, while Chinese central government departments or members of China's various opposition movements lobby for support in the USA, Japan or Europe. When you join the rest of the world, you do so on the rest of the world's terms.

And that is where Western advocates of democracy and Chinese regime reformers part company. Western democratizers look for a cultural revolution in a China where there is no place for illusions of grandeur. They do so because they fear that national conservatives in the USA may otherwise prove to be correct about China's appetite for world power status. Since it is this nostalgia that is alleged to have held China back in the past two centuries, the regime reformers' modernization project cannot succeed unless they dispense with it. Western democratizers, in other words, are almost Maoist in their desire to purge the past from China's collective memory. Whereas Mao sought to purge China of inherited attitudes on hierarchy as the prelude to his revolution, so Western democratizers seek to empty China of its collective nostalgia for an irrecuperable past. There can be no cleaner break with the past in China than by the introduction of multiparty elections across the length and breadth of the country. Regime reformers, not surprisingly, are of a different mind: since 1978, the regime has gone out of its way to revive a sense of history, of Chinese accomplishments over the millennia, and of the presence of the past in the future. This is neither a cyclical view of history, where China once again becomes a Middle Kingdom, nor a discontinuous view, where China makes a clean break with the past. China's reformers have a view of the future, recognizable to British Tories: you are sufficiently concerned about it to move towards the future looking backwards. The aim is to reconcile China's masses to the necessary transformation, but to do so one step at a time: the last step then, after establishing a market economy, allowing freedoms to develop, and creating a state of law, will be democratization. The moment and the manner, the regime reformers hint, is ours to choose.

This thesis of China's managed transformation is often suffused with a quiet optimism as to the outcome. As Singapore's Senior Minister, Lee Kuan Yew, was quoted in *People's Daily* (2000), "China has taken a major step to plug its economy into the global grid, which will make it one of the most important players in the global exchange of goods, services, capital, talent and ideas in the twenty-first century". And indeed, there are many reasons to espouse such an interpretation. The regime accepts the challenges of interdependence; it is ready to experiment and to learn from the rest of the world; it aspires to a position of co-responsibility in the counsels of the world. There is definitely no going back to false gods and failed models. The Chinese people, it is argued, would not stand to be treated like mushrooms: they have been kept in the dark and covered in ideological excrement once, and would resent being so treated again (White, 1993). Their main concern is to improve their standard of living, and they would not take kindly to leaders who failed them. The regime already lives in a proto-democracy in that it seeks acclaim in the daily plebiscite of the market economy. If it can deliver prosperity, more freedoms, better justice and eventually democratization for all, then it will have achieved its mission. China, in short, is not a threat. It may, however, be an unavoidable partner in the Asia-Pacific region. We are back to the vision of China's future as a great power and related worries about what this all portends.

We have four main visions of China's future (Figure 1.1). Fear of the regime's sudden death is a princeling's argument to secure the status quo by defending it. China's introversion as a weak regional power enables the USA, and the Western powers, to promote democratization there. The view of China's emergence as driven by ambitions draws attention to China's potential and purposes. China's "common marketization" is a pragmatic,

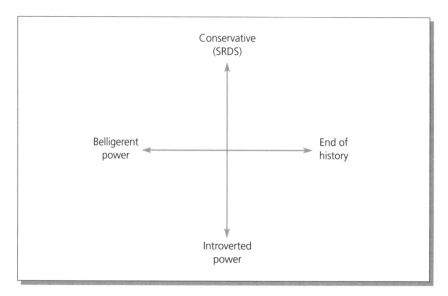

Figure 1.1 ◆ Alternative China futures

managerial strategy to lead the country to prosperity. Its watchword is: we'll deal with that problem when we reach it.

All four visions cast their shadow over China's future. Which vision will prevail? Each of these four visions of China's future adopts the same procedure, which is to pick and mix the evidence to suit the underlying thesis of China (1) as heading for disaster, (2) as a second-rank, medium-size power, (3) as an ever more assertive power with a grudge, or (4) as a cooperative and poor country giving clear priority to its social and economic development. In the following chapters, I argue that Communist China is not dying but is morphing into something else; it gives priority to domestic affairs in order to emerge in the longer term as a pillar of global society. The factor of time is thus crucial to an understanding of China, and of how to operate there. Time is at the heart of China's geopolitics, and of its irreversible inclusion in the global system – the subjects of the next two chapters. For the rest, let's deal with each problem when we reach it.

References

Morton I. Abramowitz, 1997, "China: can we have a policy?", Carnegie Endowment for International Peace, pp. 26–7.

Richard Bernstein and Ross H. Munro, 1998, *The Coming Conflict*, New York, Vintage Books, p. 42.

Sung Ch'iang *et al.*, 1996, Chung-kuo k' o-i-shuo pu, *The China That Can Say No* [in Chinese], Beijing, Chung-hua Kung-shang lien-ho ch'u-pan-she

Thomas J. Christensen and Richard K. Betts, 2000–2001, "China: getting the question right", *National Interest*, 62, pp. 17–29.

FBIS Daily Report, 1995, "Viewing China through a third eye", transl. *FBIS Daily Report, China* (supplement), 19, April.

Francis Fukuyama, 1989, "The end of history", *National Interest*, 89(16), pp. 3–18.

Jack A. Goldstone, 1995, "The coming of Chinese collapse", *Foreign Policy*, 99, pp. 35–54.

Immanuel Hsu, 2000, *The Rise of Modern China*, 6th edn, New York, Oxford University Press.

Samuel P. Huntington, 1993, "The clash of civilisations", *Foreign Affairs*, 72(3), pp. 50–67.

Samuel Kim, 1997, "China as a great power", *Current History*, September, pp. 246–51.

Willy Wo Lap Lam, 1995, *China after Deng Xiaoping*, New York, J. Wiley & Sons, pp. 385–6.

David M. Lampton, 1998, "China: think again", *Foreign Policy*, 98(110), pp. 13–28.

Kishore Mahbubani, 1995, "The Pacific impulse", *Survival*, 37(1), pp. 105–20.

William E. Overholt, 1993, *China: The Next Economic Superpower*, London, Weidenfeld and Nicholson.

Minxin Pei, 1997, "Is China unstable?", *Foreign Policy Research*, 7(8). Foreign Policy Research Institute *WIRE*, July 1999, http://taiwansecurity.org/IS/Pei-990707.htm
People's Daily, 2000, 15 June. "China to become important player in 21st century: Lee Kuan Yew".

Ho Pingti, 1959, *The Population of China*, Cambridge, MA, Harvard University Press, p. 249.

Robert Ross, 1997, "Beijing as a conservative power", *Foreign Affairs*, 76, pp. 33–45.

Stanley Rosen and Gary Zou, 1990–91, "The Chinese debate on the new authoritarianism (1)", *Chinese Sociology and Anthropology*, 23(2), p. 5.

Gerald Segal, 1999, "Does China matter?", *Foreign Affairs*, 78(5), pp. 24–37.

Jonathan Unger and Anita Chan, 1995, "China, corporatism, and the East Asian model", *Australian Journal of Chinese Affairs*, 33, January, pp. 29–53.

Gordon White, 1993, *Riding the Tiger*, Stanford, CA, Stanford University Press, p. 154.

2

China and the USA: ineluctable partners or rivals?

CHINA'S REACTIONS to the devastating September 11 attacks in New York and Washington, DC confirmed the centrality of the USA to China's external relations. On October 8, President Jiang Zemin once again expressed China's desire "to develop exchanges with the United States to ensure peace and stability in the Pacific region and in the rest of the world". China, he went on, offers to be "the partner of the United States in promoting world peace".[1] While the president's rhetoric reflected the regime's concern for status in world affairs, it also endorsed the leadership's view of the USA as an indispensable partner. The lesson being learnt is simple: China has most to gain as a status quo power – one that seeks to come to terms with, rather than to challenge, the reigning distribution of capabilities among states in the world as it is. The paradox is that if this strategy was implemented, then China's successful integration into the world system would transform it. Over time, China realizes its potential as a major world power. This prospect worries China's neighbors and evokes a variety of responses in the USA. One response is to engage with China so as to transform it into a political and business partner for the USA in the longer term. Another is to confront China, by creating a malign environment that undermines its development.

---

[1] www.chinaonline.com, October 8, 2001.

Hence the recurrent swings in US-Chinese relations between mutual efforts to ensure a benign environment for China's transformation, and mutual invective that threatens to invert the Chinese leadership's preferred ordering of its foreign-policy priorities. These run in order of precedence: status, development, security, Taiwan. Over the longer term, China both accommodates to the reality of US supremacy and resists it as best it can. Conditional cooperation with the USA is what China seeks, given that the USA is the unavoidable but not sole partner for states across the region. Nor has China much to gain from pursuing a counterbalancing strategy to US primacy through closer relations with Russia and India. So let's start by looking at how China turned to the USA in the war against Japan and then – as the cold war progressed – against the Soviet Union. The Asia-Pacific region became a US lake. For the foreseeable future, I argue, the USA is the vital partner for China – a crucial point in considering what this means for corporate strategies toward the China market.

War with Japan, civil war and cold war

In China's book, World War II broke out in 1931 when Japan invaded Manchuria. Six years later, in July 1937, Japan launched all-out war in China. Nationalists and Communists, who had been at each other's throats for a decade, made an uneasy truce to form a common front against the enemy. Then in December 1941, the Japanese attacked Pearl Harbor, bringing the USA into China's wars. Relations nonetheless proved difficult. The nationalists expected the USA to deal with Japan, while they were freed to deal with the Communists. The USA by contrast expected that the nationalists would pin down Japanese troops in China, leaving them free to deal with the rest of Asia-Pacific. In addition, US officials voiced their admiration for Communist efficiency over nationalist corruption. Even so, President Roosevelt persisted, against Prime Minister Churchill's urging, to have nationalist China, not India, hold a permanent seat in the UN Security Council. With Japan's defeat in 1945, civil war broke out anew, and ended in the Communists' victory in 1949.

In an essay written that summer, entitled "On the people's democratic dictatorship", Mao spelt out two key ideas. The first idea was to mobilize the masses in "a united front under the leadership of the working class". The second idea, more related to external relations, was to "lean to one side" – the Soviet side – in the cold war. These ideas would serve with decreasing relevance as a guide to policy over the three phases between 1949 and 1992 into which, with the benefit of hindsight, the history of the Republic may be divided.

China, the USA and the Communist bloc

From October 1949 to 1960, China was, in appearance at least, a close Soviet ally. The Sino-Soviet treaty of friendship, alliance and mutual assistance, signed in 1950, included the declaration of a military alliance against Japan and its allies. In response, President Truman's Secretary of State, Dean Acheson, made a statement that seemed to place Taiwan, to which the nationalist forces had retreated, and Korea, outside the USA defense perimeter. Both had been Japanese colonies until the war's end. When North Korea invaded South Korea to end the country's division, Beijing and Moscow were both drawn into the conflict. The USA rode in under the aegis of the UN and, in September 1951, signed a peace and security treaty with Japan. With this, the geostrategic contours of northeast Asia were firmly in place: USA predominance in the Asia-Pacific region has since provided the overarching presence of Asia's security structure.

US military positions in Japan, Korea, the Philippines and then Indochina were bound into America's global network of alliances and military bases. Nationalist China took up China's Security Council seat at the UN, and in 1954 the USA reluctantly agreed to a mutual defense pact with Taiwan. The port of Vladivostok gave the Soviet Union a presence on the Sea of Japan, next to Korea and China's northern provinces. Ever wary of his big neighbor, Mao began to edge China away from close relations with the Soviet Union. The split became an open one in 1960, when the Soviet Union terminated all technical and economic assistance to China. Mao resented Moscow's claim to leadership in the Communist movement, feared its efforts to seek accommodation with the USA, notably over nuclear weapons, and attacked the Soviet Union for reducing support for revolution in developing countries (Griffith, 1964).

China surrounded

The second phase roughly covered the decade of the 1960s, which China initiated by affirming its rights and claims along the Himalayas. China had occupied Tibet in 1950. Frontier agreements were signed with the Nepalese and Afghan monarchies, the socialist regime in Burma, and the Islamic republic in Pakistan. Dispute over borders with India escalated into armed conflict in 1962, when the PLA inflicted severe losses on badly equipped Indian forces. As China's leaders became anxious about the Soviet military build-up along the disputed Sino-Soviet 7000-kilometer frontier, massive military installations were set up in China's western provinces. At the same time, the USA extended military support to the government of South Vietnam. This sucked the two Communist powers as competing rivals into the Indochina war. China refused to adhere to the Nuclear Test Ban Treaty and later the Non-Proliferation Treaty, patronized by the two great powers, and built up a minimal nuclear weapons capability.

However, Mao and other Chinese leaders repeatedly made clear that China would not take the initiative to provoke a war with the USA. As support waxed in the USA to bring home the boys from Vietnam, Chinese enthusiasm waned for US retrenchment from the Asian mainland. A serious Sino-Soviet clash on the Ussuri river in 1969 – the first armed conflict between two nuclear powers – served to underline the danger to China of not leaning to one side. Alliance with the USA in containment of the Soviet Union spelt an

> Alliance with the USA in containment of the Soviet Union spelt an end to Chinese support of revolutions around the world

end to Chinese support of revolutions around the world; in turn, that meant the slow deradicalization of Chinese politics at home.

China's US alliance

China's geopolitical rapprochement with the USA occurred just as traditionally poor Asia-Pacific countries were swept up in the worldwide technological revolution. For Mao, the purpose of closer relations with the USA was to counter Soviet ambitions in Asia, avoid a condominium of the world between the two great powers, pre-empt Soviet nuclear blackmail, and win access to US military technologies. For President Nixon and his foreign-policy adviser, Henry Kissinger, the broad purpose was to redeploy US military power from the Asian mainland to its maritime bases in the Pacific and establish a close working relationship with the Chinese leadership on a common platform of opposition to (Soviet) hegemonism. In October 1971, the USA acquiesced in a UN vote to grant Beijing the China seat at the UN, previously held by the nationalists. Then, in February 1972, both leaders signed the Shanghai Communiqué, which acknowledged "that all Chinese on either side of the Taiwan Strait maintain that there is but one China and that Taiwan is a part of China". The USA also affirmed interest in the "peaceful settlement of the Taiwan question by the Chinese themselves" (see Mann, 1998, for an excellent account). This arrangement articulated relations between the USA and China for the coming decades.

It took until 1978, and Deng's return to power, for the arrangement to take shape. By then, the People's Republic of China (PRC) had built its credentials as a partner on the world stage, having established diplomatic relations with 115 states, belonging to twenty-one international organizations, and participating in seventy-one non-governmental organizations. It was the combination of Deng's economic opening and President Carter's efforts to align with China to curb Soviet expansion that brought about US-Chinese normalization. The USA severed diplomatic ties with the nationalists, but this created a backlash in Congress, which passed the Taiwan Relations Act on April 10, 1979, replacing the 1954 Defense Treaty.

Through subsequent swings in mood, differences in domestic structures between the USA and China were downplayed. The USA won a partner to help contain the Soviet Union around Asia. It was understood that the US would not challenge the Chinese Communist leadership, and that a continued US military presence acted in restraint of Japanese ambitions. China won a US commitment to the one China policy and direct executive-to-executive relations with the top American leaders, largely bypassing Congress. Both sides shared intelligence. The PLA purchased US weapons and technology, and cooperation was intensified on satellite development. The second part of the 1980s was the high point of the relationship. Trade boomed, with the USA becoming one of the leading foreign investors in China. Over 40,000 Chinese students in the 1980s attended US universities. Not least, the relationship helped build China's credentials as a reliable partner on the world stage. China established bilateral diplomatic relations with nearly all states, joined international organizations, applied for membership in the General Agreement on Tariffs and Trade (GATT), became an honorary member of NATO, and signed on to dozens of non-governmental organizations. China's relations with Asia-Pacific neighbors eased.

The events of June 1989 in Tiananmen Square dramatically changed the Western world's view of China. With the collapse of the Soviet Union in 1991, Peking was the one remaining major Communist power in the world. There could be no disguising the fact that Beijing's and Washington's views on politics diverged. If either tried to revive the old executive-to-executive relationship of 1972–89, Congress was there to ensure that China's record on human rights would be constantly aired in public. China was on its own.

China in a unipolar world

Alone, but in a world of states, where states are the prime political units and live in a system of self-help that keeps them divided and forever competing. They ally temporarily if any one threatens to acquire such wealth, power or prestige as to overshadow and even extinguish their own. These alliances tend to form around the great powers, so called because they are distinguished from lesser powers by their capabilities. Relations between the great powers and their alliances describe the global structure, of which there are three known types. The global structure is multipolar when resources

> Alone, but in a world of states, where states are the prime political units and live in a system of self-help

are distributed among a number of key, but unequally endowed, power centers. It may be bipolar, as during the cold war, or it may be unipolar – a world dominated by one power, which serves as a pole of attraction or repulsion to all states (Kapstein and Mastanduno, 1999). The prediction of great power behavior is that changes in the distribution of power resources lead to changes in alignment and sharpened competition for prestige.

For the past thirty years, at least, and as far ahead as the eyes can see, the USA was, is and will be the world's solitary power without equal in the pantheon of powers, and without precedent in the modern era. It was not always so. In the dying years of the cold war, American declinists were in vogue (Kennedy, 1987). They argued that the country was overextended and in retreat as a world power. The US share of world products and world exports, respectively 33% and 17% in 1950, had slipped to 25% and 11% by 1989. The US share of world monetary reserves had fallen from 50% to 9%. Yet, as Table 2.1 indicates, the USA is endowed with both "hard" and "soft" power (Nye, 1991). Hard power refers to the ability to get others to do what they would not otherwise do; soft power refers to the intangible means to influence the world's evolution in a way compatible with US preferences.

Measured in terms of traditional power resources – population and territory – and five measures of economic prowess, the USA has no equal. Decades of heavy investments across the board in new technologies have given the USA a commanding lead in high-tech warfare and in high-tech exports. America's primacy stretches across all measures of economic power resources. After the stellar economic performances of the 1990s, the US shares of world product and exports were up, by 2000, to 30.6% and 13%, respectively, as Table 2.1 shows. Its share of outward foreign investment stock is just one indicator of the range and scope of America's "extraterritorial empire" (Strange, 1988). The dollar reigns supreme. US corporations are prime players in the world energy industry. The USA is the hub of a global network of multilateral and bilateral alliances. Its corporations, universities and research laboratories are prime sites for the discoveries that drive forward the new technologies. The major institutions such as the UN and its family of organizations are imbued, at least by their intellectual origins, with the liberal vision that inspired the foundations of the USA.

Table 2.1 ◆ Shares of traditional power resources

	USA	Russia	Japan	China	India	Brazil	Germany	Britain	France
Population (mn)	282	146	127	1,262	998	170	82	60	59
Territory (x 1000 km²)	9,629	17,075	378	9,598	3,287	8,517	357	243	552
GNP per capita, 2000 ($)	34,100	1,160	35,630	840	450	3,580	25,120	24,430	24,090
GNP, 2000 (% world)	30.6	0.6	14	3.4	1.5	1.9	6.6	4.6	4.5
Manufacturing (% world)	24.7	1.2	16.6	3.4	1.7	2.7	7.8	4.4	4.5
Merchandise exports (%world)	13.0	1.4	8.1	3.0	0.6	0.9	10.3	5.1	5.8
Hi-tech exports (share of OECD)	26.3	–	21.1	–	–	–	16.2	10.7	8.7
FDI outward stock, 1999 (% world)	23.7	–	6.1	0.56	–	0.02	8.8	13.9	6.3
Military expenditure in 2000 ($bn)	294	58	44	41	14.4	17.5	28	36	34

Total FDI stock in 1996 equals 11% world GDP.

Sources: International Bank for Reconstruction and Development, International Institute of Strategic Studies, World Development Report (from the World Bank) and Organization for Economic Cooperation and Development.

By contrast, China is at best a medium-rank power. The country has fourteen neighbors, and its frontiers by land and sea are longer than the earth's circumference. China's national income is slightly larger than Brazil's, but its large population ensures that it ranks 128 on the most favorable measure of income per capita. In military terms, China accounts for 4.5% global defense spending, and a significant 25.8% in East Asia and Australasia. Its exports are three times less than Germany's, and outward foreign direct investment stock is minimal. Its domestic market is small, although it does receive 10% total inward foreign direct investment worldwide. US and EU corporate investment in China is no bigger than their stake in Brazil, and is reputedly less profitable.

> To achieve social and economic development, China needs as peaceful and secure a domestic and global environment as possible

To achieve social and economic development, China needs as peaceful and secure a domestic and global environment as possible. The USA is the best placed nation to offer or obstruct this (Gill, 1999). Forging national cohesion by creating a common national enemy is a clear temptation. As we shall see later, it is also a dead end. So let us ask what China's foreign-policy options are, with a view to showing why China always tends to come out in favor of accommodation with US power. The options involve anxious resistance to the USA, conditional cooperation and countervailing alliances.

No viable alternative to dealing with number one

US strategy is to stay number one for as long as possible. That is the post-cold-war mantra. In a Defense Department planning guidance document issued immediately after the Soviet Union's collapse, US policy is "to prevent any hostile power from dominating a region whose resources would, under consolidated control, be sufficient to generate global power".[2] So the USA must establish "a new order that holds the promise of convincing

---

[2] Defense Planning Guidance, published in abridged form in the *New York Times*, March 8, 1992.

potential competitors that they need not aspire to a greater role or pursue a more aggressive posture to protect their legitimate interests". This means addressing conflicts around the world in such as way as "to promote increasing respect for international law, limit international violence, and encourage the spread of democratic forms of government and open economic systems". Later, as conflicts multiplied in the Balkans and in Asia, Pentagon reports emphasized the need for the USA to "remain engaged in Asia, committed to peace in the region, and dedicated to strengthening alliances and friendships" (Nye, 1995). The primary objective was "to integrate China into the international order". But this view remained contested. One decade after the Soviet Union's collapse, a department strategy review concluded that "a stable and powerful China will be constantly challenging the status quo in East Asia. An unstable and relative[ly] weak China could be dangerous because its leaders might try to bolster their power with foreign military adventurism" (*Washington Post*, 2001; *New York Times*, 2001).

China's strategic community readily recognizes US all-round superiority. But how does this realization interpret into policy? It is one thing to identify the manifestations of US power but quite another to decide what to do about it. One theme running through the varied Chinese responses to US supremacy is an overpowering angst, registered in constant complaints in the press about hegemonism and great power politics as the source of threats to peace and stability.

China's leadership has much to be anxious about. Consider the PLA's condition. Its budget has risen persistently since 1990, but on the Pentagon's estimation the PLA is not thought to be in any condition to conduct an integrated operation against Taiwan in the near future – and that is probably much too favorable a judgment. As much of China's military equipment dates from the 1950s and 1960s, China has bought Russian warplanes, ships and ballistic missiles. This has prompted an upward push in India's and in Taiwan's military spending, without noticeably enhancing the PLA's ability to project power. The PLA's morale is considered poor, its organization is deficient, senior officers have minimal exposure to modern weapons, and the officer class is reported to be riven with party factionalism and family nepotism (Karmel, 2000; Shambaugh, 1999–2000).

Then there have been the stunning US-led military actions in the Gulf, in Kosovo, and then in Afghanistan. The Desert Storm campaign in January 1991 crushed Iraq's armed forces within twenty-four hours, marking the bankruptcy of Soviet military doctrine as inherited from World War II and the overwhelming superiority of Western technology. As a Rand Corporation report states: "The Gulf War demonstrated that the application of high-tech in the military has given weapons an unprecedented degree of precision and power, heightening the suddenness, three-dimensionality, mobility, rapidity and depth of modern warfare" (Burles and Shulsky, 2000). For China, this spelt maximum vulnerability of PLA weapons and the urgent need to review strategic concepts.

NATO's March–June 1999 bombing campaign over Kosovo came as an even greater shock. The NATO forces suffered no combat casualties, and Belgrade capitulated. China, which was not a belligerent, had its Belgrade embassy destroyed on May 8, when cruise missiles thoroughly devastated the building and killed some of the Chinese employees. A frightened Chinese regime released a torrent of anti-US outpourings in the media. One article accused the USA of seeking to become "Lord of the Earth", and compared US aggression in the Balkans to that of Nazi Germany (Reuters, 1999). Beijing could not help but note that a few weeks after the end of the Kosovo bombing, the election of the new President of Taiwan, Chen-Shui-bian, who defeated the ruling party, the KMT, after five decades in power on the island, indicated a further consolidation of the democracy movement in Taiwan and a further postponement of reunification between island and mainland.

NATO's Kosovo campaign hurt in other ways. What was the value of being a member of an exclusive club, with a permanent seat on the UN Security Council, if the NATO allies chose to become the world's police officer without so much as a nod in the direction of the UN? At least the USA had observed diplomatic niceties during the Gulf War in 1991. President George Bush, one of the intimates of the 1972–89 executive-to-executive relations between Beijing and Washington, had taken extensive pains to have China abstain in the UN Security Council vote on taking military action against Iraq (Dreyer, 2000), but in 1999 there were no such niceties. The NATO allies, convinced of the righteousness of their cause, attacked a sovereign country without seeking prior authorization from the UN Security Council. They acted within NATO rights according to the UN Charter, but clearly their claim to have the right to intervene in the internal affairs of states was a doctrine that the Western powers could apply against China over its activities in Tibet or Xinjiang.

The September 11 attacks on New York and Washington, DC, and the US war on terrorism, came as a further shock. Not least of Beijing's concerns was the unpredictability of the US-led war on international terrorism, the duration, scale and scope of the military campaign, and Washington's longer-term intent. What China's leadership sees is a strengthening of the US military presence in Central Asia, alongside the ongoing redeployment of US forces to the Asia-Pacific region. The USA, in short, is preparing to encircle China in order to contain its future expansion as a world power. At the same time, the consolidation of the Russian alliance as the US prime partner on the Euro-Asian continent underscores the attraction felt by Moscow to seek prior accommodation with Washington, rather than join in an alliance of the weak with India and China to counterbalance an over-mighty USA. Japan's initial rush to show solidarity with the USA pointed the same way but was followed by signs of Japanese disquiet at the prospect of worsening relations between the USA and Saudi Arabia, the world's – and Japan's – prime oil well.

China's options, short of cooperation with the USA, all have costs attached and all bring China back to its relationship with the USA. The worst way of containing the USA, the Chinese leadership realizes, is by taking on the USA in a head-to-head competition for technological leadership. That was the way the Soviets went, and little good it did them. Then there is the option of expanding China's own arms sales to enter markets such as Pakistan, Iran, Iraq and North Korea. But the disadvantage there is that much of China's technology comes from the USA. So another option is espionage against the USA by exploiting lax safeguards at US laboratories (Congress, 1999). But this also entails high risks, such as helping to enrage the US Congress. The conclusion is clear: "We must dance with the wolf", President Jiang Zemin asserts (Ching-Sheng, 1999).

That means, in practice, continuing to cooperate in multiple ways with the USA, while standing up to it whenever necessary to calm regime anxieties or to purchase legitimacy in the wider population. Development and modernization come before defiance.

China and Asia-Pacific

China prefers conditional cooperation with the USA across maritime Asia to conflict and confrontation. There is little to be gained, and much to be lost, for China to play the wrecker in the region (for a contrary view, see Kalder, 1996). That is the evidence from China's actions, rather than its words. They betoken the USA as an unavoidable but not sole partner for all states across maritime Asia. It is the relations between the states and peoples of the region, as much as US preference, that keeps the US Gulliver bound down there.

China's lips: the two Koreas and Japan

Consider the case of Japan, the most superficially quiescent of US allies. China's nightmare is of an assertively nationalist Japan. After flirting at the end of the cold war with the idea of a more autonomous strategy, Japan apparently decided to stay with its economic and security dependence on the USA. Japan's prominence in the 1990s as Asia's giant – equivalent to 80% of the Asia-Pacific economy – could be secured only by a true opening of its economy. Only by learning to live, like Edwardian Britain, off its overseas income could Japan hope to become the hub of a commercial, financial and cultural empire. That would mean running permanent trade deficits and having the yen become a reserve currency in the manner of the dollar. The challenge proved too great. Japan failed to make the necessary domestic reforms and opted in 1996–7 to renew the 1951 security arrangements with the USA. With clause IX in the Japanese constitution outlawing war as a tool of policy, the US post-1945 client relationship was a sure way for Japan of keeping Japanese military expenditures down and keeping their neighbors' confidence in the US presence up. China knows that the US presence in Japan constrains any possible Japanese adventurism.

Another area where Beijing and Washington have overlapping but far from concordant interests is in the Korean peninsula. South Korea towers over its northern neighbor and has spun a worldwide web of corporate and state relations. Seoul exchanged ambassadors with Beijing in August 1992 and ended diplomatic relations with Taipei, opening the way for investment in China by the large Korean *chaebol*. By contrast, Pyongyang, the bleak capital of North Korea, has watched its puny economy shrink by two-thirds since 1989. An unquantified number of its citizens – maybe up to three million – have starved to death. Its foreign-policy options dwindled. Two assets remained in its grasp: weapons of mass destruction and its own population. The first, developed with the help of Egyptian, Iranian and then Russian engineers, found their way on to world markets, the second developed into world headlines. When complaints were made, Pyongyang raised the stakes, bargaining food supplies and funds against promises not to develop nuclear capabilities further. Then, in August 1998 – four months after India and Pakistan had exploded their own nuclear devices – North Korea test-fired a Taepo Dong-1 missile over Japan, causing acute anxiety there. The missile turned out to have a third stage, implying that the Taepo Dong had intercontinental range, capable of striking the USA.

This transformed overnight the politics of arms control inherited from the cold war: if such a brutal and decrepit state as North Korea could launch an intercontinental ballistic missile, then the world really was becoming a dangerous place. On the spot, the US administration moved to build national missile defenses (NMD), while Tokyo, Taipei and Seoul considered what to do about theater missile defense (TMD), covering US and allied troops.

China has always regarded Korea as the lips that protect its mouth. Neither Beijing nor Washington want a withdrawal of US troops from South Korea, leaving Japan as the only country remaining in Asia with US troops and bases on its territory. Both cooperate to create an institutional environment facilitating North–South talks. Both work to prevent nuclear proliferation and seek to discourage North Korea's nuclear ambitions, much as Beijing has pledged, in accord with Washington, not to help Pakistan's nuclear program. Both encourage Pyongyang to adopt market reforms, much along the lines of China's experience since 1978. There is, however, a difference in the thrust of US and Chinese policy toward Korea: the USA is more ready to push for collapse, while China prefers evolution. Meanwhile, the paradox is that the status quo in the Korean peninsula that gives them common cause to cooperate hangs on Pyongyang's life expectancy, and on the Nordpolitik of Seoul. If and when Korean unification comes, then the interests of Beijing and Washington, as well as of Russia and Japan, will diverge in that all will be tempted to pull the peninsula into their own sphere of interest. Better for China, then, to work to keep North Korea alive as long as possible than to endanger the broader agenda of US-Chinese relations. Reason of state and humanitarian concerns are not readily reconciled in the affairs of northeast Asia.

China's foreign policy: Taiwan

China, it has been said, has only one foreign policy, and that is Taiwan. It is over Taiwan that US-China relations are most fraught with distrust. Since the Nixon–Mao meeting in 1972, and the Taiwan Relations Act of 1979, US relations with Taiwan and China's relations with both have been predicated on mutual acknowledgment of both Taiwan and the mainland forming one China. Whatever the ambiguities of diplomatic language, this acknowledgment has withstood the tests of time. One such test has been China's concern that US post-cold-war policy has consolidated rather than loosened the bilateral security arrangements between the USA and China's maritime neighbors. US-Japanese security arrangements, for instance, allow for deeper US-Japanese maritime cooperation in the Taiwan Straits, while the US offer of TMD to Taipei and Seoul threatens to cement the US alliance. Yet the fact remains that the mainland is far from having the military clout to take Taiwan by storm, even if such were ever the intention of Beijing.

Given China's military weakness, any change in the nuclear balance in the Asia-Pacific region inevitably affects Chinese-US relations on Taiwan. Japan, Korea and Taiwan are potential nuclear arms states, while India and Pakistan have taken the step to nuclear status. Given such a geopolitical context, it is not surprising that Beijing has been ready to cooperate with

Washington's efforts to promote arms-control regimes and to conduct high-level discussions on regional security (see Table 2.2).

While China, with India, has criticized arms-control regimes in the past as designed to perpetuate the supremacy of the haves over the have-nots, their value to China is to be able to maintain capabilities at minimum cost. China's is a minimal nuclear deterrent, which enables China to sit at the high table as one of the UN Security Council's permanent members – all enjoying nuclear accreditation as symbols of their status. China's deterrent has minimal credibility, being highly vulnerable, based on land, and with only twenty missiles capable of reaching US territory, compared with the US triad of launch vehicles on land, air and sea. In war, China's nuclear capability could be taken out by a lethal US first strike.

Why, then, all the fuss in China about US determination to move ahead with NMD in the wake of the Taepo Dong-1 missile test by North Korea? Here are five explanations in ascending order of importance:

◆ The least significant cause relates to abstract nuclear calculus. Development of NMD, this says, gives the USA a first-strike capability. The USA can strike a devastating blow first from behind a protective missile shield, then dictate conditions. Stated in this way, the US decision to develop missile defense is a bid for global supremacy. In fact, global nuclear affairs are less dire. The science required for NMD is at least a decade away. China's deterrence may have minimal credibility, but that is enough to make any aggressor think before attacking. Equally, the USA already enjoys first-strike capabilities against highly vulnerable China nuclear platforms.

◆ The fuss in China about NMD is to do with the effective death of arms-control regimes. The clothing made of non-proliferation fabric has been rent from the Chinese nuclear emperor's body. But no one has declared the emperor naked. Locals, like South Korea and Japan, know that he becomes irrate when shamed in public. Hence, both South Korea and Japan have not espoused the US proposals for TMD with enthusiasm. Given that Japanese public opinion is restless over the US military presence in the archipelago, and that North–South Korean relations are on the move, questions have been raised about the

Table 2.2 ◆ Chinese participation and positions regarding various arms-control and non-proliferation agreements, organizations and regimes

Agreement, organization or regime	Chinese participation and positions	Date
Anti-Ballistic Missile (ABM) Treaty	Stated support Stated opposition to revision	NA
Anti-personnel landmine (APL) ban	No	NA
ASEAN Regional Forum (ARF)	Yes	1994–present
Biological and Toxin Weapons Convention (BTWC)	Yes	Acceded November 15, 1984
Chemical Weapons Convention (CWC)	Yes	Signed January 13, 1993; ratified April 25, 1997
Committee on the Peaceful Uses of Outer Space (COPUOS)	Yes	Observer 1980; member 1981
Comprehensive Test Ban Treaty (CTBT)	Signed but not ratified	Signed September 24, 1996
Conference on Disarmament (CD)	Yes	1980–present
International Atomic Energy Agency (IAEA)	Member of the IAEA Board of Governors	Applied September 1983; member January 1, 1984
London Convention (on nuclear dumping)	Yes	Adherence took effect February 21, 1994
Non-Proliferation Treaty (NPT)	Yes	Announced intention to sign August 10, 1991; ratified December 29, 1991; acceded March 9, 1992
Organization for the Prohibition of Chemical Weapons (OPCW)	Founding member upon entry into force of CWC (April 29, 1997); member of the Executive Council, elected for two years (1997–9)	April 29, 1997–present
Outer Space Treaty (OST)	Yes	Acceded December 30, 1983
Partial Test Ban Treaty (PTBT)/Limited Test Ban Treaty (LTBT)	No	De facto participation since its last atmospheric test on October 16, 1980
Strategic Arms Reduction Treaties (START) 1&2	Stated support	NA

continuation of the US presence in the northeast Asian region, and about the possible future structure of the region's security. US troops will not engage without nuclear cover, and the USA is going ahead with NMD.

◆ The missile embroglio makes the Chinese Communist emperor vulnerable to militarist demands to invest in armaments, when scarce resources are needed for alternative uses and cooperation with the US provides a cheaper way to maintain security. Arguing the case for compromise with the USA opens the Communist emperor to criticism from regime die-hards that he is prepared to kowtow to US diktats. China, they say, has to develop a broad deterrence capability sufficient for China to say no to the USA. And it has to do so because, sooner or later, the USA will confront China's Communist emperor with a stark choice: go democratic or endure an arms race. The very future of the regime is at stake.

◆ From Beijing's perspective, the US offer of TMD to Seoul, Tokyo and Taiwan already contains all the ingredients of such a threat. If accepted, then the offer cements their alliance behind a US nuclear perimeter and places China on the other side. Taiwan receives further technology transfers that are not available to the mainland. One minor bonus for Beijing is that Seoul or Tokyo operate as moderating influences on US policy in Washington. But they could just as well decide not to sign up to a TMD seen as aimed at China. Worse, Beijing is clearly nervous that TMD strengthens the independence movement in Taiwan, in that the new democracy is a deadly threat not just to mainland China's hopes for reunification but also to the party-state. Despite the fact that no one in Taiwan is prepared to risk declaring independence, especially when the USA has given repeated statements *urbi et orbi* that it opposes such a move, the US offer in effect says to Beijing: look, if you were democratic, we wouldn't be talking about missile defense. You'd be one of us.

◆ TMD is more of a political issue than a military one. TMD casts doubt on China's nuclear capability to cover Taiwan, given that, in theory, Taiwan may be protected by TMD against possible incoming missiles fired from installations in Jiangxi or Fujian provinces just opposite the

Taiwan coastline. China is in favor of the nuclear status quo because: (1) Beijing prefers the ambiguous status quo where China points a nuclear weapon at Taiwan, which in fact is highly vulnerable to US strikes. This preserves some minimal leverage of Beijing over a Taiwan that talks of independence. Here, China's policy priority is economic development, with reunification taking a back seat; (2) China has its own specific reason for opposing NMD or TMD. It would strengthen Taiwan's deterrence capability and thereby undermine further the leverage that Beijing has over Taiwan. Of course, the most devastating of mainland Chinese options – as I suggested to a senior Chinese official – is to hold democratic elections without renouncing the goal of reunification. A democratic mainland government would be in a much more powerful position than a Leninist dictatorship to negotiate with the USA on the political form of China's unity. The official agreed.

Taiwan's democratization may be conceived as a threat to China's strategy of reunification as long as China's leadership is intent on maintaining the party monopoly on power. Hence, the concern in Beijing at the rise of the independence movement in Taiwan, associated with the political fortunes of the Democratic Progressive Party (DPP), and the emergence of other new parties such as the Taiwan Independence Party and the Taiwan Solidarity Union. But by the time that Chen Shui-bian, the DPP candidate, won a plurality of votes in the March 2000 presidential elections, he had moved away from confrontation with the mainland. The official positions of Beijing, Taipei and Washington remain as they have been: a clear preference by all parties, to paraphrase Winston Churchill, for jaw-jaw over war-war.

China's southern sea frontier

If China's neighbors in northeast Asia are an intimidating lot, then it is China that is the intimidator to its south. Since the early 1990s at the latest, the PLA has given priority to the new concept of sea as national territory, *Hai yang guo tu guan* (Kim, 1997). With its 18,000-kilometer coastline, China claims sovereignty over the South China Sea, also claimed by Taiwan, Vietnam, the Philippines, Malaysia and Brunei, as well as 6,000 islands and three million square kilometers of territorial waters. It has grabbed reefs in the Spratly Islands archipelago, and it is rumored to have put down markers for the Natuna gas fields off the coast of Indonesia. At stake are the potential oil and natural gas reserves and the vast fisheries of the region. The result has been predictable: scared neighbors, such as the Philippines and even Vietnam, have turned anew to Washington for help, either to equip their armed forces or to help promote business. Anti-US sentiments inherited from the Vietnam war or, in the case of the Philippines, from US support for the Marcos dictatorship, have been toned down.

> If China's neighbors in northeast Asia are an intimidating lot, then it is China that is the intimidator to its south

As China makes its presence felt increasingly across the southern seas, this pattern is likely to be repeated, as the maritime states beg the USA to stay as the local police officer.

Yet China's maritime assertiveness is also an expression of its growing reliance on imported oil, as it takes its place among the world's powers and seeks to integrate its economy into global markets (see Chapter 3). Japan, Taiwan, Korea and now China look to secure the oil routes around from the Gulf, through the Malacca Straits, the South China Sea, and up towards the Taiwan Straits and the Sea of Japan. All have developed their naval capabilities, and all continue to rely on the predominance of US naval power. Such considerations, combined with their thirst for foreign oil, moderate their maritime behavior.

China has sought to mend relations with neighbors through more active diplomacy in multilateral clubs. For Taiwan, as for China, extending diplomatic relations with neighbors keeps open the door to contacts with the wider world. China's neighbors have been only too ready to reciprocate. As mentioned earlier, South Korea moved quickly to renew diplomatic relations with Beijing in 1992. That summer, the member states of the Association of South East Asian Nations (ASEAN), founded in 1965 to counter Communism, launched the Asian Free Trade Area (AFTA), with a commitment to abolish tariffs and non-tariff barriers by 2008. China, Russia, Japan and the USA were invited. In October, the Emperor Akihito made an unprecedented visit to China, symbolizing Japan's tentative quest for a new foreign policy after the cold war.

Japan, too, seeks to avoid head-to-head trade and business battles with the USA by more active participation in multilateral bodies, such as the Asia Pacific Economic Cooperation (APEC). APEC includes China, Taiwan, Hong Kong and Singapore, and has been used by the USA to endorse WTO-type liberalization policies for financial services and telecommunications. Japan has consistently backed China's accession to the WTO. In 1997, APEC members, including China, signed up to early voluntary sectoral liberalization (EVSL) in areas ranging from chemicals to telecommunications and energy. Although the initiative petered out over US-Japanese differences, it nonetheless gave China a grandstand from which to proclaim its market-opening intent. China's neighbors voice consistent support for its entry to WTO, preferring to get access to its internal markets through multilateral means than to wait at the gate while the big boys from the USA, the EU and Japan help themselves through bilateral market-opening negotiations.

China's neighbors, too, dislike Western human rights lectures as much as dollar dominance. When the incoming Clinton administration in 1993 accused China of human rights abuses, Beijing found allies in Singapore and in Kuala Lumpur against "Western human rights imperialism". What they resented was the West's propensity to preach, but they were also concerned to assert a right to be different. China joined ASEAN as a consultative partner, in order – as the communiqué stated – "to safeguard shared rights and interests of developing countries". As we shall see later, China was negotiating entry to the world trade club as a developing country. With that status went the right to protect national industries. By 1996–8, the USA was shifting away from condemnation of China to engagement – a shift lubricated by an avalanche of Fortune 500 investments into China – while China was downplaying its differences as a developing country. If you want to be treated as an equal by the powers that be, the motto runs, don't ask for special treatment. Do what they do. In other words, adopt free trade first to deal with human rights complaints later.

Just as consistently, China has laid down its claims for primacy in the Asia-Pacific region. This has been enhanced greatly by the return of Hong Kong to Chinese sovereignty in 1997, giving China a de facto clout in international financial diplomacy, which it never previously enjoyed. For instance, China opposed Japan's proposal for an Asian monetary fund to counter currency instability. When the Asian financial storm broke in late 1997, it offered $1 billion to strengthen currency support in the area. In May 2000, China, with Japan, South Korea and ASEAN member states – now numbering ten – set up a currency swap and repurchase system between central banks to reduce the region's vulnerability to shifts in currency valuations on global markets. With Hong Kong's return providing the mainland with its own window over the southern Asia-Pacific region, it is clear that there is no marginalizing China in international diplomacy. In October 2001, Shanghai played host to the twenty heads of state and government of APEC member states, the most important such international gathering ever to be held on Chinese soil.

The China–Russia–India triangle

The alternative to conditional cooperation is counterbalancing US hegemony in a post-cold-war world composed of "one superpower, many strong powers". Since the Soviet Union's collapse, the structure of relationships across the Asia-Pacific region is bipolar, with China as a regional great power and the USA as world power (Ross, 1999). The predicted result is twofold: China seeks wherever possible to find partners to counter US power and influence, and US diplomacy pre-empts such action by making clear to all the risks entailed or the rewards foregone. In China's triangular relations with India and Russia, the latter predominates but does not preclude the former.

Rivals for prestige and development

In Chinese discussions on world politics, the rise of multipolarity, *duojihua*, is the greatest check on the US quest for global hegemony, *baquan*. But Beijing's relations with Moscow and Delhi bear this out only partly. All three have seen their Soviet-based military industries or strategies downgraded by the US-led high-tech revolution in military affairs. All three have felt uneasy at NATO's expansion eastwards, and at NATO's bombing of Serbia without the say-so of the UN Security Council members. All deploy their nuclear status, India being the most recent convert, to augment their standing on the global stage. All oppose NMD for specific reasons. For China, the NMD issue is highly sensitive because it touches on reunification. For Russia, NMD threatens to create an arms race that Russia would lose before its started. India's opposition on NMD is more as a diplomatic card to be played when suitable. Hence their cooperation in matters of prestige is strictly limited. Rivalry and hypersensitivity are much more evident. They are rivals in economic development, with China able to boast the most impressive performance in terms of rankings (see Table 2.2). India's and China's nuclear ambitions feed on inherited mutual distrust, with India's missile range, for instance, covering the whole of China. Their leaders are as easily sleighted as flattered: Beijing was not happy when Pyongyang treated Secretary of State Madeleine Albright with more honor than Chinese Defense Minister Chi Haotian (*Financial Times*, 2000), but there was much pleasure at China's association with the annual world economic summits among the major world economies. All three fall over each other to get invited to Washington DC, or to invite the US president to their own capital. One of the many lessons learnt from September 11 is the eagerness with which all three have trimmed their sails to US winds.

The same ambiguity holds with regard to frontiers and minorities. Withdrawal of Soviet troops from Indochina and Afghanistan brought to an end the Chinese leadership's nightmare of encirclement by an expansionist Soviet Union, and greatly contributed to facilitating both powers' agreement to lower tensions along their 7,000-kilometer border. Russia supports China's case on Taiwan and Tibet in the face of Western pressures, while China backs Russia's case in favor of the war in Chechnya and against NATO's eastward expansion. China and India both seek to reduce their differences over Tibet, while China acts as a moderating force on Pakistan's nuclear ambitions and in its territorial claims on Kashmir. All three powers, furthermore, are concerned, as is Iran, about the explosion of Islamic fundamentalism across Pakistan, Afghanistan and central Asia. All three have their own Muslim communities – in Chechnya, Xinjiang and across India – sensitive to the call for action against atheism. All three are therefore sensitive to

US actions in central Asia and around the Gulf. That is where their material interests are difficult to reconcile, while their occasional aspiration for a countervailing alliance to US primacy founders on a sharp competition for prestige and status in world affairs.

China and the Gulf

A key feature of China's relations with Russia and India is its integration into the global energy system – a matter to be discussed in the next chapter. From the viewpoint of China's geopolitics, the key point regarding energy supplies is that the overwhelming source of China's oil imports is, for the foreseeable future, the Gulf, far and away the world's largest oil and gas reserve. As the USA is the dominant power in the region and controls the sea lanes, China has opportunities to cooperate with US policy when interests converge and challenge them when they diverge.

> China either supports the US position, at the risk of alienating one or other of the local states, or it supports local challengers, at the risk of alienating the USA

In the longer term, as its dependence on oil imports from the region grows, so does China's exposure to political risk. As a senior Chinese petroleum geologist was quoted in the *Straits Times*, (2001), "The Middle East is a powder keg." China faces an awkward dilemma: it either supports the US position there, at the risk of alienating one or other of the local states, or it supports local challengers, at the risk of alienating the USA.

In the first case, supporting the USA in the Gulf can have its rewards. In the glory days of the Reagan years, when the Chinese-US alliance stood firm against Soviet hegemonism, and China seemed bound for market democracy, the USA and China both backed Afghanistan's freedom fighters against the Soviet Union. China helped Pakistan and Iran – both impeccable in their anti-Soviet credentials – in their nuclear industries and supplied weapons to Iraq. Then came the end of the Iran–Iraq war, followed by the Soviet Union's collapse, and then the Gulf war. China's relations with the USA went into deep freeze over Tiananmen. But by adopting a cooperative stance in the UN, where it voted for eleven Security Council resolutions against Iraq, China's diplomacy won concessions from the USA on trade policy. China abstained on Resolution 678, authorizing the forcible expulsion of Iraqi forces from Kuwait, and opposed ideas to overthrow Saddam Hussein. In 1997, China joined France and Russia to soften the UN embargo on Iraq, and gained access to an Iraqi oilfield. But in October of that year, when President Jiang Zemin visited Washington, he pledged not to engage in nuclear cooperation with Iran and also not to support Pakistan's nuclear program. In counterpart, China won renewed nuclear business with the USA and a revival of discussions on WTO entry. After September 11, the USA turned to China as one vital stabilizer and crucial partner in the war on terror across the vast area of Euro-Asia and the Asia-Pacific region.

In the second case, China fears the consequences of the USA losing power in the Gulf. Hence, China's leadership has looked for an alternative source of oil and gas supply in Siberia, the Russian Far East, and central Asia. But efforts at cooperation between China, India and Russia have foundered on the depths of their mutual suspicions: Russia fears Chinese intentions on Siberia and the Russian Far East, where Chinese migration is escalating while Russian demography is in precipitous retreat. When India successfully tested its intercontinental ballistic missile in January 2001, Delhi singled out China as India's main security threat. And that on the final day of a state visit to India by Li Peng, former Prime Minister and key figure in China's Politburo Standing Committee. The measure was not criticized by Washington, more concerned with establishing good relations with India to counterbalance Russia and China. Then came September 11. China, Russia and the central Asian states had all signed the Shanghai accords that summer against Muslim activism in the region, but there was little sign of close cooperation to counterbalance the world's major power once the USA declared its war on international terrorism. Russia and China both jumped at the opportunity to thump their own separatists, in Chechnya and in Xinjiang. Russia gave conditional backing to a US presence in the central Asian republics, while Beijing fretted at the prospect of a permanent US presence in Afghanistan. The fear in Beijing was that the USA might exploit its opportunity to complete China's encirclement in

Asia-Pacific by consolidating its position in Afghanistan, in Central Asia and with Russia.

China's challenge to the USA

In conclusion, wherever China turns, there stands the USA, or the global market with the USA at its center. This is the world that China has to come to terms with. Year by year, China's interdependence deepens. Little is to be gained by confrontation, and the rewards for counterbalancing alliances are remote while the risks of a policy of defiance are great. China offers cooperation, but conditionally in order to preserve distance, extract legitimacy from confrontation, and as part of the policy of status. But cooperation is clearly seen as preferable to conflict and confrontation. The paradox is that to reduce its vulnerability to the global power structure, the regime must accelerate reforms and deepen China's interdependence. A harsher verdict is that the regime must saw off the Marxist-Leninist branch on which it is perched (Segal, 1999).

And there lies the rub. A benign environment, to a considerable extent supplied for the foreseeable future by US global policy, is an indispensable condition for the Chinese leadership's ability to cleave to the ordering of its foreign policy priorities. For if that benign environment is supplied, and the Chinese leadership, through all the dramas and difficulties ahead, manages to transform China along the lines, say, of a greater Singapore (see Box 2.1), then the world's balance of power is forever altered. In other words, the leadership's strategy for China as a status quo power for the foreseeable future holds a revolutionary connotation for the longer term. It is this expectation among neighboring states, and in particular among US proponents of a much less accommodating US policy to China, that colors present attitudes. Better, say the neighbors, to come to terms with the rising giant so as to pile up favors in his metaphorical bank, than to defy him now on the dubious assumption that the USA may be relied upon as an ally. Better, say the US hawks, to challenge the rising giant now by not providing the conditions required by China's leadership to fulfill their longer-term plans.

It is these different timetables in the minds of the Chinese, and much of the US leadership, that ensure that China's central relationship with the US

Box 2.1 The Singapore Model

Singapore, formerly a British naval base, is a city-state of three million people, mainly Chinese, Indians and Malays. They have been ruled since 1959 by one political party, the People's Action Party (PAP), and under the leadership of one man, Lee Kuan Yew. After a bitter internal struggle, the English-educated, more pragmatic wing of the party triumphed over the pro-Communists in 1961 and went on to an unbroken string of electoral victories. The PAP has regularly won 60–70% of the popular vote. In 1963, the Singapore Association of Trade Unions was banned and its leaders arrested as pro-Communist subversives. Lee Kuan Yew was convinced that a city-state without natural resources could not afford the luxury of partisan politics. He acted after 1965, and the split from Malaysia, to crack down on corruption. Singapore is run as a meritocracy in which position is gained by skill, performance and demonstrated loyalty to the leaders and their policies. Successive PAP governments have delivered high growth and a high standard of living, taking the city-state from developing-world to first-world status. Obligatory contributions have kept savings high, while providing funds for rapid development of the infrastructure. Since 1971, the city-state has gone out of its way to attract high-tech investment. Present strategy is to promote Singapore as a knowledge centre. Per capita income is $36,000, placing Singapore number four in the world, about 20% above the very high US average.

as the world's current great power will continue to be divisive in domestic US debates about what constitutes correct China policy. Conversely, the imperative of preserving the Chinese leadership's current order of priorities in policy will require cool heads in Beijing, accompanied by timely concessions to US demands.

Presently, Beijing's legitimacy depends to an extent on anti-US rhetoric, at least domestically. But its legitimacy depends even more on economic development, and that in turn requires cooperation with the USA. The present paradox of China's leadership runs thus: the more China integrates into the global system, the more the existing power structure of the regime is challenged. So the future paradox runs thus: were China's leadership to accelerate the country's democratization in order to ensure a continued favorable US policy stance, this would represent a revolutionary strategy to transform the world's power structure in the longer term. Such a development would require postponing a verdict on whether democratization leads to a more peaceful world. In the meanwhile, let's turn to China's incorporation in the global economic system.

References

Mark Burles and Abram N. Shulsky, 2000, "Patterns in China's use of force: evidence from history and doctrinal writings", Rand Corporation, http://www.rand.org/publications/MR/MR1160/

Yu Ching-Sheng, 1999, "Jiang Zemin repeatedly expounds China's domestic and foreign policies in three internal speeches", *Ching Pao (Hong Kong)*, 264, pp. 24–6 [in FBIS, July 9, 1999].

105th Congress, 2nd Session, House of Representatives, 1999, "The Cox Report. Report of the Select Committee on US National Security and Military/Commercial Concerns with the People's Republic of China", May 25.

June Teufel Dreyer, 2000, "The PLA and the Kosovo conflict", Strategic Studies Institute, http://www.army.mil/usassi/welcom.htm

Financial Times, 2000, November 27.

Bates Gill, 1999, "Limited engagement", *Foreign Affairs*, 78(4), pp. 65–77.

William Griffith, 1964, *The Sino-Soviet Rift*, Cambridge, MA, MIT Press.

Kent Kalder, 1996, "Asia's empty tank", *Foreign Affairs*, 75(2), pp. 55–69.

Ethan B. Kapstein and Michael Mastanduno (eds), 1999, *Unipolar Politics: Realism and State Strategies After the Cold War*, New York, Columbia University Press.

Soloman Karmel, 2000, *China and the People's Liberation Army: Great Power or Struggling Developing State*, London, St Martin's Press.

Paul Kennedy, 1987, *The Rise and Fall of the Great Powers: Economic Change and Military Conflict from 1500 to 2000*, New York, Random House.

Samuel K. Kim, 1997, "China as a great power", *Current History*, September, pp. 246–51.

James Mann, 1998, *About Face: A History of America's Curious Relationship with China, From Nixon to Clinton*, New York, Alfred A. Knopf.

New York Times, 2001, May 17.

Joseph S. Nye, 1991, *Bound to Lead: The Changing Nature of American Power*, New York, Basic Books.

Joseph S. Nye, 1995, "The case for deep engagement", *Foreign Affairs*, 78(54), pp. 90–103.

Reuters, 1999, 'China says US wants to become 'Lord of the Earth' ", June 22, http://taiwansecurity.org/Reu/Reu-990622.htm

Robert S. Ross, 1999, "The geography of the peace", *International Security*, 23(4), pp. 81–118.

Gerald Segal, 1999, "Does China matter?", *Foreign Affairs*, 78(5), pp. 24–37.

David Shambaugh, 1999–2000, "China's military views the world: ambivalent security", *International Security*, 24(3), pp. 52–79.

Straits Times, 2001, "China set to be a bigger player in oil arena", *Straits Times*, February 16.

Washington Post, 2001, March 17, "2025 visions a China bent on Asian dominance", Robert G. Kaiser.

3

The land of the rising dragon: China's economic growth[1]

IF CHINA RUNS SMARTER in the future, it can still catch up with the richer countries. Running smarter means reforming economic structures and systems to fit global markets. Mao's China had run hard to stay very poor. That was the bad news. The good news was, and is, that east Asian countries have demonstrated that better living standards are fast entering the reach of millions of people. The new Asia is going to be driven not by Japan but by China, ruled by a Communist Party with a deservedly radical reputation. The party, after all, is the heir to Mao Zedong, a man with a justifiable claim to being the greatest of all tyrants in the annals of the world. He sought to introduce a socialist utopia to China, to build up its industrial base, to make the country self-sufficient, to prepare it for wars with either or both of the two world powers, to consolidate his political power base, to transform Chinese people, to promote revolution in developing countries, and to abolish class differences. At the end of his life, he admitted that much of his life's activities had been in vain, and that the old China he had sought to drag kicking and screaming into the modern

> The new Asia is going to be driven not by Japan but by China

[1] Stephen Roach, 1998, "Land of the rising dragon", *Financial Times*, March 4.

world was still alive and well. Over a quarter of a century since his death, China's economic performance is feted by unabashed China bulls such as Ken Courtis, vice-chairman of Goldman Sachs, Asia-Pacific, who expresses his approval of China's financial market and corporate reforms in superlatives. China, says the world-renowned, financial dealmaker and European Institute of Business Administration (INSEAD)-trained pundit, is a capitalist El Dorado.

In this chapter, let's set out to answer some questions: what has China's economic performance been, and what is it likely to be? This involves us in tracking Mao Zedong's record and inheritance, and how China has become deeply embedded in the world economic structure. One point worth noting here is that there is no *deus ex machina*, such as the Will of the People or the Class Struggle, which propels the China saga forwards through time. Better policy in China, as elsewhere, is a matter of discretion. In the next chapter, we ask why policy has been such as it has been, and consider the likely future thrust of policy.

Mao's utopian economics

The promise of a socialist world never seemed more probable than in the years following the triumph of Stalin's Red Army in 1945, the defeat of Germany and Japan, the independence of India in 1947, and the entry of the Communists to Beijing in 1949. Nowhere was confidence in the ability of government to set wrongs to right more widespread than where Communist Parties ruled. The prime fact of human history, they had learnt, is ownership and therefore control of the means of production. Hence, class struggles being the engine of history, injustices will be remedied when owners have been expropriated by the masses of people, organized in a political movement. The full program called for the abolition of the market, confiscation of property in the name of the people, and a monopoly of political power for the CCP. Of course, this proved to be a recipe for exclusion from global trading arrangements. Abolition of the market as a decentralized mechanism for the creation and distribution of wealth was simply incompatible with prevalent international ideas about making markets operate in support of broadly shared objectives. Autarky was the consequence, and poverty the result.

The new government in Beijing was particularly eager to set past wrongs to right. First came a harsh assertion of China's sovereignty. Sovereignty was a treasured and tangible acquisition, bought in blood and tragedy after a century marked by internal turmoil, invasion, civil war and inflation. Exercising sovereignty would enable the party-state to establish a command economy along the lines of the Soviet Union, and to reject China's incorporation into world markets, where the capitalist powers called the shots.

For Mao, the lessons of the past were clear: China had to modernize while borrowing and adapting to local circumstances the best of Western science and technology. But China also had to be master in its own house: that meant intrusive Party control over the daily lives of the Chinese people, the elimination of capitalists and landlords at home, and China's withdrawal from world markets. Commercial relations were sustained with the Soviet Union until 1960, when the two Communist giants fell out, while the USA imposed a trade embargo on China that lasted from 1950 to 1971.

Mao ranks with the greatest of utopian tyrants. His was a vision both of a renovated China and of a Communist society peopled by human beings whose natural goodness had been released by discarding their feudal and capitalist chains. All measures were framed in terms of this desired destination. A number of devastating consequences followed as night follows day (Murrell, 1992). The first was for government to Wipe the Slate Clean of inherited social arrangements, which were considered intrinsically worthless precisely because they were old. The second was to have the population collectively make a Great Leap Forward in order to put as much distance as possible between the past and the desired objective. The third was to place trust in theoretical and abstract reasoning as the primary input for the design of society's new arrangements. The fourth was to consider that once policy had been adapted, and changes introduced, they were irreversible. And finally, because utopian thought and action was theoretical by derivation, the prime source of inspiration was the knowledge held by Party theorists and technicians. There was little appreciation in Mao's China that much valuable knowledge was disseminated through Chinese society about how to procede, and even less that once that knowledge was dispersed or destroyed, then the law of unintended consequences was likely to take over.

As Angus Maddison, has argued, Chinese Communism involved risky experimentation on a grand scale (Maddison, 1999). He identifies four major sets of measures that were implemented with a view to interpreting the Communist vision into reality:

◆ The first fundamental change to be introduced was to expropriate landlords, the national bourgeoisie and foreign interests. The aim was to abolish property rights as the definitive feature of a class society, and thereby to enable the Party to expropriate the agricultural surplus and to do away with class enemies. In 1958, all private property disappeared and 123 million peasant households working in cooperatives were dragooned into 26,000 giant people's communes. Private enterprise was then eliminated in the Great Leap Forward, during which up to thirty million people are thought to have lost their lives. In the 1960s, Third Force industries were decentralized in fulfillment of Mao's concerns about the imminence of war. The number of people engaged in retail trades fell to six million.

◆ The second fundamental change was to run a command economy. This meant securing finance for investment through corporate taxation as the prime source of government revenues, and allocating them to industrial purposes through the plan. Consumption was held low, and in 1972 measures were taken to limit family size. The policy of one child per family was really only implemented as of 1978–9. As we shall see, this has had far-reaching effects. In Mao's time, about 50% of people of working age were in the workforce, but rigid control over labor movement – the counterpart to political control and job security – trapped people in low-income employment. Because management faced a soft budget constraint – in other words, they had near automatic access to finance – they tolerated worker absenteeism. A major success, despite the anti-intellectual thrust of the Cultural Revolution, was the sharp improvement in literacy from 20% of the population in 1949 to 60% by the late 1970s, and a rise in life expectancy from 38 to 65 years.

◆ The third fundamental change was to cover the country with a dense
web of regulations. These covered investment funds and physical
inputs, the movement of labor, and fixed prices and wages. The central
planning mechanism was alternately strengthened then weakened as
local self-reliance was encouraged. Welfare provision was delegated to
enterprises that provided housing, education or health services to
employees. By 1978, per capita income had trebled over 1952.
Industry, particularly the heavy sort, overtook agriculture as the prime
sector in terms of aggregate production, and employed over half of the
industrial labor force. The government raised the rate of investment,
but – as in the Soviet Union – resources were used inefficiently.

◆ Foreign trade was a state monopoly, the aim being to make China net
self-sufficient. Such goods as were imported came mainly from other
Communist-ruled countries and were essentially producer goods not
available at home. In the 1960s, as the population continued to grow in
absolute terms and farm output was disrupted, China began to import
grain from Canada and Australia. Foreign direct investment almost
disappeared, and foreign borrowing was held to a minimum. In effect,
China was not quite so isolated as appeared. Relations with the UK were
conducted on a pragmatic basis, so that China could enjoy a substantial
injection of foreign currency earnings from the sizeable trade surplus
with Hong Kong. There were also trade agency connections abroad,
and a high-profile channel for special trade diplomacy. Japan was an
important trade partner.

What was Deng's 1978 economic inheritance from the trials and tribula-
tions of China over the decades following Mao's entry to the Celestial Palace
in Beijing? Firm control over the levers of a command economy had been
the Party's chosen path to China's revival (Lin, 1995).

On the plus side, the centralized system established under Mao had shown
that it could mobilize massive resources, that China had established an independent industrial system and had moved towards food self-sufficiency.
Growth had resumed after the disastrous years of the early part of the century.

On the minus side, the command system had delivered neither control
nor efficiency. When the dynamics of the private sector became too evident,

Mao accelerated the growth of the planned system. When the planned system became too top-heavy, he sought to decentralize it, even to dismantle it. Mao conceded at the end of his life to President Nixon that all he had managed to achieve was to change a few place names in the neighborhood of Beijing (Kissinger, 1979).

In 1978, China was a desperately poor country. Per capita income was 7% of the USA's; 60% of the population survived on less than $1 a day, and international trade at 10% gross domestic product (GDP) was the lowest out of 120 developing countries. What people wanted was better living standards, not great leaps or clean slates.

East Asia's economic miracle

Better living standards were fast entering the reach of millions of people throughout east Asia. Under US protection, states across the Asia-Pacific region pursued variants of a dual strategy: one element was political, relating to the nature and priority of governments; the other informed outward-oriented economic policies.

First and foremost, state facilitation of economic growth was conceived as an anti-Communist strategy (Rustow, 1960). Nowhere more than in the Asia-Pacific region was America's anti-Communist crusade carried into the structure of the allies' domestic politics. Harsh anti-Communist governments laid the foundations for Asia-Pacific's successful authoritarian capitalist states. Preferential access to US aid, markets and know-how was granted for security reasons to the USA's Asian allies and their firms. The 1960s proved to be the crucial decade, as Mao's China blundered from one manmade tragedy to another. The answer to Marxist class war, all Asia-Pacific governments proclaimed in their own way, was modernization. Integration of states into the world economy would bring democratization in the wake of economic development. East Asia's model proved attractive: strong government, a public drive for literacy, support for agriculture, and rapid transition to low rates of population growth, along with prudent fiscal policies, high rates of saving, export-led growth, and openness to inward direct investment. States had to procede by stages, first meeting their peoples' basic needs, and then, once those were satisfied, developing a more sophisticated political system. The more "well-to-do" a nation became, and the larger was its "middle class", the more democratic it was likely to be (Lipset, 1960).

Second, east Asian growth strategy drew on the "flying geese development paradigm" (Akamatsu, 1962), whereby lower-wage countries followed Japan up the value-added chain of production and exports. This model held that leader countries would phase out production in areas of activity where they were losing competitiveness, and replace local production with imports from "followers", which succeeded in building up a competitive industry in that product. Once a product matured on the market, the comparative advantage of producing it would pass to the follower country, while the leader launched into the production and sale of a new product. Applied to east Asia, the model described the shift of labor-intensive production among US electronics firms, followed by Japanese then European corporations to low-cost production platforms. Taiwan, Singapore and Korea in the 1960s, then Malaysia in the 1970s, were swept into the worldwide electronics revolution. China joined in the 1980s and at accelerated pace after 1991 and the Soviet Union's collapse. East Asia's high growth pattern thus charted a shift out of agriculture into export-oriented light industry, driven by technology transfers through direct investment from leading industrial countries.

The result was a leap in human welfare for millions of east Asians. Economic growth drove this transformation. East Asian per capita income grew faster than anywhere else in the world. Life expectancies rose sharply, and income inequalities narrowed – indicating the growth of opportunities for poorer people. This is one significant difference with mainland China's more recent experience. Mainland China also followed east Asia's example as a manufacturing export champion. East Asian countries doubled their export share on world markets as their manufacturing base expanded. In the 1990s, east Asia again led the world, with growth rates twice those in Latin America and the Mideast, and nearly four times those in Africa. The major contrast, though, was between dynamic east Asia and the shrinkage of the Russian Federation at an unprecedented rate of 4.8% per annum (see Table 3.1).

Table 3.1 ◆ GDP growth: China and selected countries, 1980–2000 (%)

	1980–1990	1990–2000
China	10.1	10.3
Other low-income countries	4.4	3.2
India	5.8	6.0
Indonesia	6.1	4.2
South Korea	9.4	5.7
Russian Federation	–	–4.8
East Asia	7.9	7.2
Japan	4.0	1.3
USA	3.0	3.5

Source: China State Statistical Bureau (SSB) and World Bank, 2002.

China's economic performance: 1978–2002

China could climb on board the East Asian economy only by turning its back on Mao. The deed was done at the Third Plenum of the eleventh Chinese Communist Party Congress held in December 1978, where the Party announced its shift away from focus on the class struggle to economic development. Hua Guofeng, Mao's chosen successor, proposed to follow "whatever instructions Chairman Mao has given", to which Deng countered with the slogan "practice is the sole judge of truth". This shift in ideology paved the way for reform, the essence of which was to introduce more market around the plan (Naughton, 1996). Subsequently, China bought into the Asia-Pacific growth package, promoted exports, encouraged inward investment, developed special economic zones, attracted investment, and opened up infrastructure for development.

When China began to open to world markets in 1978, the measures in retrospect were less than bold. Ideologically, they were justified in terms of reversing a "premature attempt at transition to communism" (Qian, 2000): pragmatically, they were founded on a realization that economic success was more urgent for the regime's long-term survival than trying to get the "real world" – that elusive concept of utopian thinkers – to conform to ideology. Conservative empiricism, as we shall examine in the coming chapter, was the way chosen. The results were remarkable: over the next two and a half decades, China's GDP per capita rose at an annual average of 8%, 200 million people were lifted from poverty, and China became the world's second largest economy, overtaking Japan, at least as measured in purchasing power parities (PPP) – exchange rates calculated on a basis to take into account the local prices of goods and services that are not traded internationally. As China prospered, the Soviet Union collapsed.

China's growth was comparable only to Korea's and far exceeded that of other large developing countries, such as India and Indonesia. It accounted for nearly two-thirds of the increase in total income of low-income countries. Equally notable is how wide this growth has been spread across China. When income growth of the thirty provinces is measured over the period 1978–95, China held twenty of the world's fastest growing economies in those years (World Bank, 1997). Even so, China's per capita income in PPP at the end of the period was 11% that of the USA, 14% of Japan's and 20% of Taiwan's. It was still evidently a low-income country with low productivity per head and therefore in a good position to achieve a rapid catch-up. Indeed, its abundant human resources, if deployed well and utilized in an increasingly competitive economy, could continue to drive China's super-growth forwards for decades.

Before we get carried away, we should pause to ask what to think of China's statistics. With a pinch of salt is the straightforward answer. The consensus view is that real growth rates have been considerably below the official rates (Yeh, 2001). As a rule of thumb, observers such as the Asian Development Bank (ADB) deduct two points from China's official growth rates. About 3% may be accounted for by the regular inflow of underemployed rural labor to higher-productivity jobs in towns and cities. Another 3% is accounted for by stockpiles, as much of state enterprise output cannot find a market. Worst of all, the World Bank estimates that the costs of pollution may be as high as 8% of annual national income and output. If all these costs are added together, a negative verdict is that China may have had negative growth since the mid-1980s (World Bank, 1997).

There is no doubt that China has a major pollution problem on its hands, but the improvement in China's use of resources suggests that the pessimistic scenario is considerably exaggerated. What can be retained is the existence of some serious impediments to growth. After all, with such a huge laborforce and pent-up demand, there should hardly be any restraint on the country's growth potential. There are also other contributing reasons for these lower recorded growth rates. One is that China's statistical service had to be almost completely revamped after its near disappearance during the Cultural Revolution. Then there have been problems of incomplete coverage in the small business sector, overreporting of output increases, and underreporting of inflation. Nonetheless, over the 1990s, most prices were freed, allowing for more accurate market-based statistics, which recorded a regular annual decline in growth rates. Over time, China's statistical apparatus is improving.

> There is no doubt that China has a major pollution problem on its hands

China in the global structure

China's interdependence with a US-dominated global structure has, is and will continue to deepen. This process may be traced through changes in structural power, defined by Strange (1994) as "the power to shape and determine the structures of the global political economy within which other states, their political institutions, their economic enterprises, and (not least) their scientists and other professional people have to operate". The US non-territorial empire (of corporate investment, financial institutions, the media, the dollar markets, the military bases, the alliance networks, the oil pipelines) is its epicenter. So let's see how China's 1972 alliance with the USA has blossomed into its Open Door policy, prompted improvements in China's resource allocation, tied its national money and credit system more closely into global financial markets, and made China increasingly dependent on imports of energy resources to keep its economy turning. There is no going back to autarky.

The China trade

One of the major events during the prolonged contest between the USA and the Soviet Union was the opening of US diplomacy to China, confirmed at the February 1972 Mao–Nixon summit. A delayed effect came in

December 1978, when Deng had the Third Plenum of the eleventh Chinese Communist Party Congress condemn Mao's "leftist mistakes" and announced the implementation of his mentor Zhou Enlai's Four Modernizations. Deng needed little convincing that countries open to trade tend to have faster growth rates than those with closed economies. The evidence was all around the Asia-Pacific for those with eyes to see and appreciate. At the time, China's trade was less than 1% GDP, and the trade deficit was widening. Initially, the aim was to increase exports of raw materials, such as coal and oil. Given the very low starting point, exports grew at twice the rates of world trade. Even so, China's per capita export level by the turn of the millennium was still very low at about 13–14% of the world average. Assuming that these rates may be maintained easily – a not unreasonable proposition in view of the fact that over half of China's manufacturing exports, which now account for 90% of the total, are made by efficient foreign investors using cheap mainland labor – China's world export market share could double by 2010–15 to about 6% of the world total. By 2020, China could become one of the world's top three exporters, alongside the USA and the EU and well ahead of Japan. This is why wrapping China into the WTO is so important: China has no experience of being a voluntary and supportive pillar of a global trading system.

> One of the major events during the prolonged contest between the USA and the Soviet Union was the opening of US diplomacy to China

China's trade policy developed very much along the lines of other Asian countries, promoting out and protecting in. Tariffs were lowered over the 1990s; export firms were allowed to keep a proportion of their foreign exchange receipts and to import components for re-export after processing at zero tariffs. The currency was slowly devalued from 1978 to 1994, and the state monopoly on trade was abandoned. Meanwhile, foreign investment rates grew consistently until the boom years of the late 1990s, when inward investment came to account for up to 13% of total investment for one year. Trade policy and inward investment proved highly complementary (Lemoine, 1999). Trade policy encouraged local production for export markets, and foreign investors sought to escape higher wage costs at home. In addition, China rediscovered the benefits to be derived from a long coastline, and deep-water ports that served to link inland and east Asian markets. Given the underdevelopment of its transport infrastructure – China's eight big ports handling 80% of China's seaborne trade were 20% over capacity by the early 1990s – Deng's Open Door strategy created prime incentives for China to bid eagerly for soft loans from the World Bank.

Four special enclaves were set up in 1980 opposite Hong Kong in Guangdong province, and opposite Taiwan in Fujian province. The best known of these special zones was initiated when the PLA Construction Corps erected a barbed-wire fence around Shenzhen village. The aim was to attract investment from ethnic Chinese businesspeople in Hong Kong and in Taiwan by offering to isolate their operations from local mainland Chinese regulations on ownership, tax, labor relations and materials. So successful was the experiment that, in 1984, Deng had similar privileges extended to fourteen coastal cities on the grounds that "we should create several Hong Kongs". The advantages of their coastal infrastructure, proximity to markets and availability of skills was compounded by the business-friendly environment, the dynamic spillover effects on surrounding areas, and the ability to pull in immigrants. Locating these zones on the coast opened up wealth gaps with the internal regions of China, prompting Beijing to extend the privileges to five inland provinces – Anhui, Jiangxi, Hunan, Hubei and Sichuan. The zones provided platforms for the emergence of a mainland Chinese business class. A considerable proportion of investment there originated as funds siphoned offshore from state enterprises, and then recycled via Hong Kong for location in the zones to benefit from the various tax or labor privileges.

The key to China's Open Door policy is Hong Kong, one of the destinations to which Shanghai's business community had fled following the Communists' takeover of the mainland (Sun, 1991). The Chinese provided the low-wage workforce in a free market economy operating under British law and administration. Exports boomed, while the city's importance grew as the mainland's entrepôt and as a center for corporate headquarters and financial services throughout east Asia. Corruption was stamped on, and when the mainland opened up in 1980 Hong Kong's sophisticated mercantile culture seeped into southern China. Rich business houses met powerful mainland political barons: both needed each other, the first to exploit the mainland's near-inexhaustible supply of cheap labor, and the second to secure foreign capital and technology. Shenzhen, in 1978 a rural township of 30,000 inhabitants, grew into a three-million-strong hinterland for Hong Kong industrialists. By the time of Hong Kong's reversion to Chinese sovereignty in 1997, its population of six million in effect supplied China's prime capital market, accounted for about 50% of the mainland's trade with the rest of the world, provided two-thirds of inward investment there, and represented about 25% of China's total gross national product (GNP). State enterprises were lining up to list on the stock market as a stepping stone to their emergence as corporate players on world markets. Hong Kong in short was a gleaming example of what Chinese people could accomplish in a market society under the rule of law. For Beijing, the return of Hong Kong meant an acceleration in the learning process about running a market economy, while keeping Hong Kong citizens' democratic aspirations under wraps.

While trade policy encouraged the processing and export of imported intermediary products, Asian-Pacific firms thundered into China to take advantage of cheaper labor costs and favorable policies. Export industries were promoted through special regimes designed to keep low tariffs on imported components to assembly and re-export. A major stimulus to exports was the provision for export firms to keep a portion of their foreign exchange receipts. Joint ventures between state firms and foreign corporations were encouraged through tax exemptions and export requirements, while the yuan's exchange rate was slowly devalued by 70% between 1980 and 1993. The currency then began to revalue as the inward direct investment boom gathered force in response to Deng's call to his fellow Chinese, and to overseas compatriots, that "to get rich is glorious".

By the turn of the millennium, China had risen up the ranks from number thirty-two world exporter in 1978 to number six worldwide, behind the USA, Germany, Japan, France and Britain but ahead of Canada, Italy, the Netherlands and Hong Kong. Exports grew at double-digit rates, and the structure of exports shifted from half of total exports in the 1980s in primary goods to 90% in manufacturing goods (see Table 3.2).

Table 3.2 ◆ Structure of China's foreign trade (%)

	1985	1990	1995	1997	2000
Exports					
Primary goods	50.6	25.6	14.4	13.1	10.2
Manufactured goods	49.4	74.4	85.6	86.9	89.8
Imports					
Primary goods	12.5	18.5	18.5	20.1	20.7
Manufactured goods	87.5	81.5	81.5	79.9	79.2

Source: *China Statistical Yearbook*, 2000. Compiled by National Bureau of Statistics, People's Republic of China. China Statistics Press, Beijing.

Foreign investors accounted for 40–60% of total exports. One reason for this surge in trade was the growth in the number of trading firms from less than twenty in 1978 to hundreds of thousands. Another was the strategy of Taiwanese, South Korean and Japanese investors who saw the mainland as an assembly platform to supply the rich markets of the West. Trade between the mainland and the home countries remained in balance, while huge surpluses piled up on the export business to the USA and the EU. The immediate result was a statistical skirmish between Beijing and Washington about the real size of the surplus – US statistics recorded trade deficits with China that were twice as large as China counted in its bilateral trade surplus with the USA (Fung *et al.*, 2001).

A more significant consequence of these surpluses with the rich world was that China's credit-worthiness on global capital markets soared as dollar reserves piled up. Because flying-geese investments into lower-value-added assembly in China spelt the displacement of relatively unskilled labor in the USA and the EU, the size of China's trade surpluses with the two trading giants quickly moved up their scale of concerns. Both the USA and the EU moved to bring China into the WTO with a view to encouraging Beijing to accelerate market liberalization. To say the least, China has learnt how to play the modern game of state-corporate diplomacy very quickly.

China's resource allocation

The Open Door policy spelt major changes in economic structure, as the market spread and more and more business activity had to become geared to what customers in China or abroad were ready to buy. Quite simply, opening up the economy meant that resources were used more efficiently. We shall look more closely at demography and agriculture and the state enterprise sector in the next chapter. For the moment, the simple point to record is that labor and capital inputs were used much more efficiently as a result of the Deng reforms, non-state-sector enterprises grew much faster than state enterprises, consumer products became available to widening sections of the population, and China's production system became tied closely into that of the booming Asia-Pacific region. A resolutely civilian bias in production meant that, unlike in the Soviet Union, resources were not skewed to military purposes.

> China has learnt how to play the modern game of state-corporate diplomacy

The conventional technique to account for the sources of growth is to measure the contribution of labor, capital and a residual that indicates a ragbag of factors – called total factor productivity – such as management, the application of technologies or the improved use of resources. For the post-1978 reformers, the results of these studies are relatively favorable. The contribution of labor inputs has tended to increase since the 1978 reforms, indicating that labor markets have become more flexible. About half of China's growth is explained by capital inputs. Indeed, capital inputs have increased, but their productivity has declined and stocks per capita have risen sharply. This is a clear sign that capital has not been used as well as it might have been and that a large amount of output has accumulated unsold in warehouses. Nonetheless, the residual measure – total factor productivity – rose sharply from –0.78% growth rates in the years 1952–78 to +2.23% thereafter (Hu, 2001). What this spells is that resources have been much better used, and that changes in China's corporate structure will enable them to be used much better again in the future.

In the secondary sector, industry by 1999 accounted for 49.3% of the national economy and employed over 23% of the working population (Table 3.3). This is divided into heavy and light industries, the latter being the biggest absorber of labor.

The industrial sector is also segmented statistically into state and non-state sectors, characterized as consisting of town and village enterprises (TVEs), urban collectives, foreign-funded enterprises and privately owned

Table 3.3 ◆ China's industrial structure, 1952–2000 (% GDP)

Industries	1952	1965	1978	1985	1989	1992	1995	1997	2000
Primary	50.50	37.94	28.1	28.35	25.00	21.77	20.51	19.09	15.9
Secondary	20.88	35.09	48.16	43.13	43.13	43.92	48.80	49.99	50.9
Tertiary	28.62	26.97	23.74	28.52	31.95	34.31	30.69	30.93	33.2

Source: China Statistical Yearbook, 2002.

Chinese firms and small business. China has protected its state enterprises, but the source of dynamic growth lies in the non-state sector. State-owned enterprises (SOEs) accounted for 77.6% of industrial output in 1978, but this fell to 26.5% in 1998 (Figure 3.1). The non-state sector (collective and 'other') overtook the state sector in the mid-1990s, accounting for 73.5% of industrial output in 1998. The non-state sector tends to be in the faster-moving consumer goods markets, while the state sector is in heavy industry, utilities, banking and transport. The private sector's share of industrial output – included in other – has risen from next to nothing in 1978 to 16% in 1998, employing 81 million people.

The main point to note here is that this industrial structure in China created highly competitive markets. The non-state sector, tied closely into the

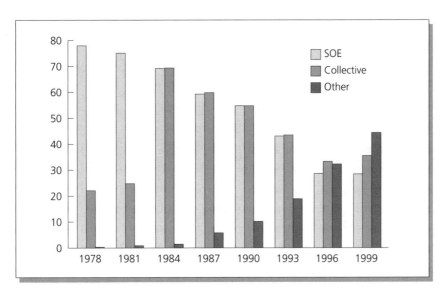

Figure 3.1 ◆ Output of industrial sector by ownership
Source: China Statistical Yearbook, 2000.

metamorphosis of the party-state under Deng, fed on *guanxi*, or relationships between business and political entrepreneurs, but was also subject to
strong competition, hard budget constraints, open markets and low taxation. Deng's careful policy of "feeling the stones as you cross the river"
essentially comes down to this gradualist approach to freeing up the non-
state sector. Here was a crucial difference between China's experience
combining growth and reform and the Soviet Union's experience of having
to introduce reform in a stagnant economy. But the absence of clear property rights has allowed for the emergence of a very uneven playing field, a
crucial matter in the regime's future evolution. The very success of the non-
state (but still Party-related) sector also made ever more urgent an effective
reform of the SOEs.

As Deng was quoted in the *Economic Daily* (1993), "The greatest
achievement that was totally out of our own existence is that rural enterprises have developed." The story of the TVEs 'collectives' in the statistics of
Figure 3.1 opened in July 1979, when the central government allowed
provinces to grant tax holidays to their enterprises and also to enter consumer goods production. The bigger step came in March 1984, when the
former commune and brigade enterprises were renamed TVEs, and business
in the countryside was in effect liberalized. There, numbers shot up from
1.4 million in 1983, to 6.4 million in 1984, to 24.5 million in 1993. As a
result, China accelerated into the reforms, with more goods in the shops,
more jobs being created, and greater incentives for Party members to
become entrepreneurs, in contrast to the Soviet Union where reform was
introduced while the economy stagnated, without adequate provision of
consumer goods, and where most Soviet workers pretended to work and
the state pretended to pay them, as the joke went. When Soviet officials
rushed for the exits from the collapse of the state sector, they became "biz-
nessmen" rather than entrepreneurs.

If TVE expansion was the story of the 1980s, then the growth of the
private sector has been the main feature of China's economy since 1992
(World Bank, 2000). Until then, private business in China developed in a
context of unclear property rights, extensive local government patronage,
and much regulatory and political uncertainty. Deng's call in his southern
tour in 1992 for an acceleration of market-oriented reforms signalled to
entrepreneurs that party-state attitudes to private enterprise were more

welcoming. It was in the course of the 1990s, as the conditions of state enterprises worsened that the party-state converted more completely to the virtues of entrepreneurship. The shift in official attitudes was confirmed at the fifteenth Party Congress held in September 1997, when private enterprise was recognized as an important component of the economy. The forum also emphasized the rule of law and its key role in a modern market economy. Private ownership and the rule of law were incorporated into the Chinese Constitution in March 1999. By the late 1990s, private enterprises were the main source of new employment, were more efficient in the use of resources, and were present in all sectors. The majority are in services. Well over 90% of retail outlets and restaurants are in private hands, as is well over 50% of the wholesale trade.

China and global financial markets

One of the most abundant resources in China is the very high rate of savings, both domestic and foreign. Domestic savings rose from $76 billion in 1978 to $894 billion in 2001, or a rise from 38% savings in a much smaller economy where consumers had little to no choice to a 43% savings rate in an economy over four times the size and with rapidly expanding consumer markets. Households are the prime reason for the increase. Once Chinese ancestral traditions were allowed to flourish, whereby parents worked and saved in memory of past and for the benefit of future generations, family savings soared. The urban population, which is recorded as saving more than the rural population, rose from 196 million people in 1980 to over 400 million at the turn of the millennium, while in the countryside people entered industrial or service sector workplaces where there was no social security coverage of any kind. Over these two decades, inequalities grew: by 2001, 80% of total bank deposits were held in 20% of total accounts (*Washington Post*, 2002). The incentives to save a larger fraction of income proved all the greater. *La Chine profonde* had multiple reasons for thriftiness: the rise in per capita incomes, smaller families, children's education, longer life expectancy, old age, insurance against illness. However, in the future, the population will be aging so saving will decline.

In addition to domestic savings, China receives a large contribution of foreign savings, which come in the form of inward direct investment in plant and equipment. These investments constitute upwards of 70% of inward capital flows, making China the prime developing country destination for foreign direct investment. In turn, this inward flow has deepened China's integration in the production and trade networks of Asia-Pacific. Over the 1990s, mainland China became the single largest recipient of inward investment in the developing world, equivalent to about $250 billion during the decade. Japan, Taiwan, Hong Kong, Singapore and Korea accounted for 70%, the rest coming from the USA and the EU. The largest inward investors were the overseas Chinese. By 2001, the 145,000 foreign invested enterprises were reckoned to account for 10% of the urban workforce, 17% of industrial output, and – variably from one year to the next – 40–50% of annual exports (*Oxford Analytica*, 2001).

Deng's deeper message on foreign direct investment in China was to the Chinese overseas diaspora, the more than fifty million Chinese people who had made their homes anywhere between British Columbia and California to Taiwan, Singapore and Southeast Asia. In Thailand, Malaysia, the Philippines and Indonesia, Chinese businesses are prominent far beyond their numbers. In the Philippines, for instance, the Chinese represent 1% of the population but hold 35% of the sales of domestically owned firms. In Indonesia, ethnic Chinese account for 2% of the population but hold 70% of private capital. In Malaysia, overseas Chinese business is associated closely with Prime Minister Mahathir's power structure. Together, the Chinese diaspora's combined overseas liquid assets in 1990 have been calculated as equivalent to about two-thirds of Japanese bank deposits at the time (*The Economist*, 1992): "Bring your expertise, technologies and savoir faire, Deng told them in so many words, and let us work together to build a modern China, indeed a greater China, rather than continue fighting the civil war from the 1930s and the 1940s."

His call was heard. Of the $250 billion investment flooding into China over the decade of the 1990s, about half came from Taiwan, Singapore and Hong Kong (see Chapter 8). Two-fifths of Taiwan's overseas investment went to the mainland, making it the second source of inward investment after Hong Kong. As the mainland continued to expand through the Asian downturn in 1997–8, its attraction for Taiwanese business grew. To the original reasons for choosing the mainland as an export platform, such as low labor costs, flying-geese investments such as assembly and subcontracting work, or proximity to seaports, came the additional attraction of China's market size: compared with the vulnerable, smaller east Asian economies, China sailed through the east Asian *tsunami* like an unsinkable ocean liner (see Box 3.1). China's reputation as the number-one emerging market destination for investors stood confirmed.

One major attraction for foreign investors is its relative immunity to the swings and roundabouts of global financial markets. China generates its own vast supply of savings and is not dependent on short-term, volatile cap-

Box 3.1 Unsinkable ocean liners

Epic films of China's civil wars, which featured Mao and his chief lieutenants in heroic pose, are no longer popular. Old hands at Beijing film studios, short of government cash, have been working increasingly for Taiwan or Hong Kong money. As Mr Yang, a film technician in China, told me, his fear is that Western films have tremendous appeal for the younger generation. *Titanic*, for instance, appeals for its love story of a penniless artist and an heiress pledged to marry wealth and privilege. The hero, too, dies a hero's death, which is more than can be said about the many who scramble to save their own lives at the expense of others.

ital flows to compensate for the lack of funds at home like nearly all other developing countries. But China's national money and credit system is tied ever more into global financial markets, as shown by the size of cross-border flows: according to the World Bank, the mainland attracts 40% of foreign direct investment flows to developing countries, 10% of bank lending, 10% of portfolio equity flows, and 5% of bond flows (World Bank, 1997). In part, this was encouraged by the opening of a securities market in China in 1991, in Shanghai and Shenzhen. Foreign investors were given access to buy B shares in enterprises seeking to raise capital in the markets. In part, the growth in cross-border flows was driven by state enterprises, which responded to the prospect of heightened competition from inward investors on domestic markets by seeking foreign alliances. They also borrowed heavily from overseas, notably from Korean and Japanese financial institutions. One favourite transaction was for state enterprise managers to stash away funds in Hong Kong banks, or to buy the stocks of Hong Kong corporates with significant mainland assets. The weaknesses of this money and credit system will be discussed in Chapter 7. For the moment, suffice it to say that the 1997–8 Asian financial crisis made them much more visible. Most importantly, it became evident that if overseas investors were to continue to buy into China's economy, then the reform of the whole system would have to proceed apace. Improved business conditions would be vital for the further integration of China's markets with the global system.

China's thirst for energy resources

China is at the early stages of converting from coal to oil or gas for fuel, raising its sensitivity to political conditions in supplier countries and to the urgency of its earning dollars as the world's key commodity currency. The signs were already on the wall that demand was exceeding supply when China's State Planning Commission decided in 1986 that the country must move away from oil self-sufficiency and import foreign oil. Meanwhile, major investments were sunk in exploration in Xinjiang province and offshore in the South China Sea, but with meager results. The International

Energy Agency reckons that China, which now consumes 9% of global energy, will raise its share to 20% by 2010. China, turned a net oil importer in 1993, is the fastest growing importer and by 2010 is expected to import over 50% of its oil (see Table 3.4). By 2020, China may be importing two to three times as much as it produces locally. Up to 90% is expected to come from the Gulf. The same goes for other Asian oil importers, where local oil production has failed to keep pace with demand.

Developing Asia, particularly China, accounts for the overwhelming rise of demand for energy among developing countries. Here are some of the reasons:

Table 3.4 ◆ World oil consumption by region, 1990–2020 (million barrels per day)

Region/country	History			Projections					Average annual percentage change 1996–2020
	1990	1995	1996	2000	2005	2010	2015	2020	
USA[a]	17.0	17.7	18.3	19.5	21.2	22.7	23.7	24.7	1.2
Western Europe	**12.5**	**13.5**	**13.7**	**14.4**	**14.8**	**15.3**	**15.6**	**16.0**	**0.7**
UK	1.8	1.8	1.8	1.9	2.0	2.1	2.1	2.2	0.7
France	1.8	1.9	1.9	2.0	2.1	2.1	2.2	2.2	0.6
Germany	2.7	2.9	2.9	3.0	3.1	3.2	3.3	3.3	0.6
Italy	1.9	2.0	2.1	2.1	2.3	2.5	2.6	2.8	1.2
Japan	5.1	5.7	5.9	5.6	5.7	6.0	6.3	6.6	0.5
Former Soviet Union	8.4	4.6	4.4	4.4	4.5	4.7	4.9	5.2	0.7
China	**2.3**	**3.3**	**3.5**	**4.6**	**5.0**	**6.4**	**8.1**	**8.8**	**3.8**
India	1.2	1.6	1.7	1.9	2.6	3.1	3.5	4.1	3.8
South Korea	1.0	2.0	2.2	2.1	2.8	3.4	4.0	4.7	3.3
Brazil	1.3	1.5	1.5	1.6	1.9	2.3	2.8	3.4	3.4
Total developing	**17.0**	**22.2**	**23.1**	**26.2**	**31.4**	**37.0**	**42.9**	**48.7**	**3.2**
Total world	**66.0**	**69.9**	**71.5**	**77.1**	**84.8**	**93.5**	**101.8**	**110.1**	**1.8**

[a] Includes the fifty states and the District of Columbia. US territories in Australasia are included.

Totals may not equal sum of components due to independent rounding.

Sources: **History**: Energy Information Administration (EIA), 1998, *International Energy Annual 1996*, DOE/EIA-0219(96), Washington, DC.

Projections: EIA, *Annual Energy Outlook 1999*, 1998, DOE/EIA-0383(99) Washington, DC.

◆ China's demand for oil, 25% of total demand for energy, is driven by high rates of industrial production, the automotive revolution, the surge in air travel, and complex pricing controls that lock in end-users. Like India, Indonesia, Korea and Thailand, energy use is inefficient relative to industrialized countries (Ishiguro and Akiyama, 1995).

◆ Natural gas is just over 2% of total demand but is planned to rise rapidly. Its advantage is that gas is a clean fuel, it is needed as industrial feedstock, and it lies in vast quantities under the top soil of Siberia (eight fields in western Siberia alone) and in the central Asian states.

◆ Over three-quarters of China's energy consumption is provided by domestic coal supplies, of which China has 11% of global reserves. Much of this is of low quality, dangerous to mine, highly sulphuric, and very polluting. If China were to industrialize on the back of its brown coal, it would asphyxiate.

◆ China's energy policy is influenced by Japan's focus on security of supply. Development of national resources, maintenance of fuel stocks, and government-to-government deals come before considerations of price. China's leaders swing between emphasizing the need for security of supplies and the urgency of choosing the most cost-efficient energy.

◆ Such policies have a number of attributes: they invite huge investments in mammoth projects, such as the Three Gorges Dam project to harness the waters of the mighty Yangtse river; they are dangerous in that they promote the diffusion of nuclear capabilities as is now happening around Asia; and they flourish on government-to-government deals between consumer and supplier states.

In China, the two instruments of state policy are China National Petroleum Corporation (CNPC) and PetroChina, which spearhead efforts to source for oil and gas around the world. With encouragement from Japan and Mideastern states, CNPC has diversified into overseas purchases of fields.

As mentioned already, the overwhelming source of China's oil imports is for the foreseeable future from the Gulf, far and away the world's largest oil and gas reserve. But the whole region is a political powder keg and creates major difficulties for Chinese diplomacy: should China continue to tilt to support of the US position there, or should China put its weight behind backing local interests hostile to the USA? The most urgent requirement being security of oil supplies, China's leadership looks for an alternative source of oil and gas supply in Siberia, the Russian Far East and central Asia. Russia needs the exports, US influence is minimized, and China is thirsty for oil and gas. Russia and central Asia have huge reserves. In addition, there are distinct advantages for China: despite central Asian wariness about China's intent, China has signed border pacts with Russia, Kazakhstan and Kyrgyzstan, but not with Tajikistan. Kazakhstan is the key state in terms of location and reserves. In 1997, CNPC purchased a 60% stake in Kazakhstan's Aktobemunaigaz; and in September, then Premier Li Peng signed $9.5 billion contracts for the oilfields in western and northern Kazakhstan, and to help fund pipelines through to China and Iran. Chinese trade with Russia, now only 2% of total trade, would rise as the Russian, Siberian and central Asian network of pipelines was extended to reach China.

> Should China continue to tilt to support of the US position there, or should China put its weight behind backing local interests hostile to the USA?

For all the geopolitical excitement about a continental energy strategy to reduce overdependence on the Gulf, there are considerable problems involved. One is that Russia's oil and gas industry is in a poor state, oil wells in Siberia are depleted, and reserves are expensive to exploit on account of Siberia's climate and terrain. Another problem is the financial cost of extending pipelines across China and investing in exploration and development across such a huge area. Indeed, CNPC had to turn to the world financial markets for funds and therefore fell under critical scrutiny of financial analysts: without the backing of the Western oil companies, it is doubtful that CNPC's flotation would have been picked up by investors. In other words, the other dimension of energy strategy to security is price, and there is a strict limit as to how much China can afford to pay for the energy it consumes. Were China's leadership relaxed about the country's deepening integration in the global system, then they might bring themselves to recognize that their dilemma is self-imposed.

Let us imagine China's emergence in the coming decades as a market at least the size of that of the USA. Whatever problems China faces as it becomes ever more dependent on world markets, there can be little doubt that its energy markets will be too big to ignore. And as global energy markets are more efficient than ever, they will be able to ensure secure supplies at the best price available. Oilmen everywhere will want to be in China. The fact is that China's leadership is not relaxed about China's integration into the global system and is not yet prepared to trust the country's future energy supply to an impersonal world market. The players, like BP, Shell, Texaco, Elf and Petrobas, and their own new champions, are all too visible, too impressive, for the leadership to believe that these corporations are driven by price competition alone.

In short, just as there is no exit for China from the global system, so there is no going back for China as a member of the global economy. The Communist party-state is in charge, but it has little option other than to supervise the country's transformation to a market society. China's deep embedding in the global economic structure has fundamentally altered the balance in China between authorities and markets. The driving forces behind this process will continue to operate, such as the innate animal spirits of the Chinese and foreign business community, the hard work of the Chinese people, the growing flexibility of the economy, and the opening of the economy on to world markets.

China is poised for a very long period of growth. China's low per capita income means there is enormous potential for catch-up, albeit at a slowing pace over the following three decades. High savings rates will tend to fall off as the population ages, and return on capital will tend to show decreasing returns. But the Chinese economy is likely to wing along on an abundant supply of labor, its continued attractiveness as a venue for foreign investors, and the development of its service sector. Wages are likely to stay low as far as the eye can see, making China a favored destination for assembly and subcontracting work. As China joins the WTO, east Asian countries will find that the competitive pull of China on foreign investors obliges them to accelerate their own market-friendly reforms. Failure to do so could have dire consequences, as we shall see, for their future evolution, and for the stability of east Asia.

Much conventional wisdom holds that China will overtake the USA as world number-one economy anywhere between 2006 and 2025, depending on the mix of assumptions made. This, in my judgment, is very unlikely. Such expectations are built on the wobbly statistical foundation of purchasing power parities: the world in effect trades in real, current greenbacks. Using current dollars at 1990 prices, catch-up time for China arrives around 2040–60. That is all the more credible because what happens in the future depends in large part on the direction taken by economic policy reform, and intimately linked with that is China's political development. Richer, better educated Chinese people will not always tolerate unelected officials telling them what they should or should not do. China's domestic transition holds the clue to China's future position in the WTO. These are the subjects of the following three chapters, starting with economic policy reform, moving to China's political underdevelopment, and finishing with WTO membership.

References

K. Akamatsu, 1962, "A historical pattern of economic growth in developing countries", *The Developing Economies*, 1(1), pp. 3–25.

Economic Daily, 1993, June 13.

The Economist, 1992, "The Overseas Chinese", *The Economist*, July 18.

K.C. Fung, Lawrence J. Lau and Joseph S. Lee, 2001, *US Direct Investment in China*, Washington, DC, American Enterprise Institute for Public Policy Research.

Anhang Hu, 2001, *The Chinese Economy in Prospect*, Santa Monica, CA, Rand Corporation, p. 106.

International Bank for Reconstruction and Development, 1997, "China engaged" in *China 2020: Integration with the Global Economy*, Washington, DC, World Bank.

Masayasu Ishiguro and Takamasa Akiyama, 1995, "Energy demand in 5 major Asian developing countries: structure and prospects", World Bank Discussion Papers, no. 277, Washington, DC.

Henry Kissinger, 1979, *White House Years*, Boston, MA, Little Brown.

Françoise Lemoine, 1999, "Les délocalisations au coeur de l'expansion du commerce extérieur chinois", *Economie et Statistique*, 6/7(326–327), pp. 53–70.

Cyril Z. Lin, 1995, "The assessment: Chinese economic reform in retrospect and prospect", *Oxford Review of Economic Policy*, 11(4), pp. 1–24.

Angus Maddison, Chinese Economic Performance in the Long Run, Paris OECD, 1999.

Seymour Martin Lipset, 1960, *Political Man*, London, Doubleday.

Peter Murrell, 1992, "Conservative political philosophy and the strategy of economic transition", *Eastern European Politics and Societies*, 6(1), pp. 3–16.

Barry Naughton, 1996, *Growing out of the Plan: Chinese Economic Reform, 1978–1993*, Cambridge, Cambridge University Press.

Oxford Analytica, 2001, "China: foreign investment", *Oxford Analytica*, February 5.

Yingyi Qian, 2000, "The process of China's market transition (1978–98): the evolutionary, historical and comparative perspectives", *Journal of Institutional and Theoretical Economics*, 156(1), pp. 151–71.

Walt Rustow, 1960, *The Stage of Economic Growth: A Non-Communist Manifesto*, London, Cambridge University Press.

Susan Strange, 1988, *States and Markets*, London, Pinter, pp. 24–5.

Yun-Wing Sun, 1991, *The China-Hong Kong Connection: the Key to China's Open Door Policy*, Cambridge, Cambridge University Press.

Washington Post, 2002, "In China, the rich seek to become the 'big rich' ", *Washington Post*, March 17.

World Bank, 1997, *China 2020*, Washington, DC, World Bank, p. 3.

World Bank, 2000, *China's Emerging Private Enterprises: Prospects for the New Century*, International Finance Corporation.

K.C. Yeh, 2001, "China's economic growth: recent trends and prospects", in Shuxun Chen and Charles Wolf, *China, the United States, and the Global Economy*, Santa Monica, CA, Rand Corporation.

4

Riding the tiger: China's economic policy reform

EMPIRICISM HAS BEEN CHINA'S method of exiting from the command economy. "It doesn't matter", Deng famously stated in 1962, "whether a cat is black or white as long as it catches mice." Preconceived ideas are out and pragmatism is in. This has translated into the party-state demonstrating a commendable capacity to deal with the unintended consequences of its own actions. By contrast to Russia, China's reform has been managed well. Whereas Russia wallowed in stagnation over most of the 1990s, China's economy has gone from strength to strength. Yet Russia is at least a semidemocratic polity, a step that China's leadership has yet to take (Buruma, 2001). Failure to take it could destroy the prospect, now open to China, of re-establishing its

> The CCP has gone about as far as it possibly can in economic reform without bolder political reforms

central place in world markets. As the Chinese saying goes, once you're on a tiger, it is hard to get off (*qi hu nanxia*). Clearly, the CCP prefers to keep riding to running the risk of ending up in the tiger's abdomen. So let's start by specifying how a market-opening exercise in a socialist command economy leads rather quickly into the initial stages of regime change. We can then introduce a comparison of the transformation in economic policy between China and Russia. The takeaway is that the CCP has gone about as far as it possibly can in economic reform without bolder political reforms – the subject of the following chapter.

The process of changing regime

As Vaclav Klaus, the former Czech prime minister, has said, all transformation processes are multidimensional (Naughton, 1995). This is particularly so of the transformation out of a socialist command economy, whose original creation has entailed the destruction of capitalist economic institutions, the adaptation of command economies to local conditions, and the creation of socialist institutions. Exit from socialist command economies requires no less destructive, adaptative and creative activity. But there is one major difference: entry to a command economy requires destruction of the trust upon which market exchanges depend, whereas exit into a market economy requires the construction of trust between public official and market agent and between market agents. Destruction of trust is an exercise in ham-handed brutality; the construction of trust requires sensitive cultivation, especially – as in the case of China – when trust is a very scarce commodity, in view of the fact that many marketeers are Communist Party officials.

Now let's assume that our story of China's transformation begins at year zero and moves towards some time in the future. This point in the future we shall label convergence, because the way the story is going to be told is biased towards demonstrating that the process of transformation from a command economy leads to convergence of Chinese norms, rules and institutions on those of the developed world. The flaws in this functionalist story are self-evident: all participants have to be agreed on how to interpret market signals, on the procedures to follow, and on the ultimate objectives. This is a very bold assumption to make. At each one of the decision points along the path, people have a quiverful of choices, which they select for a host of reasons related to their understanding of their own situation, their desires, their loves and their hates. Real-world participants are made of blood, prejudice and passion, by contrast to the bloodless calculating machines in our stylized story.

Given our predictable calculating machines, once launched the process of China's transformation takes on its own dynamics. Chen Yun, one of Deng's rivals in the 1980s, expressed a similar view with his "bird-cage economy" theory, whereby the cage of state planning has to control the bird of free market forces. "The bird", his policy aphorism ran, "should fly but only within the cage: without a cage it will fly away." His preference was for keeping the bird firmly regulated, controlled, supervised. The nuance in Chen Yun's expression is its emphasis on the importance of political discretion: birds are freed only because the owner opens the cage.

There are two variations on what force drives the transformation from command to market economy: one comes from below, the other from above. If we trace the origins of the transformation from below, we focus our attention on the discontented in society, how organized they are, what their appeal may be, and the capacity of the state to crush, concede to, or convert them. When we focus on reform from above, we assume that reform ushers forth from the brow of public officials, as it were, by rational choice; we take for granted that the state can implement its policy. In both cases, the political authority of the state, and its financial and administrative capability, is the key to success or failure.

Top down is where we can begin. Exit from the command economy is generally segmented into four related parts: liberalization, stabilization, privatization and democratization. This is where regime change comes on stage. China's is a party-state, the essence of which is to claim a monopoly over political power, economic resources and the truth. Traditionally, Communist Parties take over the state by force or ruse, crush all opposition, rule in the name of the masses, and mobilize public enthusiasm for its projects. As we recalled in the previous chapter, they soon get round to abolishing private property, an independent judiciary, and the open market for goods and services. Communist revolution is "a sweeping, fundamental change in political organisation, social structure, economic property control and the predominant myth of social order, thus indicating a major break in the continuity of development" (Neumann, 1949). The agent for this transformation is an autonomous state: change in the economy comes as a consequence of its autonomy.

If fundamental, systemic change is the way into revolution, then regime change is the way out. Regime change implies a substitution of the old for new norms, rules and institutions. The problem is that the state is captured by the economy it has taken over. The center has to strive to re-acquire the autonomy it forewent, and to unravel the multiple bonds that tie it down. Separating politics, law, markets, business and society – all fused under socialism – becomes a prime consideration for public officials. This has two consequences: first is the struggle over sequencing – what priority between stabilization, liberalization, privatization or democratization? Second is the struggle over control of the agenda and its content. The advantage lies with public officials, who enjoy a vast domain of policy resources to liberate in the future precisely because the state is engaged so deeply in the whole procedure of resource allocation. Public officials can choose when, how and under what conditions to relinquish controls or to build up a new resource base.

> There is always the prospect that the state loses control over the agenda and is overwhelmed by the process that it has initiated

With such resources at its disposal, the state can retain mastery over the process of controlled opening for an indefinite period. But mastery is managed, not inherited. There is always the prospect that the state loses control over the agenda and is overwhelmed by the process that it has initiated.

Chinese and Russian exits from socialist planning

Let us introduce our matrix, which serves as a prop to chart our way through the maze of factors that we have to consider (see Figure 4.1). Our date is 1978, when China's command economy starts to become something noticeably different but genetically identifiable. We can then run briefly through the dates in the chart to remind ourselves of key moments in both the Chinese and Russian exits from a command economy. Our focus here is the horizontal axis labelled market-corporate; the next chapter will concentrate on the vertical axis, charting a state-administration path from dictatorship to consolidated democracy.

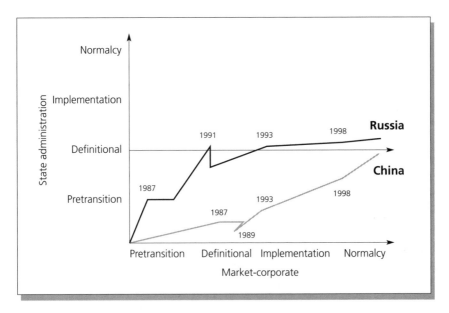

Figure 4.1 ◆ The Chinese and Russian transformation paths
Source: adapted from Tsuyoshi Hasegawa, 1992

The matrix of economic and political transformation

As a way of introduction, let us define some terms that may serve as guide-posts to help us think about sequencing in the transformation process. *Ex post*, we can study historical examples and compare them by dividing them into broad phases and listing some of the regularities that tend to occur over the whole cycle as a state or a market system transforms from one system to another. That path may be presented in the form of a circle or illustrated in a straight line, as in our matrix, that starts at point zero and tends in the market-corporate or the state-administration direction. If it takes the shape of a circle – as Chinese historiography has interpreted the rise and fall of dynasties – then the phase labelled "normalcy" fades into a pretransition story; if it is presented as a straight line, then the challenge for the powers that be is to preserve this happy condition labelled "normalcy" for as long as possible. We should beware, though, that, whether as circle or line, dividing time into phases is only a device to help us chart China's path into the future. It should not be allowed to trap us into forgetting our arbitrary division of time into segments, our assumption that the tasks are manageable, and that the destination is a Chinese "economic society" – a term yet to be defined.

The pretransition phase

First comes the pretransition phase, of indefinite duration depending on the circumstances. The proximate condition for breakdown of the old order is that the incumbent power is unable to resolve a growing list of problems. Consider the late-eighteenth-century Qing dynasty. China's troubles are often dated from the late eighteenth century, when a sharp rise in population prompted land hunger, serious disturbances, and a sharp decline in morale at the court. The Qing dynasty failed to adapt to the external challenge as Western merchants and missionaries tested the restrictions placed on them by the imperial authority. Over the coming century until the collapse of the empire in 1911, China experienced wars, famine, disorders, economic stagnation and social dislocations on a vast scale. Broadly speaking, two contending parties emerged, those traditionalists who defended the idea that Chinese civilization had to be preserved, and reformers who proposed that to survive China had to adopt the best technologies – political, legal or industrial – that the West had to offer. In the language of regime change, two contending coalitions formed, led initially by hardliners in the regime against any change and softliners who argued the case for a dialog with moderate opponents (O'Donnell and Schmitter, 1986). They deploy exclusive symbols and appeal to different mobilized factions within or outside of the regime.

The hour of decision

The hour of decision strikes as we move away from the pretransition phase and a new leadership takes over from the old. The Qing dynasty's fall, for instance, began when revolutionaries accidentally exploded a bomb in the Russian concession in Hankou, one of three cities in Wuhan. The police discovered the names of the agitators, soldiers mutinied, the governor and his family were slain, and loyalist troops were defeated in December in Nanjing, the nation's capital in the fourteenth century. By January 1912, Sun Yat Sen, the founder of modern China, became provisional president of the Chinese Republic. A similar moment of decision struck in December 1978, when the Third Plenum of the eleventh Chinese Communist Party Congress announced the shift in party focus from class struggle to economic development. Hua Guofeng, Mao's chosen successor, insisted that "whatever instructions Chairman Mao has given, we all follow". Deng countered with the slogan "practice is the sole judge of truth". The shift in ideology paved the way for Deng's market-oriented reforms.

The definitional phase

The definitional phase is characterized by a struggle between contending parties over the norms of the new regime. Leaders distance themselves from, or cling to, previous policy paradigms. Reformers may conceal their ultimate objective, which is to transform the inherited regime into a different entity. Whether policy proposals for reform succeed or fail depends much on the weight of the constituencies that reformers can win over in support of their cause. Any one set of proposals is not doomed a priori to meet insuperable resistance. If it fails, then the way is open for a reign of the radicals, and the transition moves away from regime change to revolution, where the definition of norms becomes the main dividing line between the contending camps. The outcome is determined by the fortunes of war. All participants are aware that such a development is ever present, and may be expected to go some way to sacrificing the purity of their own convictions in the interests of achieving a liveable consensus. The propensity for caution is going to be particularly marked where memories of disaster and tragedy are fresh. Hence, the definition of norms is a central stake in the reform process: winning the high ground in the intellectual battle for ideas is essential to the new governors' ability to shape specific policies. Every step along the way has to be negotiated with discrete policy communities of interests, composed of incumbents from the old regime and interests that have been recent entrants to the policy arena. Just as the final form that norms take is a result of negotiations between interested parties, so are the rules and their implementation.

This is because the leadership has to feel its way to establishing the boundaries separating permissible behavior and dissent, where bargaining and concessions become routine. Consider, for instance, the Chinese party-state's definition of what it was up to in economic policy during the decade of the 1980s: China was "a commodity economic structure integrating a planned economy with market regulation". Not very helpful as a definition for China's negotiators seeking entry to world trade talks (Yongtu, 2000), but definitely helpful in establishing some common ground between Party reformers and Party conservatives over the central issue of what policy to adopt to state enterprises.

This definitional phase is particularly delicate because uncertainty is rife about the sustainability of what all know to be an interim situation, and because there is an inrush of new participant groups to the arena of public policy (Shain and Linz, 1995). Where the boundaries of the permissible are located remains a matter of discretion, explored tentatively only by risk-takers. Both reform path and boundaries depend on the predispositions of the leaders, the calculation they make about the future payoffs of concessions or suppression, and the balance of forces. It also depends on the participants' relation to the past, whereby participants in the policy process will seek to retain certain reserve domains for the future (in the police, armed forces or state enterprises), and whether the eventual winners show moderation towards their former rivals at the expense of sacrificing the expectations of their more militant followers. In the case of the Chinese party-state, the boundaries of the permissible became very clear following the crackdown of June 1989: the party tolerates no threat to its hegemony. But, as we shall argue, it is a political hegemony that is shrinking as China's natural pluralism is emerging fast.

Implementing the new norms

The third phase overlaps in reality with the second in that norms become accepted, the central task is more one of interpreting the norms as rules and implementing the rules. Public policy moves into more pragmatic channels. The excitement of negotiating the new settlement abates. Compromisers and trimmers are in the ascendant, and the regime's personnel becomes a mixture of relics from the old regime, erstwhile radicals, and technocrats.

One of the features of such a stylized phase is that populations that have experienced revolution and disaster in a recent past may not like the regime, but they most likely prefer to live with the devils they know rather than risk another disaster on the promises of devils they do not know. Both the regime reformers and the population know all too well that the silken threads of habit and tradition have been broken in the revolution and have to be revived in novel form. For this, acceptance of the iron chains of dictatorship may be the price people are more than ready to pay – on condition that the regime delivers stability and economic improvement for a large majority (Brinton, 1965). The public's skeptical attitudes to the regime complement the focus of regime reformers on implementing detailed policy rules for such central functions as the financial system, labor markets, accountancy practice and bankruptcy. In effect, the recently agreed settlement becomes "the only game in town" (Schedler, 1998).

Bedding down into standard operating procedures

The third phase then fades into a fourth phase, when the regime becomes established in its new format. For a market-opening regime, such as China's, achieving such a condition entails importing methods of governance from developed countries and adapting them to local conditions. To use an analogy, there is no need to reinvent the legislative wheel after it has been discovered elsewhere. In addition, there is the cost attached to delay in clinging to failed policy formulas; intelligent reformers aim not to store up problems for the future, but rather to create a functioning market economy as soon as possible. The long-term goals of institutional change are clear and are found in the economic models of existing market-based economies, where public officials can define policies independent of lobbies, markets once again operate, private property rights are entrenched, the judiciary is independent of political authority, and the population has acquired a trust in the workings of the polity. We are in *economic society*, one of the five conditions for a consolidated democratic state, the other four being a vibrant civil society, the rule of law, legitimate political procedures, and a viable state bureaucracy (Linz and Stepan, 1996). Economic society constitutes "a set of socio-politically crafted and socio-politically accepted norms, institutions, and regulations" that mediate between state and market. Relative to the state, market agents have to enjoy a degree of autonomy and ownership rights to be able to produce a lively civil society, while market agents need an effective state to elaborate norms, promote institutions, and enforce rules. The existence of a lively civil society is a sure sign that individuals do not stand against an all- powerful state but can pursue all types of varied associative activities.

Anywhere along this path, breakdown and disaster is a present prospect. This is especially the case in China, where the regime is introducing economic society norms but where the Communist Party is barely out of the pretransition phase in terms of political change, along the state-administrative transformation path, as illustrated in the matrix in Figure 4.1. Hence we may legitimately ask the question: what happens if the Communist Party seeks to hold the fort at this point in its transformation? And what happens if the Communist Party decides to change its governing norms – particularly the leading role of the party in state and society? The degree of economic society achieved under a party dictatorship is clearly restricted in terms of civil society, the rule of law, political legitimacy or bureaucratic viability. It is, by definition, not consolidated, other than as an interim status of ill-defined duration. It is an economic society, bis, in a party-state monopoly, where all procedures become standard, and there is another game in town – more dictatorship or more democracy. The danger is, as North (1991) argues, that there will tend to be increasing returns to groups that have nestled into the fabric of the original settlement and an incentive for them to preserve the existing constraints. That is why any set of norms, if they are to be adapted to changing circumstances, have to be accompanied by an adaptive mechanism: a standard operating procedure to change standard operating procedures. Otherwise sclerosis sets in, only to be undone by war, revolution or free trade (Olson, 1982). The party-state, in other words, is riding a tiger (*qi hu nan xia*) and cannot get off for fear of the consequences. Let's go back to our point zero in 1978 for China and in 1985 for the Soviet Union.

Comparing Mao's and Brezhnev's legacies

There were some similarities between the inheritance that Mao left behind in the late 1970s and Brezhnev's legacy to Gorbachev in the Soviet Union in the mid-1980s. Command economy structures had abolished the market as a decentralized mechanism for the creation and distribution of wealth. Central authorities allocated financial and physical resources, administered prices, sustained monopoly structures, and limited transactions on the world market to a minimum. There was monopoly control by the Party of all aspects of life, a fusion of Party, state and economy at the level of firms, and a system of organized social dependence. Managers did not face a hard budget constraint, shoddy work was rewarded, innovation was stifled, and workers were mollycoddled. Rewards went to whoever was best at extracting and hoarding scarce resources from multiple layers of bureaucracy. These generated constituencies within the party-states that became resistant to change and often ignorant of anything that moved outside of their immediate bailiwicks.

One major difference between the reform histories of China, Poland and Russia has been the Chinese Communists' aversion to policies with unknown outcomes (Woo, 1994). China's Communist Party leadership had too much experience of Big Leaps and Clean Slates to be tempted again. The Big Bangs that Western economists recommended in Europe and Russia were reminiscent of Mao's utopian economics because they suggested that present conditions should be aligned as soon as possible on the desired state of things. In Poland, for instance, the Big Bang took the form of a simultaneous move to free prices, overture of the country to international trade, the adoption of non-inflationary monetary policies, and legalisation of private economic activities. And just as Mao had done away with capitalists, so the hidden agenda behind the Polish shock therapy in 1990 was for the anti-Communists to sweep away as many Communist public officials as possible. Their pretext was that Poland's command economy suffered from high and rising inflation, budget and external deficits, and spiralling foreign debt. So apply Big Bang. This yielded two lessons for

China's conservative Communists: keep in office, and avoid financial melt-down like the plague.

Another major difference was that after 1978, gradualism became a deliberate strategy of China's Communist Party leaders, and for two distinct reasons. First, they were convinced that the best way to proceed was by "feeling the stones to cross the river", in other words, that socioeconomic constructs are best built through a process of accumulative, small changes. Second, they were not agreed, or clear, about the ultimate destination of policy. So they allowed experience to speak to them. As Gao Shangquan (1997) of the State Council says:

> *The method of reform achieves gradual advances through popularizing experiences gained at pilot units. That is, prior to implementing any reform measure on a nationwide scale, it must go through a stage of experimentation at a pilot unit, to accumulate experience. Reform measures are carried out boldly at the trial stage, and daring breakthroughs are encouraged.*

Thus, by the century's end, a curious inversion of roles occurred: Communists in China practiced politics as if they were Burkean conservatives, tentatively feeling the ground before venturing into an unknown future,[1] while Western liberal economists adapted a global Leninist vision, which dictated that there was only one policy fit for all, and it was "made in the USA". China's conservative Communists are Leninists by default; they are not to be convinced by Western Leninist liberal economists in a hurry to apply their recipes.

There was a further particularity of Mao's legacy. Mao left a weakened central bureaucracy and well-entrenched provincial governments – the unintended result of his violent swings in policy. As Mao Zedong (1977) said in his 1956 speech "On ten important relationships", "We must not follow the example of the Soviet Union in concentrating everything in the hands of the central authorities, shackling the local authorities and denying them the right to independent action." Subsequently, local governments were given

---

[1] On conservatism versus utopia, see Peter Murrell, 1992, "Conservative political philosophy and the strategy of economic transition", *Eastern European Politics and Societies*, 6(1), pp. 3–16.

powers to supervise all but the large state enterprises, while the country was divided into 24,000 people's communes and production was decentralized further. Then, during the Cultural Revolution, which lasted from 1966 to 1976, Mao established all-embracing "revolutionary committees" and purged 60% of officials, including the head of state and the defense minister. His phobias about centralized bureaucracy left the country organized along territorial lines but also vertically by sector in a dual structure of overlapping and competing authorities. The consequence was a nominal central planning authority and a de facto devolution of powers to local governments (see Box 4.1). This "federalism, Chinese style" allowed for multiple experiments regarding agriculture, fiscal measures and free trade zones (Montinola et al., 1995). By contrast, Gorbachev faced powerful, centralized bureaucratic resistance to his reform measures.

Another differentiating factor was historical norms. China has fifty-six different nationalities and ethnic groups: the Han nationality accounts for 93% of the population. So as reforms began, there was no historical or constitutional rationalization for provincial secession. The Soviet Union, by contrast, was an empire composed of nationality groups, of which the Russian group was the largest. Up to 50% of the population of the Soviet Union was composed of nationality groups, compared with 7% of China's inhabitants. This had at least two implications for reforms of the party-

Box 4.1 Local reform initiatives

It is scarcely an exaggeration to say that agricultural reform was initiated by the peasantry. Peasants took control rights over all production, except for the right to dispose of the land. This practice, initiated in December 1978 by the Xiaogang Production Brigade of Fengyang County in Anhui Province, soon spread to other parts of the province and received strong support from the provincial governor. Twenty peasants representing twenty households put their fingerprints with their own blood on a "contract" to divide the brigade's land among the households. By doing so, they also promised to fulfill the procurement quota of grain to the state. This was the "household responsibility system", which the Party agreed to only reluctantly.

states: one was that administrative or economic policy measures of decentralization did not mingle with nationality in any central way in China, whereas in the Soviet Union economic reforms inevitably cut across ethnic and nationality lines. The other was that China experienced no major clash between opposing forces to challenge the foundations of the party-state. When Boris Yeltsin was elected President of Russia in the country's first direct and open election to the office of head of state, there was no prospect of his being won round to recognize the inherited appointment of Gorbachev as the Soviet Union's secretary-general. Here was a direct clash between two irreconcilable claims on power, one bureaucratic in origin, the other democratic. The closest that China has come to such a confrontation, as we shall see in subsequent chapters, is between the expected beneficiaries and losers of China's entry to the WTO.

Not least were the significant structural differences between the economies of China and Russia. In retrospect, it proved easier to reform the agricultural sector in China than was the case for both the farm and the industrial sectors in the Soviet Union. In 1978, 75% of China's workforce was employed in agriculture. Only 20% of the population worked in state enterprises, so the government could afford to make repeated attempts at reform in the industrial sector without bringing down the whole system. Welfare provision, furthermore, did not extend to the countryside. Once agriculture was decollectivized in the early 1980s, an economic dynamic based on family enterprises was unleashed. As Whyte (1995) has argued eloquently, Chinese "entrepreneurial familism" is structured around trust and can operate with a minimum of explicit contracts in what amounts to a spontaneous market mechanism. By contrast, up to 90% of Soviet citizens worked in state enterprises – whether farm, industrial or service – which provided them with an all-encompassing welfare. Given the lack of incentives, organizations ran at a loss, subsidized by the Soviet Union's vast energy sector. Not surprisingly, resistance to reform in the Soviet Union was massive. Gorbachev's downfall may be ascribed in large part to the depth of damage inflicted on Russian society by Lenin and Stalin, whereas Deng's good fortune lay in the limited time available to Mao to inflict his tyranny on China.

The three key characteristics over the cycle of exit from a command economy, and the exploratory path to economic society, are destruction, adaptation and creation:

◆ Liberalization measures in exit from command economies are *destructive* of the existing regime. They include measures to abandon fixed prices, restrictions on trade, barriers to the entry of new firms to contest incumbents, through to tight control over financial markets – the most delicate of all mechanisms. Firms are allowed to go bankrupt. As information becomes much more abundant, it excedes the capacity of any group of public officials to control. Society is now the repository of a vast and decentralized web of knowledge, which firms must tap if they are to compete effectively.

◆ Winners begin to separate from a pack of losers, requiring *adaptation* of bureaucratic procedures and rights. This entails a major reduction in the center's command over resource allocation and a redistribution of decision powers to market agents regarding production and distribution of goods, services and incomes. The budget has to be separated from the capital market, and firms, banks or trading companies must no longer be branches of ministries. If markets are to fulfill their function as the ultimate arbiters of what is made, what is bought and how wealth is distributed, then the pricing mechanism must be allowed to operate as a decentralized information system linking buyers and sellers. That requires taking vigorous action to prevent abuse of market power by firms, and to ensure price stability.

◆ This all prompts institutional *creativity* on the part of public officials: labor market legislation has to be introduced or revised completely, savings must be allowed to flow through financial institutions whose agents decide on investment opportunities, and markets in corporate assets must be allowed to develop. That in turn requires the introduction of property rights and the substitution of court procedures and the rule of law for the discretion of public officials. Central bankers, anti-cartel authorities, and supreme courts have to be allowed to establish their autonomy over and against political authorities.

Let us now follow the Russian path, starting in 1985 at Russia's point zero on the graph, the year when Gorbachev was appointed secretary-general of the Communist Party. The Chinese reform, of course, started earlier and was under way for over a decade before the Gorbachev lesson could be learnt. *Ex post*, Russia's story is replete with lessons for a Chinese leadership anxious to extract China from failed policies. In particular, the Russian experience confirmed Chinese conservatives in their intent to preserve a strong party-state and to keep power.

Russia's transformation path

Unlike Deng in China, Gorbachev did not have the luxury of starting with economic reform first. Brezhnev had cemented bureaucratic inertia into stasis. Gigantic organizations spawned dependent clients, while omnipresent red tape secreted unofficial markets. Corruption prospered. One of Gorbachev's first measures was to accelerate economic growth. But the Soviet command economy was too atrophied to respond. When Soviet export revenues shrunk as world oil prices fell abruptly, Gorbachev in 1987 announced perestroika, or restructuring of the Soviet system, involving devolution of powers from the center to provincial authorities and to corporate organizations. Then, in 1988, he announced radical reform of the political system, alongside the policy of glasnost – openness. Glasnost had the unanticipated consequence of giving voice to latent nationalisms and awakening aspirations that had lain dormant for decades. All reforms merged in a political process that escaped Gorbachev's control. In quick succession, Boris Yeltsin succeeded in being elected by universal suffrage as Russia's first ever president. The August 1991 putsch to preserve the socialist system collapsed ignominiously, and on December 25, 1991, Gorbachev resigned. Soviet Communism and its dream of a socialist world was dead. Applied to China, the lesson is clear: do not do everything at once. In particular, do not launch political reforms that then dislodge the Communist Party from power.

In January 1992, President Yeltsin appointed Russia's first post-Communist government with a mandate to transform the Soviet command system into a market economy. Here, the difference with China was not quite so great as it may seem: Russian reformers such as Yeltsin and Gaidar had been active members of the Communist Party, while it was the Chinese Communist Party itself that supervised the country's transformation towards a market society. The aim in Russia was to create profit-seeking private corporations owned by outside shareholders. The Gaidar program gave priority to reducing inflation. It had four key features: liberalization of prices, the freeing of the foreign exchange markets for import purposes, sharp reduction of central budget expenditure to control the growth of money, and the break-up of state monopolies through a privatization program, under the direction of Anatoli Chubais, a convinced economic liberal. The broad program was outlined in the Memorandum of Economic Policy approved by the International Monetary Fund (IMF) in February 1992. In June Russia joined the World Bank, and in July she became a member of the IMF. The policies contributed to a reduction in monthly inflation, a much lower budget deficit and a collapse in real wages. Meanwhile, privatization proceeded apace.

Gaidar's Big Bang was, in effect, never applied. The Communists retained control of parliament, the central bank, the state enterprises and collective farms. Local governments took to spending more than they taxed. Mayors built up their big-city political machines, while old-guard Communists hung on to their power bases in rural areas. With the printing press operating at full throttle, inflation soared to 2000%. By summer 1993, insiders had acquired two-thirds of Russia's privatized and privatizing firms, state subsidies accounted for 22% of Russia's GNP, and little restructuring was under way (McFaul, 1995). In order to consolidate democracy Russian-style, Yeltsin bombed the parliament into submission, won the general elections, and had a new constitution confirmed by referendum. Presidential powers were strengthened further when Yeltsin took control of "power ministries" – defense, the interior and foreign affairs – as well as the committees for espionage, the security services, frontier troops, information, television and radio. But success in implementing his economic strategy continued to elude him. As his popularity shrank to a bare 3%, he struck a deal with seven leading bankers to swap loans for equity in return for their backing in the presidential elections of June 1996. Their media swung into action, helping Yeltsin to victory against the odds. The seven bankers went ahead to create a corporate oligarchy, accounting for up to 50% of the Russian economy. In parallel, the government implemented a hard-currency strategy with the backing of Western institutions. But in August 1998, Western investors on Russia's capital markets voted with their feet in a desperate rush out of rouble assets in the wake of the Asian financial crash. The rouble's devaluation, and an unexpected windfall in the form of a rise in the level of world oil prices, soon stimulated economic revival. Russia's market economy, and the country's post-Communist elites, were both firmly in place.

China's transformation path

The key political detonator was the initial consolidation of Deng's position in 1978 and the ideological sleight of hand that defined Mao's leaps towards socialism as "premature" (Qian, 2000; Ma, 2000). The main impetus to economic growth, alongside the Open Door policy and the September 1984 settlement with the UK on Hong Kong, came from agricultural reforms and the easing of constraints on communal enterprises. Market-oriented measures were then extended to the state enterprises in 1984: dual-track market liberalization allowed for the coexistence of two market prices, one for the liberalized market and the other for output still falling under the plan. The contract responsibility system allowed managers to negotiate the distribution of excess cashflow between their units and government. On the plus side, these measures stimulated competition as new players entered the China market; consumer goods production rose sharply, and state enterprise industrial output and value added per capita shrank relative to "other" – the TVEs and the ill-defined private sector (see Table 4.1).

The number of people living below the poverty threshold in China fell from 250 million to under 100 million. On the negative side, politically inspired bank-lending surged and inflation jumped. With corruption more visible, demands for more thoroughgoing reforms culminated in the movement for democratization, Zhao Ziyang's efforts to prevent confrontation, and finally the brutal crackdown on the students demonstrating in Tiananmen Square in June 1989. Victory in the inner-Party struggles over economic policy went to the gradualists rather than the Big Bangers, for whom Gorbachev was a likely model, and their supporters outside of the

Table 4.1 ◆ Industrial performance by type of ownership

Year	Millions employed in SOEs	Millions employed in other enterprises	Gross value added per person in SOEs*	Gross value added per person in other enterprises
1952	5.1	7.3	101.5	98.9
1978	31.4	29.5	150.6	46.2
1996	42.7	66.6	72.8	117.4

*Per cent of average value added
Source: Angus Maddison, Chinese Economic Performance in the Long Run, OECD, 1998.

regime. Thereafter, there was some talk of conservatives seeking to reverse reforms, but resistance proved too great, and it soon became evident that achieving growth without inflation was priority number one (for a good account, see Fewsmith, 2001).

The years 1989–92 were truly anxious ones for China's leadership. First, Japan's boom turned to bust in the summer of 1989; Germany moved fast to unity, pulling up global interest rates to fund the cost of reunification; the Soviet Union disintegrated; and the so-called Washington Consensus paved the way for the internationalization of the new, American way of capitalism. All of this was important to China because it raised the central question of which of the different models among capitalist states was most appropriate for countries in transition from command to market economies. Should it be US-type shareholder capitalism, French-type state-led capitalism, or German-Japanese national cross-shareholding structures under managerial control? In the early 1990s, policy advice for China's transition tilted clearly in favor of Japan – the model of the anti-Communist state-led capitalisms of east Asia. In the words of Leipziger and Thomas (1993) of the World Bank, east Asian success was due to "the positive role of government in charting a development course". Such business-friendly public policy yielded positive results: superior rates of accumulation of physical and human capital; rapid integration into the world economy; industrial expansion via growing export market shares; and red-carpet treatment for inward direct investors.

China's leadership opted for the Korean model – close enough to Japan's without being Japanese, state-led, and national capitalist. Party-state thoughts were elaborated in the "Decision on issues concerning the establishment of a socialist market economy", drawn up under the direction of the then Party Secretary-General Jiang Zemin, and adopted at the fourteenth Party Congress in November 1993. This is one of the key documents in China's transition. All components of the reform, which together form the basic framework of the socialist market economy (SME), are considered by the leadership as comprising one "interrelated and mutually conditioning" organic entity (see Box 4.2).

Box 4.2 The SME structure

The socialist market economic (SME) structure is linked with the basic system of socialism. The establishment of this structure aims at enabling the market to play the fundamental role in resource allocation under macroeconomic control by the state. To turn this goal into reality, it is necessary to uphold the principle of taking the publicly owned sector as the mainstay, while striving for a simultaneous development of all economic sectors, to further transform the management mechanism of state-owned-enterprises, and to establish a modern enterprise system which meets the requirements of the market economy and in which the property rights and responsibilities of enterprises are clearly defined, government administration and enterprise management are separated and scientific management is established. It is necessary to establish a nationwide integrated and open market system ... to transform the government's functions in economic management and establish a sound macroeconomic system which chiefly relies on indirect means to ensure the healthy development of the national economy. It is necessary to establish an income distribution system ... while adhering to the road to common prosperity. It is also necessary to establish a multi-tiered social security system ... so as to promote economic development and social stability. It is necessary to establish a legal system and to adopt down-to-earth measures to push the overall reform forward actively step by step and promote the development of the social productive forces.

Decision of the CCP Central Committee on some Issues Concerning the Establishment of a Socialist Market Economic Structure. Adopted November 14, 1993. *Beijing Review*, November 22–8, 1993.

Zhu Rongji, former mayor of Shanghai, was appointed as *Lao Ban*, loosely translated as economic policy supremo. He promptly recentralized control over the financial system, bringing down inflation from an average 22% per annum to 1% by the time of the east Asian financial crash in 1997–8. This thereby tightened budgetary constraints on the 350,000 or so state enterprises. Command economy structures had ensured a considerable expansion of employment in the state sector from ninety-five million employees in 1978 (amounting to nearly 10% of the active population) to 148.5 million in 1994 (almost 20% of the active population) (Asian Development Bank, 1997). Indeed, China's industrial growth in the period had resembled that of Japan and Korea in the cold-war years, when both countries invested into industry at very high rates but with lowering rates of return. China's heavy industries devoured raw material and energy inputs, as well as squandering the country's abundant savings. At least half of these large and medium-sized industrial enterprises were bleeding money, their managers engaged in widespread asset-stripping, and their workers pushing for above-productivity wage rises.

In the years 1993–8, China's leadership fought out their battles behind closed doors. Even so, two broad and contradictory strands of policy were visible. One was identified with Zhu Rongji, who tended to adopt a more market-oriented posture, and the other with Premier Li Peng, more identified with the heavy-industry brigade. In fact, both strands of policy overlapped around China's version of the Korean model. The leadership prompted a policy described as "grasp the large and let go the small" (*zhua da fang xiao*), involving the identification of pillar industries, such as petroleum and automobiles, the formation of joint-stock enterprises, the reduction in ministerial controls, and the de facto privatization of the smaller state enterprises. Joint ventures between state enterprises and foreign corporations was encouraged with a view to promoting technology transfer. Foreign investment rose in the energy, telecommunications, transport and construction sectors, as well as in retail and consumer goods sectors.

What really attracted investors was market size, the country's potential, and the aspirations of China's Communist emperor as measured in the Pharaonic nature of his large-scale projects.

The best known is the Three Gorges Dam project for a 640-kilometer lake to create hydropower, pumping and storage facilities along the middle and upper reaches of the Yangtze River. The project is to be ready by 2009 and is expected to provide up to 8% of the country's electricity needs. Chinese officials estimate that the reservoir will partially or completely inundate two cities, eleven counties, 140 towns, 326 townships and 1,351 villages. The reservoir will displace 1.9 million people. The initial cost in the late 1980s was set at $6 billion; in late 1998, the Chinese government calculated the total cost by 2009 at $25 billion; the real likely cost is closer to $75 billion. Environmental groups have campaigned against the project, relocation monies earmarked for the one million locals to be displaced have helped finance thriving bordellos, and expected costs continue to rocket skywards. But the project attracts in Western corporations like bears to honey.

In 2000, the State Council – China's Council of Ministers' equivalent – set up a high-level interministerial Western Development Committee, charged with the task of charting long-term, fifteen-year development strategies for China's western provinces including Tibet and Xinjieing. The project includes new trunk railways, roads, gas pipelines, and communications hubs. Funds come through government fiat and from the Asian Development Banks or World Bank. Here, in the poor interior, the attractions to foreign business are less obvious, so the incentives would have to be that much more attractive.

Meanwhile, in January 1998, the bottom fell out of the Korean currency, the won, and a number of major conglomerates (*chaebol*) went bottom up. Imagine the Chinese leadership's dismay. There had been the horror at events in the Soviet Union, followed by the creeping realization that Japan's old formulas did not work in a global market, to the interest in the Korean ways of doing things only to see the Korean collapse in early 1998, through to the anxious observation that the US way offered a way forward only to observe its vulnerability to corporate-led under- and overinvestment cycles.

The collapse of the Korean won sounded the knell of the Japanese model in east Asia and opened the sobering prospect for China's leadership that the only option in a global economy was to learn as much as possible about the US ways of doing things and then to seek how to introduce such changes in the very special context of China (see Box 4.3).

Box 4.3 A China model?

Beijing once aspired to learn from South Korea's development but has now disbanded its study groups. Instead, the boot is on the other foot, with voices in Seoul calling for a special taskforce and other measures to meet the Chinese challenge. The *Chosun Ilbo*, Seoul's leading conservative daily, ran an editorial on August 15, 2001 headed "China More Capitalist than Korea"; the paper concluded: "Now it is our turn to learn from China."

The thought began to circulate among the world's policy wonks that maybe east Asian governments had not been so far-sighted after all. The new tone was summarized in Paul Krugman's (1997) pithy statement that the east Asian miracle was no miracle at all: growth in Asia was "mainly a matter of perspiration rather than inspiration – of working harder not smarter". The true comparison for east Asia growth, Krugman argued, was not with Western countries but with the Soviet Union. Just as the Soviet Union had thrown resources into the struggle for expansion in capacity, so had east Asia's anti-Communist regimes. But they were using resources inefficiently, as indicated by a secular fall in their rates of return. Furthermore, their markets were too distorted for the price mechanism to play its central part in bringing consumer demands and corporate supply into line with one another. The east Asian states had traveled blind in the past. In a global market, they did not have a clue how to procede.

What to do? China clearly had its own peculiarities, but it was also part Soviet Union, part east Asian tiger. The government in effect underwrote business risk, market discipline was weak on subsidized firms, non-performing bank loans were said to be equivalent to 25% GNP, and all the incentives were in place for Chinese corporations to diversify into all types of unrelated business activities. Credit was readily available to the politically well-connected, and corporations had easy access to tax-efficient credits (World Bank, 1999).

The answer came in March 1998. Zhu Rongji moved to the premiership, while Li Peng moved to head the National People's Congress (NPC).

The thrust of policy was to accelerate the pace of marketization, withdraw the government further from the market, upgrade private property rights in the Chinese constitution, reform the bureaucracy, and move decisively to join the WTO. Thereby, global norms would be incorporated into Chinese legislation and practice, while central government control over recalcitrant provincial or city governments would be reinforced. The agenda was made public when, in November 1998, major newspapers published the speech of Joseph Stiglitz, World Bank Chief Economist, to Beijing University, delivered in July of that year. In "Second generation strategies for reform for China", Stiglitz recommended further, deeper institutional restructuring and a completion of its move to markets. Stiglitz in effect sketched the program for China's future economic reforms: the need to enhance government revenues through tax reform, welfare policy, reform of the financial system and of state enterprises, and entry to international organizations. Membership of the WTO, Stiglitz pointed out, was bound to restrict the state's freedom to direct credit. This was clearly one linchpin around which future political battles would turn.

So what can be said about China's transformation path compared with Russia's? And what can be said about China's likely future path? Clearly, step-by-step conservative reforms are a constant of China's reform style. Equally, China's economy has grown, while Russia's has shrunk – many would argue that given the overdevelopment of a heavy-industry sector geared primarily under the Soviet Union to the production of military equipment, Russia had no option. Nonetheless, Russia introduced democratic norms if not practices of government, while China's leadership has talked of democratization but prefers to cling

> **Step-by-step conservative reforms are a constant of China's reform style**

to the party-state monopoly hold on power. Marketization has reduced direct control over economic resources in both China and Russia and has highlighted the importance to both states of developing effective and efficient institutions and instruments of indirect control over markets. In China, the Leninist state is afflicted by an explosion in corrupt practices and interests, while establishing trust in the state, law, finances and administration has become a vital precondition for further success in the transition.

China, like Russia, is one of the worst polluted countries in the world, with air and water pollution levels many times those of international standards. Air and water pollution has incurred an economic cost, according to the World Bank and the Asian Development Bank, equivalent of 3–8% GDP per annum.

In short, China looks two ways from the vantage point of its Chinese-style market economy: back to a very successful transformation out of a command economy, and forward to an economic society, one of the five conditions to achieve a consolidated democracy. That may only be achieved by a party-state decision to change its norms and embark on the path to China's political transformation – the subject we turn to now.

References

Asian Development Bank, 1997, *Emerging Asia: Changes and Challenges*, Manila, The Philippines, Asian Development Bank, p. 117.

Crane Brinton, 1965, *The Anatomy of Revolution*, New York, Vintage Books.

Ian Buruma, 2001, "What Beijing can learn from Moscow", *New York Times Magazine*, September 2.

Joseph Fewsmith, 2001, *China Since Tiananmen: The Politics of Transition*, Cambridge, Cambridge University Press, pp. 21–71.

Tsuyoshi Hasegawa, 1992, "The connection between political and economic reform in communist regimes", in Gilbert Rozman (ed.), *Dismantling Communism Causes and Regional Variations*, Washington, DC, The Woodrow Wilson Center Press, pp. 59–113.

Paul Krugman, 1997, "Whatever happened to the Asian miracle?", *Fortune*, August 18, p. 27.

Danny M. Leipziger and Vinod Thomas, 1993, *The Lessons of East Asia: A Overview of Country Experience*, Washington, DC, World Bank.

Juan Linz and Alfred Stepan, 1996, *Problems in Democratic Transition and Consolidation: Southern Europe, South America, and Post-Communist Europe*, Baltimore, Johns Hopkins University Press.

Shu-Yun Ma, 2000, "Understanding China's reform: looking beyong neoclassical explanations", *World Politics*, 52, pp. 586–603.

Michael McFaul, 1995, "State power, institutional change, and the politics of privatisation in Russia", *World Politics*, 4, pp. 210–43.

Gabriella Montinola, Yingyi Qian and Barry R. Weingast, 1995, "Federalism, Chinese style: the political basis for economic success in China", *World Politics*, 48(1), pp. 50–81.

Barry Naughton, 1995, *Growing Out of the Plan: Chinese Economic Reform, 1978–1993*, Cambridge, Cambridge University Press, pp. 3–5.

Sigmund Neumann, 1949, "The international civil war", *World Politics*, 1, pp. 333–4.

Douglas C. North, 1991, *Institutions, Institutional Change and Economic Performance, Political Economy of Institutions and Decisions*, Cambridge, Cambridge University Press, p. 99.

G. O'Donnell and P. Schmitter, 1986, *Transition From Authoritarian Rule: Tentative Conclusions about Uncertain Democracies*, Baltimore, Johns Hopkins University Press.

Mancur Olson, 1982, *The Rise and Decline of Nations: Economic Growth, Stagflation and Social Ridgidities*, New Haven, Yale University Press, pp. 141–4.

Yingyi Qian, 2000, "The process of China's market transition: the evolutionary, historical and comparative perspective (1978–98)", *Journal of Institutional and Theoretical Economics*, 156(1), pp. 151–71.

Andreas Schedler, 1998, "What is democratic consolidation", *Democracy*, 9(2), pp. 91–107.

Yossi Shain and Juan Linz, 1995, *Between States: Interim Governments and Democratic Transitions*, New York, Cambridge University Press.

Gao Shangquan, 1997, "China's economic restructuring, structural adjustment and social stability", *China Economic Review*, 8(1), pp. 83–8.

Martin King Whyte, 1995, "The social roots of China's economic development", *China Quarterly*, 144, pp. 999–1019.

Wing Thye Woo, 1994, "The art of reforming CPEs: comparing China, Poland and Russia", *Journal of Comparative Economics*, 18, pp. 276–308.

World Bank, 1999, *China: Weathering the Storm and Learning the Lessons*, Washington, DC, *World Bank*, p. 30.

Long Yongtu, 2000, "On the question of our joining the World Trade Organisation", *Chinese Economy*, 33(1), p. 16.

Mao Zedong, 1977, *Selected Works of Mao Zedong*, Vol. 5, Beijing, People's Press.

5

Feeling the stones as you cross the river: China's political policy

THE PARTY-STATE IS A RELIC of the past century, not a herald for the next. Since the events of May–June 1989 on Tiananmen Square, China's party-state has entered an implicit pact with the population: rough and tough politics carry on within its precincts, but people enjoy much greater freedom than before. The problem is that the Communist dynasty can no longer give a satisfactory response to the fundamental political question: by what right do you rule? It can no longer answer with any credibility that it rules on behalf of workers and peasants. Yet the genie of market reforms is out of the bottle, and its twin, the genie of political reform or revolution, is struggling to escape. Either regime reformers lead the country through market-Leninism to market-democracy, or economic policy becomes impaled on an untenable status quo. That is when the opportunity opens for revolution from below, with the regime cast in the role of the Romanian dictator Ceauşescu and his wife, acclaimed one

> Either regime reformers lead the country through market-Leninism to market-democracy, or economic policy becomes impaled on an untenable status quo

moment by the crowd and killed the next. Let us follow the political transformation path sketched in the previous chapter, noting some reasons why China's leadership has been on the ideological defensive since 1989. We can then look at the dynamics of revolution from below and some of the regime's key political features, and then assess the path that China's market-Leninists have yet to tread. Without such an assessment, corporate operations in China will be flying blind. The reason is simple: the essence of business is to have to deal with a future where risk and reward lie but about which we know little. This chapter will isolate some central features of what we know and do not know about China in the coming years.

No alternatives to market-democracy

China's leadership has been constantly on the ideological defensive since 1989. With the disappearance of the Communist system, market-democracy reigns supreme with no contestant in sight. An easy expectation is for convergence of the world's population on common norms of governance, incomes and life expectations. But convergence is only one prospect among many, and a fragile one at that. We can see why this is so if we consider China in the US-dominated global structure introduced in the previous chapters. Changes in control over some of its key elements of security, credit and knowledge have worked to fundamentally alter the relation of authorities to markets in China. We shall be looking more closely at production and credit in Chapter 7. Meanwhile, the simple point to retain is that China's nominally monopoly party-state has to share powers in what is fast becoming a pluralist polity.

China on the ideological defensive

Consider China's security. From the regime's perspective, this is not purely a geopolitical concern. It is also ideological. The regime conquered power in China nearly half a century ago with an ambitious socialist program, and failed. Now China confronts market democracy, the policy package stamped

"Made in the USA", and that assumes a one world as driving towards shared prosperity, democracy and better living conditions for all. The vision is inspired by Anglo-American liberal ideals, suggesting the removal of all constraints on individuals' pursuit of self-fulfilment, except where the exercise of one person's freedom limits the freedom of another. From this follows the idea of a government with a limited mandate to manage public affairs, renewable through regular elections, and a broad obligation on society to assure all individuals equality of opportunity but not of reward. Two key institutions of liberalism are property rights, transmissible over generations from parents to children; and the market, which spontaneously coordinates the decisions of millions. Any attempt by government to eliminate inherited inequalities by legislation, classical liberalism holds, destroys the incentives inspiring individuals to excel. Government is to be limited to ensuring external security, law and order, and public investment projects.

For Deng, and his successors, this is a vision that is only partially applicable to China, at least for the foreseeable future. "In the China of today", Deng Xiaoping (1991) declared, "we can never dispense with leadership by the Party." The Party's task, he added, is to provide the authority to create a "socialist market economy". The substance of this is spelt out clearly in the "Decision of the CCP Central Committee on some Issues Concerning the Establishment of a Socialist Market Economic Structure", a key quote from which is cited in the previous chapter. The political intent of the decision is to create a state of law, not a Western-style democracy. China's leaders clearly fear the consequences of introducing universal suffrage, multiparty elections, one man one vote, and freedom of expression into a huge country with only minimal experience of democracy. Indeed, giving Chinese people the vote in elections to all levels of the state is far from being a surefire recipe to ensure the rule of law, a separation of powers, and checks and balances throughout the polity. Corrupt practices are widespread, and leaders or potential leaders are always looking for ways to entrench their privileges indefinitely. Democratic elections offer one way to do so. But an early move to introduce direct elections across the length and breadth of the country could ensure that China becomes just one more "illiberal democracy" (Zakaria, 1997), alongside the many law-free states in the world that have held elections "for the eyes of the Americans", to paraphrase the cynical

Brazilian expression of the nineteenth century about the need to write a constitution in order to float a bond in the London markets.

The problem is that however dazzling China's economic performance, Western opinion is not prepared to condone the regime until it satisfies Western criteria of democracy. Why should we believe, the rhetorical question runs, a Communist party-state with the CCP's record when its leaders say that they intend to introduce the rule of law to China? Monopoly control over power resources inevitably leads to abuse and is incompatible with any reasonable concept of democratic government. While we may agree with this, it is equally true that it took centuries for the rule of law to evolve in Western countries and is likely to take a very long time indeed for Chinese society to gain a consciousness that law may be there to protect against arbitrary government. Furthermore, the key question is: rule of law for whom? Is it the rule of law for corporations or for individuals? In Singapore, in some ways a model for the CCP vision of China, the legal system does quite well at protecting foreign investors and is arguably less concerned with protecting individuals.

In fact, China appears relatively well placed in various performance league tables published by Western institutions (see Table 5.1). To little avail.

Table 5.1 ◈ China in selected world rankings out of nine states

Country	GNP 1999 ($)	GNP per capita PPP, 1999 ($)	HDI * 1999	FDI	Corruption	Political rights	Economic freedom	Weapons suppliers	Total index ranking
China	3	6	6	2	5	7	6	3	4
India	5	8	9	7	7	2	8	8	8
Russia	6	3	3	5	8	5	7	2	5
Indonesia	8	7	7	4	9	3	5	4	7
Brazil	4	4	4	3	3	3	4	5	3
Turkey	7	5	5	–	4	4	3	6	6
Vietnam	9	9	8	–	6	7	7	9	9
Japan	2	2	2	6	2	1	2	7	2
USA	1	1	1	1	1	1	1	1	1

Sources: International Bank for Reconstruction and Development, United Nations, Corruption Index, Freedom House, Stockholm International Peace Research Institute, Heritage Foundation, United Nations Development Program, Organization for Economic Cooperation and Development, International Monetary Fund, and Transparency International.
*HDI = Human Development Index

China's leadership has to endure constant attacks in international organizations, through Western parliaments and press, or via non-governmental organizations such as Amnesty International on Chinese Communist human rights practices (Box 5.1).

Chinese diplomacy may get the backing of Russian, African and Asian states, or at least have a sympathetic hearing in Western capitals when it declares that human rights for poor countries are primarily about the struggle against poverty. However, as shown by the long diplomatic struggle to bring China into the WTO, or to have Beijing stage the Olympic Games, the industrial democracies will confer prestige on China only as part of a wider package. As George Will (1997), a US political commentator, entoned: "The strategic aim of US policy is, and must be, the subversion of the Chinese regime."

Box 5.1 China's human rights practices

An Amnesty International Report 2001 for China claims that 2000 saw continued repression of peaceful dissent throughout the country. Thousands of people were detained arbitrarily for peacefully exercising their rights to freedom of expression, association or religion. These included political dissidents, such as members of the banned China Democratic Party, and anti-corruption and environmental campaigners. Some were sentenced to long prison terms after unfair trials under national security legislation; others were detained without trial and assigned to up to three years' "re-education through labor". Torture and ill-treatment of prisoners continued to be widespread. Evangelical Protestants and Roman Catholics who worshipped outside the official "patriotic" churches were the victims of a continuing pattern of arrests, fines and harassment. The limited and incomplete records available showed that at least 1,511 people were sentenced to death and that 1,000 were executed; the true figures were believed to be far higher. In the autonomous regions of Xinjiang and Tibet, religious freedom continued to be restricted severely and people suspected of nationalist activities or sympathies were subjected to particularly harsh repression.

China in the global knowledge structure

Paradoxically, the USA has a part ally in the regime itself. The global information revolution has helped to promote more market-based competition for values, products and services. This has deepened the gap between the party-state's claim to monopoly power and the pluralist reality of China. Propaganda is no longer an easy option, as the regime has to provide credible information in an ever more open society (Keohane and Nye, 1998). Its policy stance so far is ambiguous: the government never ceases to toot China's trumpet as the El Dorado for producers of TV sets (there are over 320 million sets installed), for mobile operators (the mobile phone market in China is outgrowing that of the USA and Japan), or for Internet firms (by 2005, China will have 300 million Internet users, 100 million more than the USA). But the military, the police, the Party and the Ministry of Information Industry – a giant composite ministry brought together in 1998 – have invested massively in telecommunications and data-processing to centralize control and monitor the population better.

As a result, the party-state's monopoly on information has shrunk. The population is better informed than ever before. Chinese readers in 1978 had 930 magazine titles to choose from; by 1998, official statistics recorded 2,053 newspapers, 7,999 magazines and trade publications, and 7.24 billion copies of books representing 7,999 titles. The US government has introduced a plan to establish a computer network to help Chinese residents circumvent their government's controls over use of the network (*New York Times*, 2001). By contrast, the Saudi government's censureship is supported strongly by the USA, an excellent example of US selectiveness in exporting its values. The Party is desperately battling to preserve its censureship powers through its "administrative buro for internet propaganda", and laws are passed making it illegal to transmit materials that "incite the overthrow of the government". But whatever it tries, the diverse sources of information oblige the party-state to remain credible with the public. Old-style propaganda does not suffice; reliable news is a necessary resource for an ever more open society.

China and the Asian developmental state

The CCP is much attracted by the example of the Asian developmental state modeled on the Leninist doctrine of Kuomintang Taiwan or the dominant party-state of Singapore. The developmental state has demonstrated ability to drag populations out of poverty in the space of a generation (Wade, 1990). Central controls over society run through the hands of a governing elite, chosen through a rigorous process of selection. Leaders here are not servants of the electorate's whims. Corruption is punished by disgrace, or worse. The legal system provides justice, subject to political discretion. At its heart lies state control over the capital allocation process. Funds are distributed authoritatively to corporations that are required to compete on protected domestic markets and to win market shares abroad.

Learning from the Asian development model is not so straightforward, however. The 1997–8 Asian crash dealt a deadly blow to state-led financial arrangements in the region. More importantly, by the turn of the millennium, the model is dated as Taiwan and South Korea have become market-democracies, and Singapore is too small for large China to imitate in detail. That leaves China's leadership with an apparent option: either of consolidating a Chinese-style socialist market economy under the rule of law, or of incorporating the main elements of Western-style political systems. In fact, this dichotomy of monopoly state or Western democracy to which the leadership often refers is specious. China is special by definition, as is every other people and state. There is nothing special, therefore, about being special. This is not the same as saying, with President Clinton, that the Internet will bring democracy to China. Rather, China's political system is bound to take shape through a prolonged learning process from the rest of the world. As a senior official told me in Beijing, the ideas inspiring him in the drive for China's financial market reform are rooted in his reading of Paul Samuelson's textbook, *Economics*, which the Ford Foundation provided for China's economics students in the early 1980s. Uncle Sam's reach is long and deep.

Why the trend to market-democracy?

Market-democracy as a governance form may have swept all competitors before it, but the reasons remain controversial. There are two types of explanation from an earnestly progressive view of history's ways. Modernizers see people mounting the staircase of history from a lower to a higher form of existence. Marxists see history driven by class struggles, resulting from technological progress. Now the Chinese party-state is both a modernizer, and officially Marxist-Leninist-Maoist in inspiration. So it is a fit subject for a modernization/Marxist analysis. This predicts a variety of possible destinations – democracy, fascism or communism – and a passage to modernity, contingent on relations between classes – peasantry, landowners and urban bourgeoisie (Moore, 1972). Substitute landowners for party officials and we have the foundation for a witch's revolutionary brew; stir in economic growth as a surefire predictor of instability (Olson, 1963), add the erosion of traditional solidarities, throw in widening wealth gaps, sprinkle multiple sources of dissatisfaction, and pepper with a layer of political decay (Huntington, 1968). We are in the heartland of the determinist sudden-regime-death-syndrome school of thinking.

Marx on the farm

Consider how this story plays in China's countryside. The arithmetic is straightforward: officially, China's population is 1.3 billion, including 800 million peasants who live in the countryside, often in Malthusian conditions of rising population, limited arable land, and diminishing returns (Goldstone, 1995). As we have seen, this population is expected to rise by 2015 to about 1.5 billion. In many provinces, land per farm worker is less than in Bangladesh, and the quality of land under the plough is declining due to land erosion, deteriorating organic content, and salinization of the soil. This provides China with its primary challenge: it has to feed 20% of the world's population with 6% of the world's arable land.

We have seen that market reforms attributed to Deng began as local initiatives in Anhui province. There were a number of reasons for reforms starting first in the rural areas: after Mao's years, China's peasantry was seething with discontent, bureaucratic resistance to change was weak, and China was failing to feed its growing population. The initial step was to free farm prices and then to allow farmers to sell their surplus in the market. Next, rural communes established in 1958 were replaced by the household responsibility system, whereby farmers leased land (from the party-state) for a period of fifteen to fifty years in return for contracts to deliver supplies at fixed prices. The result was a sharp rise in output and a return of China to food self-sufficiency. Yet farm output per worker by the mid-1990s was still $296, compared with $343 in India, $355 in sub-Saharan Africa and $745 in Indonesia. By 1998, the farm population of 370 million, representing just under 50% of the workforce, produced 18% of the GDP. With labor productivity in farming under 1% of that in the USA, there is enormous scope for a continued and rapid drop in the farm population.

Where will all this population go? Looking backwards, the farm work-force fell from 76% of the total in 1975 to just under 50% at the turn of the millennium, while the farm workforce rose slightly from 365 million to 370 million (see Table 5.2). Furthermore, the traditional preference among peas-ant families for male rather than female children encouraged a cruel culling of female infants. Perhaps the one-child policy, enforced most effectively in the cities, also played its part. Whatever the complex of causes, China at the

Table 5.2 ◆ Employment and sectors' proportion of the national economy (%)

Industry	Year					
	1985	**1990**	**1995**	**1996**	**1997**	**2000**
Primary						
Employment	62.4	60.1	52.2	50.5	49.9	50.0
Proportion of the national economy	28.4	27.1	20.5	20.4	18.7	15.9
Secondary						
Employment	20.9	21.4	23	23.5	23.7	22.5
Proportion of the national economy	43.1	41.6	48.8	49.5	49.2	50.9
Tertiary						
Employment	16.7	18.5	24.8	26.0	26.4	27.5
Proportion of the national economy	28.5	31.3	30.7	30.1	32.1	33.2

Source: China Statistical Yearbook, 2001.

turn of the millennium has a male to female ratio in the order of 1.35 to 1. One prognosis suggests that so many randy males will only be too ready to turn to violence. The regime's temptation would be to turn that violence outwards against foreign enemies (Hudson and den Boer, 2002).

The last quarter-century witnessed not a massive flood of population to the cities but rather a regular stream and a natural increase in the number of urban dwellers, rising from 18% of the total to 30%. Surplus rural labor was absorbed in TVEs. They provided the main engine driving China, in Naughton's (1995) terms, to grow the market out of the plan. By the end of the period, two-thirds of rural output was accounted for by TVEs. Rural labor productivity soared as human resources were used to more effect. This went with sharp rises in income and savings rates. Rural industrialization also went with unprecedented pollution. TVEs, as often as not under the management of Party members, sprouted like mushrooms in China's huge countryside, where infrastructure for water, energy, waste disposal and communications is bare to nonexistent. For the party-state, this suggests the need to concentrate the migrating rural population on medium-sized townships, where infrastructure is affordable.

Maintaining rural economic growth while keeping political control there is a crucial determinant in China's future evolution. But problems have multiplied. Up to 175 million workers in the countryside cannot be absorbed in work on the farms or in the townships and therefore have no option but to try their luck in the cities. Such a huge army of the unemployed is potentially a major source of trouble for the regime. The regime has relaxed rural-to-urban migration, but this is likely to pull more people to the rich rural development areas along the coastline, where TVEs account for 80% of rural incomes, compared with 8% in China's far west. Central and western areas of the country are where 60% of the population live, often as not in crushing poverty. Add to that the facts that rural enterprises devour scarce water resources, are major polluters, and often operate outside the formal economy. Meanwhile, local officials have become more burdensome in their exactions on local populations, just as the

> Maintaining rural economic growth while keeping political control there is a crucial determinant in China's future evolution

government has cut back on subsidized housing, health, education and transport. This has resulted in violent outbursts and attacks on Party officials, including the burning of their homes and even their assassination. Banditry has returned with a vengeance in many provinces of China. Reformers within the Party argue that without the extension of direct elections, the party-state will lose control of the countryside.

Marx in the towns and cities

The party-state has also been challenged in the cities. We can get at this through returning to demographics. China's population is likely to increase by 25% over the next fifteen years or so, so the total population may number about 1.5 billion – maybe 1.6 billion – by 2015. Here is the source of the bulge theory of economic development – "bulge" because of the size of the active population relative to the dependent population. China has seen an enormous rise in the working-age population, much like the rest of east Asia, and a sharp decline in births. This is due, respectively, to improved health provision and the regime's one-child policy, introduced in the late 1970s to curb the population growth. As mortality rates have fallen, the average number of children per woman has fallen, despite a 95% marriage rate of Chinese women. This created first a bulge of the young, now a bulge of the employed population for the period 1990–2025, and thereafter a bulge in the old. Such a demographic structure holds a number of implications:

◆ One is that at least 700 million people will have to be living off incomes earned outside of agriculture. If the peasantry were to shrink to the one-third represented by the farm contribution to output at the turn of the millennium, then up to 1.1 billion people would have to find jobs in the non-farm sectors. In other words, the party-state faces the task of creating an economy that supports between 400 and 700 million additional jobs within the next fifteen years.

◆ Another is the financial implications of such a rapidly aging population. Fortunately, the habits of abstinence required in the past to maintain a large family presently carry over to a working couple with one child. Small wonder that savings rates in China are 43% of national income – the world record. Those savings for old age and ill health will come in

useful as a wealthier, urban Chinese population puts aside savings
between now and 2025.

◆ It is very important for China to raise the quality of its labor supply if it
is to prepare well for the retirement bulge after 2025, when returns to
capital will be falling in any event. Yet China's human capital is
under-developed: while China has 22% of its population living on less
than one dollar a day, compared with India's 47%, the average children
spend in school is 5.6 years, the same as in India. China ranks number
119 in the world league for per capita spending on education.

The implications of China's demographics are clear enough: only a
dynamic, privately owned market economy can hope to generate the jobs
needed in China over the coming decades; China's abundant savings will
have to be channelled efficiently in order to raise the productivity of labor
and capital to levels where the economy can readily carry the growth in
pension and health costs of an aging population; and to ensure that wealth
grows rapidly if not evenly, China's potential in human capital must
be developed.

Now one of the prime effects of Deng's reforms in the 1990s has been
the creation, in Marxist terms, of new classes in society. State functionaries
represent the shock troops of China's *nomenklatura capitalism*, a phenomenon well known in former Communist party-states moving out of the
command economy. Over the past decade, the Party cadres were the
largest social group to establish businesses, alongside workers and peasants. They have also benefited as insiders in the sale of party-state assets to
financial institutions held by other party-state institutions. Quasi-private
entrepreneurs, with unclear claims to property, emerge from the TVEs or
the larger corporations to have listed since the early 1990s on the country's major stock markets. Conversely, marketization in China has
stimulated the rapid growth of a private entrepreneurial class, whose
members are clamoring to create their own associations and to participate
in public policy. Jiang Zemin's decision to open membership of the Party
to business people is thus part of a larger redefinition of policy to widen
the Party's reach to embrace new social groups created in China's ongoing
transformation (see Box 5.2).

> ## Box 5.2 Jiang Zemin's "Three Represents" Theory
>
> In February 2000, Jiang Zemin announced a new concept, *san ge dai biao*. The concept declares that the CCP represents "the most advanced mode of productive force, the most advanced culture, and the interests of the majority of the population". What this theory indicates is the Party's efforts to open membership to new social forces and classes. Undoubtedly, this is a significant step to pluralism within the Party structures.

Meanwhile, China's workers stay entrapped in a Marxist-Leninist prison. Not for them the new freedoms open to China's businesspeople. The party-state retains the monopoly over worker representation (Chan and Senser, 1997), and has no intention of allowing an independent trade union movement to emerge along the lines of Solidarity in Poland. Free trade unions also complicate management's task within enterprises. Indeed, many companies in southern China depend on bonded labor, in that workers surrender their papers and pay a deposit on recruitment. They thereby become the captives of management. They have no protection against arbitrary layoffs and no social net to ensure a minimum standard during illness, unemployment or old age. Hence, the party-state's efforts to channel worker discontent against "foreign devils", rather than against abuses in its own backyard. Working people are the sacrificial lambs of China's present arrangements.

Here we have all the ingredients of our Marxist story: class war in the countryside, harsh conditions for the urban poor, the creation of new social classes, and a well-entrenched ruling class. Future direction of policy is clearly to promote the private sector across the whole economy in order to absorb the new entrants to the labor markets, the unemployed from failed firms, and the underemployed from the countryside. That in turn implies boosting the prestige of businesspeople and of granting them security in the enjoyment of their property. In turn, this stimulates civil society, prompts demands for the rule of law, fosters the need for a better-trained bureaucracy, and promotes the circulation of information. In addition, the spread of mobile phones and the Internet facilitate communication among the discontented and the means to discuss what to do about it.

Organization of opponents is the point where the economics-drives-politics school of thinking runs into trouble. People do not rebel just because they are discontented. A prerequisite to rebellion is that rebel leaders mobilize the discontented into a collective, organized force able to take advantage of the political opportunities on offer (see Box 5.3). In short, it is opposition elites that organize discontent rather than discontents that mobilize people. The economics-drives-politics argument thus transmutes into an observation of the primacy of politics.

From here on out, the Marxist story becomes more diluted. The reason is simple: opposition and incumbent elites interact in a political logic with its own dynamics. The essential point is that what matters is perceptions of

Box 5.3 Social discontent

Signs of social discontent in China include peasant demonstrations, laid-off workers joining criminal gangs, and *Falun Gong* sect members gathering to be arrested in Tiananmen Square. In June 1999, the official *People's Daily* newspaper noted that "some party members and officials who pursue personal gain have been deeply involved in worshipping Buddha and practicing astrology, divination, geomancy and physiognomy". Since *Falun Gong* was banned in July 1999, at least ninety-three adherents are believed to have died in police custody. Li Hongzhi is the sect's guru; he lives in the USA. But these disparate movements have a long way to go before they pose a major threat to the regime. Democracy advocates, Tibetan independence proponents, Islamic militants and disgruntled workers have little in common, other than dislike of the regime. Democracy advocates are often Han chauvinists, laid-off workers can find little comfort in *Falun Gong* teaching about the ills of the world as stemming from homosexuality and rock 'n' roll, and Islamic fundamentalists have little in common with Tibetan Buddhists. Not least, there is deep popular support in China for continuity, and this is strengthened by fear of chaos – only too vivid in the collective memory of the Chinese. The perception in Chinese public opinion is that there is no viable alternative to Communist Party rule. This is not the same as saying that the party-state leadership has a coherent view about how to provide institutional representation to accommodate the natural pluralism of Chinese society.

both the rulers and the ruled about policy and performance (Linz and Stepan, 1996). Governing elites may differ about appropriate policy, while significant sections of the population judge performance in the light of their beliefs about the legitimacy of the regime. They ask the governors: by what right do you rule? Governors may reply that they govern by consent or by force, or some combination. Constitutional democracy enables governments to combine both over the long term: governments may enjoy popularity when the going is good, but when the going gets tough electorates can vote them out of office for past errors. Disenfranchised people do not have that elementary right; if they wish to kick out the ruling incumbents, then they have three options: endure, rebel or negotiate. It's time to look at China's political transition.

Feeling the stones as you cross the river

Let's start at point zero on our transformation matrix from Chapter 4. In the jargon of political science, totalitarian regimes have four key characteristics: a total absence of pluralism; a unified, utopian ideology; intensive mobilization of the people; and a leadership ruling in undefined limits and great unpredictability for all concerned. Recruitment to the top leadership depends on success in Party institutions. Applied to Mao's China, the CCP state asserted a monopoly over political power, economic resources and the truth. Initially, the Party took over the state by force or ruse, crushed all opposition, ruled in the name of the masses, and mobilized public enthusiasm for its projects. It soon got round to abolishing private property, any sign of an independent judiciary, and the open market for goods and services. Businesses were expropriated, press freedoms quashed, and foreigners kicked out of the country as aliens. This is the point where totalitarians of the world unite in their similarities. Concentration camps are opened, where inmates serve as forced labor, if lucky. Limitless power accrues to the leaders, who soon enough, having dispatched real or imaginary enemies earlier than their time to the next life, turn on each other. Eventually, one leader emerges who purges any remaining foes. With a terrified, ill-informed and easily manipulated public at their beck and call, the tyrant reigns supreme.

The secret police – in the case of Mao's rule, the role of the secret police was played by the PLA – fall directly under the leader's command (see Box 5.4).

Nothing lasts for ever here below, definitely not dictators. They age, and as they do so they rail against the fate that has not granted them long enough life to implement their utopias. Once dead, their successors place some constraints on leadership. Consider Hitler's brief twelve years in power, Stalin's paranoia about alleged failures among his lieutenants, and Mao's Cultural Revolution. Andrew Nathan (1997) has aptly crowned him emperor of all tyrants: "No other leader in history held as much power over so many people for so long as Mao Zedong, and none inflicted such a catastrophe on his nation." With such a ghastly record, the regime was no longer able to legitimize its rule by appeals to a vision of a Communist utopia. Party leaders, many of them victims during the Cultural Revolution, were eager to ensure against unpredictable leadership concentrated in the hands on one man, while the masses had little to no faith left in the regime.

Reflecting on Mao's achievements in 1979, Chen Yun, inventor of the bird-and-cage analogy of economics, stated: "Had Mao died in 1956, his achievements would have been immortal. Had he died in 1966, he would still have been a great man. But he died in 1976. Alas, what can one say?" Paraphrasing, we can consider that had Deng died in 1976, his name would have been soon forgotten. Had he passed away in 1988, he may have been celebrated as the man who sidelined the "reds" for the "experts" in the party-state and put China on the express train to market-democracy. But he

Box 5.4 Li Ji on Tyranny

According to the Li Ji, a Confucian classic, Confucius and his students were walking through the forest and came across a woman sitting near an open grave. She was weeping profusely. When one of the students asked her why she was crying, she replied: "First my father-in-law was killed by a tiger. Later the tigers ate my husband. Now they have eaten my son as well." Confucius asked her why she did not leave the forest. The women replied: "At least there is no oppressive government here." Confucius turned to his students and said: "Remember this: oppressive government is more terrible than tigers."

died in 1997, with the experts in charge steering towards market-democracy, China-style. That is, with the shadow of the Tiananmen massacre hanging over the future.

Political scientists call the first step away from the Great Dictator's regime "early post-totalitarian" rule. "Mature post-totalitarian" rule emerges as Party members settle down to enjoy their privileges, with less fear of a knock at the door at dead of night. Party rule transforms into a vast political market for preference. The privileged few keep the people at arm's length but declare the constant war against them to be over. This is received with some relief, but not too much affection by the masses, whose expectations begin to rise for better living standards and less arbitrary treatment at the hands of officials. Hence, mature post-totalitarianism is little more than a temporary staging post on the way to more political pluralism.

This is where China is presently located on the transformation matrix in Chapter 4, still within the pretransition period on the political axis and on the market axis in the period labeled "normalcy". In other words, the economic society achieved so far is conditioned by the party-state monopoly on power. Consolidation of a state under law means that consciousness of laws and rights must spread through society, and that the leadership must promote local elections, reform of the bureaucracy, and the development of a civil society. Regime change is a more fundamental step: it means the leadership challenging the party's monopoly through contested general elections, and the granting of universal suffrage. Once embarked on regime change, one destination would be a consolidated Chinese democracy, located up the vertical path labelled "normalcy". But there could be many intermediate staging posts, as well as a disastrous relapse to the revolutionary conditions that engulfed China for nearly 200 years. As I shall argue, China's conservative Communist Party envisages making the country a state under law. That postpones China becoming a fully consolidated market-democracy. At issue is not if but when the leadership takes the plunge. The regime's preference is clear enough as to the when: later, rather than sooner. The chosen method is pragmatism.

Let us look at the five key features of such a consolidated market democracy (Linz and Stepan, 1996):

- The existence of civil society, where organized groups are able to express their values and objectives autonomous of states. Such a civil society is packed with churches, clubs, associations, trade unions, cultural happenings, and homes for retired professional golf players.

- The existence of political society, where the core institutions of a democracy such as political parties, election rules, parliamentary procedures, press freedom, and alternance in power of contesting teams for control over public powers have become rooted deeply in public practice.

- The existence of the rule of law, where the freedoms of citizens are ensured. The conditions for this are many: both civil and political society must flourish, and there has to be public consensus over a constitution, a commitment to abide by the rules of the game, an independent judiciary, and a strong legal culture.

- The existence of an effective and efficient bureaucracy that is usable by government of any particular party coloring. That requires a sound tax base, firm financial control over expenditures at all levels of the state, a functioning bond and money market, and civil servants answerable to the courts.

- The existence of economic society, by contrast to a market system or a command economy. In order to function, such a society requires a set of safeguards and widespread acceptance of common norms, institutions and regulations. In fact, these have to be very strong indeed because market imperfections are major sources of contention.

Contrasting the key features of a consolidated democracy with China as it is indicates what tasks lie ahead for such a reform to be implemented in full. Without any doubt, they are many, complex, and very difficult to achieve. The regime has to assure civil rights, dismantle its own political privileges, establish an independent court and judicial system, transform the bureaucracy, and build a market society. That means ensuring property rights and separating the party-state from business. It means putting distance between political arbitrariness and markets subject to the rule of law. Let us look first at political reform and then at developments in civil society, the law, bureaucratic reform and markets. The simple conclusion is that the regime lives, but rules by different policies and methods (Zhao, 2001). China has experienced regime change short of redefining its key political norms.

Towards a Chinese civil society

When Deng moved into power in 1978, he inherited a lawless polity, where the institutions of mass participation under Mao had been deployed for mob rule (Pei, 1998). If under Stalin political defeat spelt death, then Mao was that little bit more selective: his direct opponents such as Lin Biao and Liu Shaoqi met early deaths, while Deng was banned to the countryside twice. One of Deng's first actions was to announce, in February 1980, new rules on internal Party politics designed to ensure some degree of personal security to the ruling elite. Future political losers were not liquidated. Hu Yaobang was forced out of the Party leadership, but he remained in the Party and active in Party politics. Zhao Ziyang – who openly stated his opposition to martial law and his willingness to negotiate with the students in May–June 1989 – was placed under house arrest and purged. Deng sought to avoid becoming another Mao, restricting himself to relatively modest official posts and reaching decisions among senior Party figures by consensus. Hence, the tentative and inconsistent economic reform process. Deng's own succession passed smoothly, as have the preparations for the succession to Jiang Zemin. Deng also introduced mandatory retirement of Party and government officials, thereby accelerating the change in the Party elite from peasants to college-educated technocrats. The threat of a takeover of the regime by the "princelings" – the fate of Ceauşescu's Romania or Kim Il Sung's Korea – was avoided by the simple device of having more names put up for election to the Party congress than there were positions.

   Deng's constitutional reforms of 1982 sought to consolidate the greatly weakened state apparatus by reaffirming the Four Cardinal Principles, guided by Marxist-Leninist-Mao-Zedong thought: party-state hegemony, the leading role of the party, a unitary state, and the concentration of powers and democratic centralism in the Party. When the 1978–9 "democracy wall" became too free-wheeling, Deng rescinded some of the concessions the regime had made initially for citizens to indulge in the four bigs, including "big debates" and "big posters". Over time, though, much wider but undefined freedoms were granted to citizens than before, while the party-state shifted from mass repression to selective repression (see Box 5.5). An example is the Ministry of Security's policy to infiltrate religious "cults", and then to "arrest all members in one blow" (Shixiong, Fu, 2002).

Media censureship eased up and market reforms eroded Party controls. In the countryside, the ending of Mao's communes in the early 1980s dealt the Party a deadly blow from which it has not recovered: Party members

Box 5.5 China's religious policy

The Constitution provides for religious freedom, but religious activities are supervised closely. There are five officially recognized religions – Catholicism, Protestantism, Buddhism, Islam and Taoism. Practitioners must register a meeting place, regular attendants, a governing board, a minimum number of followers, a set of operating rules, and a legal source of income. According to official figures published in late 1997, there are over 180 million religious adherents and 3,000 religious organizations. Approximately, 8% of the population is Buddhist, 1.4% is Muslim, 0.4–0.8% belong to the unofficial Vatican-affiliated Catholic Church, an estimated 0.08–1.2% are registered Protestants, and 2.4–6.5% worship in house churches that are independent of government control. China so far has refused to establish diplomatic relations with the Holy See, and there is no Vatican representative in China. Weekly services of the foreign Jewish community in Beijing have been held uninterrupted since 1995, and the foreign Jewish community in Shanghai began holding services in a local hotel in 1998. Approximately 3,000 Tibetans enter Nepal each year to escape conditions in Tibet, according to the UN High Commissioner for Refugees. According to some estimates, a large percentage of the population practice some form of traditional folk religion (worship of local gods, heroes and ancestors). There is also a very active "house church" movement, where Protestant groups are particularly active. These often hold apocalyptic doctrines. The leader of Eastern Lightning claims to be Christ. These house churches have ties to missions abroad. President Bush, himself a born-again Christian, brought up the issue of religious freedoms in his visits to China (Kindopp, 2002).

Source: US State Department's Annual Report on International Religious Freedom for 1999, http://www.uscirf.gov/

there are aging and often illiterate and they lack budgetary resources and so resort to extracting fees from the peasants. Clashes have multiplied, such as the incident in Mao's native province of Hunan, when peasants in January 1999 went on the rampage after one of their number committed suicide because he could not pay an arbitrary tax on the slaughter of pigs, which a local official had levied to coincide with the Chinese New Year. Thousands of angry peasants marched on Party headquarters, overturned official cars, and burned officials' homes. And that was only one of the anti-Party riots in Hunan that year.

There have also been revolts by industrial workers, who have little adequate representation in state enterprises, much less in the TVEs, and next to none in the burgeoning private sector. Deng's response to the evidence of China's growing pluralism was to encourage the NPC to challenge the Party leadership, draw up its own bills, make amendments, and vote down appointments. In 1994, the NPC introduced a comprehensive labor code. A similar measure, aimed to bring dissent back towards the Party's institutions, was the extension of universal suffrage to village elections. But civil society has been growing much faster than the regime's efforts to provide it with some institutional expression.

Laying the groundwork for a legal system

Since 1982, too, the party-state has been developing a legal system. This is in effect a truly radical departure for a country where a fundamental maxim over the millennia has been government by men, not by laws (Mei, 1992). Marxist-Leninist-Maoist doctrine fitted readily with this tradition, as it placed law at the service of the dictatorship, just as law was supposedly at the beck and call of the bourgeoisie. With Deng's opening of China to international business, a more developed legal system was required than provided by the party-state. Rule of law, rather than of public officials, ensures greater protection of property rights, the enforcability of contracts, and freedom of citizens from arbitrary acts by others. The rule of law requires the creation of a level playing field, the development of an independent judiciary, and the subordination of public officials themselves to the law. In effect, policy continues to take priority over the law, but nonetheless there has been a great leap forward in the definition of legal norms, involving the NPC's passage of 327 laws, the State Council's issue of 750 regulations, and the emission of about 6,000 local laws and regulations by provincial authorities (Kevuan, 2000). China's new laws borrow extensively from Western traditions, concepts and procedures – a process that is bound to accelerate as China enters the WTO, and business and other relationships multiply.

Indeed, in March 1999, Jiang Zemin had the Constitution altered to incorporate private ownership and rule of law. Article 11 of the Constitution now places private business on an equal footing with the public sector: "The non-public sector, including individual private businesses, is an important component of the socialist market economy" (*China Daily*, 1999). Article 5 was amended to include the principle of "governing the country according to the law". These amendments, introduced at a crucial period in China's negotiations with the USA on WTO entry, demonstrated China's commitment to a full market system based on the rule of law. They also meant, formally at least, that the law is above both Party and state, and therefore constraining on officials rather than being an instrument at the service of officials to discipline citizens. The number of lawyers had risen sharply from 31,000 in 1988 to 150,000 by 2000, and their services are in high demand as Chinese citizens grow more accustomed to seeking redress through the courts. But their numbers are woefully inadequate, while the courts often fail to enforce their own judgments. Although the growth of the legal system will benefit private business and foreign investors, it is unlikely to be able to make much difference to the life of workers and peasants.

Administrative reforms

Deng also moved to restructure the institutions of the central state, but failed to create a lasting federal structure capable of durably absorbing routine center-local tensions over taxation, personnel, local protectionism and banking. Indeed, as the incompatibilities between the old system and the market-oriented reforms grew, China experienced an evolution out of Maoism to *nomenklatura capitalism*. What has been marketized, it is maintained, is not so much corporate assets as political power: up to a third of

Party and state officials are active business people, alongside their official jobs (Unger and Chan, 1995). A sort of fusion has taken place whereby bureaucracies are linked through networks at all levels – state, province, region, city, towns and villages – to entrepreneurs and other non-party elites. Who co-opted whom is no easy question: has business co-opted the bureaucracy, or has the bureaucracy, both Party and state, co-opted business? Definitely, the fusion has expanded hugely the opportunities in the political marketplace for favors and money – in short, corruption has exploded. Hence, the urgent need to shrink the bureaucracy and separate business from officialdom. In April 1998, Premier Zhu Rongji announced an administrative reform to cut the state bureaucracy by four million, or by 50%, within three years, to reduce the number of ministries at the center from forty to twenty-nine, and to separate ministries from their business enterprises. Autonomous business enterprises are one essential condition in the creation of an economic society. Another is forcing the PLA to abandon its businesses: economic society and large swathes of business under military command are not compatible.

A political marketplace

Economic reform and maintenance of the party-state's monopoly are not readily compatible. It is not just that the Party's hold over labor markets, the countryside and the media has weakened as civil society has become more active. Rather, China's is an incomplete transition, where the command economy is dominated increasingly by a competitive market economy, yet the legal system is in embryonic state and political markets flourish. Because informal arrangements associated with the policy of marketization have developed alongside formal structures, formal structures have eventually had to be brought into line with them. This has sapped the resources of the party-state as they have flowed out into private hands, brought criminal gangs into insider positions, and entrenched vested interests in informal networks. The only way forward, as Joseph Stiglitz (1998) reminded his audience at Beijing University in July 1998, was the "establishment of entirely new national institutions and programs". This meant, of course, going beyond the party-state's modest efforts to allow for dissent, through village elections and a more combative NPC. But the leadership is reluctant to do so. In the regime's favor is the population's fear of chaos, the fragmentation of the opposition, the co-optation of business elites, and the general ease with which Communism and nationalism in China blend. Politically, the regime is the same, not having changed beyond recognition.

A post-totalitarian regime

China's present condition is one of mature post-totalitarian rule, which holds four key features:

◆ Institutional pluralism within the party-state becomes more evident than it was when the dictator lived. Interministerial battles, differences of opinion within the regime over policy, or center-province tensions become better known. Oppositional groups outside of the regime try to create new forms of representation.

◆ There is an ever-widening gap between the official utopian ideology and reality. Party cadres grow less ideologically committed, and more criticism becomes audible from non-Party members. The party-state comes to rely more on performance as a source of legitimacy.

◆ Party institutions deployed in the past to mobilize enthusiasm atrophy. Membership generates boredom, and careerists take over. There is, at best, a minimum of associational life outside these organizations.

◆ Leadership remains constrained in loose, ill-defined ways, but recruitment to senior positions still runs through Party institutions. Because non-Party elites are nonexistent, or organized very weakly, they cannot be readily co-opted. In general, post-totalitarian regimes experience a lack of flexibility in recruiting new talent. This is one area, and a significant one, where China is diverging quite significantly from the type: non-Party elites have grown in a more pluralist China, and the Party has gone out of its way to recruit them.

Except for this last point, all the characteristics listed above apply in abundance to contemporary China. The first characteristic, *institutional pluralism*, is only too visible: take, for instance, the sector of telecommunications, where – until the ministerial reforms of 1998 – the list of political players included state commissions, the Ministry of Post and Telecommunications, its provincial and local post and telecommunication administrations, the Ministry of Electronics, the PLA, the Ministry of Radio, Film and Television, the Ministry of Foreign Trade and Economic Co-operation, the Ministry of Railways, of Electrical Power, of Coal, of Water Resources, banks, and aerospace organizations with quasi-ministerial status (Story, 1997). Then, central government has had the problem of reconciling the contrasting demands for more market in, say, Guandong province, as against more state subsidies in rust-belt areas such as Jilin province. Cross-regional alliances have been formed between the northeast, the Pearl River and the Lower Yangtze, weakening the center. The lesson is that foreign powers and corporations should predicate policy towards China on a recognition of devolution, rather than on an assumption that the center is the head of a unified superpower (Lary, 1997).

Even more notable are the signs of institutional pluralism in the regime's coercive apparatus. Post-Tiananmen debates within the regime have helped to develop a reasonably coherent strategy to suppress dissent. This includes measures to prevent link-ups between discontented groups; more centralized control over police forces; pre-emptive moves against independent labor unions, human rights monitors, underground religious movements, and ethnic separatists; isolating the apolitical majority of the population from dissident ideas by offering them prosperity and more personal freedom, short of striking political poses in public; and holding key security areas, such as the major cities, Tibet and Xinjiang province.

The problem has been in implementation: China's security apparatus is relatively small, numbering about 1.2 million in all. This is one of the smallest professional police forces in Asia. Overall, the coercive system includes the Public Security and State organs, the People's Armed Police, the courts and procurators, the prison and labor reform system, and the PLA. In addition, the system is highly decentralized and therefore dependent on local Party officials and tax sources. It draws for active support on citizenship defense committees – committees whose members could be sympathetic to local protesters, are often ill-trained, and have to earn their livings in other occupations. Beijing's orders are often lost, while nation-wide responses to common security threats are difficult to achieve. Mao's inheritance of powerful local administrations may have had its advantages in allowing a variety of economic experiments, but it is far from ideal for a regime facing so many challenges as the CCP.

Then there is a gap, nay a gulf, between the Party's official ideology and the reality of China: China has taken the capitalist high road with a vengeance. Three-quarters of Chinese workers are in private employment, small and medium-sized state firms have been privatized by Party managers at a frantic pace and corruption has exploded. Hence, Jiang Zemin's adaptation of Party policy as representing "three forces" essential for China's development: advanced productive forces, advanced cultural forces, and the fundamental interests of the largest number of citizens. This redefinition of the Party's task as opening the regime to the new social forces at work in the country goes with the grain of what reformers and regime critics can agree to, and as long as it continues to do so the regime has a good chance of remaining legitimate among a majority of people. But the regime has to continue to pro-

> There is a gulf between the Party's official ideology and the reality of China

vide a steady majority with reasons to be optimistic about their futures, and to improve its performance in key policy areas, such as inflation and minimizing the gap between rich and poor. This conditional popular support is nonetheless accompanied by a widespread sense of acute fear of the consequences of social chaos. Ninety-three per cent of respondents prefer to live in an orderly society than in a freer society that is prone to disruption (Chen *et al.*, 1997). In other words, many people in China – probably a very large majority – conclude that China needs an authoritarian regime for fast and stable economic growth (Zheng, 1994).

That the Party's institutions such as collective farms, state enterprises and TVEs have shrunk, atrophied or morphed into private businesses is not in doubt. Clearly, the Party no longer represents the interests of peasants and workers, but rather faces widespread apathy, and popular antipathy, in addition to a small but active dissident community. Even more worrying for the

Party is the spread of social groups and movements, filling out the space left by the retreat of the Party's own organizations from civil society. Worse, the triads – China's homegrown mafia – were discovered to have taken over the municipality of Shenyang in the northeast, while an illiterate peasant pocketed enough money to buy the Party, army, police and customs officials in Xiamen, the main port of the coastal province of Fujian.

Recruitment to senior positions still runs through Party institutions: the Party still holds to the Leninist principle that "the communist party controls the cadres" (Hellman and Kirchberger, 2000). Following the official declaration to move China to a socialist market economy, new guidelines were defined for recruitment to leadership cadre position at the level of counties and upwards. Between 1992 and 1998, 323,600 new cadres were appointed out of a total leadership cadre of 508,000. Of these new cadres, 60% were younger than forty-five, and 80% had completed university education. In other words, the party-state holds *nomenklatura* power and has used it forcefully to rejuvenate senior membership. The younger cadres are there to implement the economic policy reforms that are rapidly awakening China's civil society.

Given such a contrast between the inherited features of the regime and the social changes fostered by its own policies, it is hardly surprising that Jiang Zemin and his Politburo colleagues have experimented on political reforms (Lam, 2001a). They have dabbled with direct elections, but their heart is in creating a well-educated, Singapore-type elite under CCP supervision. At the fifteenth Party Congress in September 1997, Jiang Zemin pledged to "extend the scope of democracy at the grassroots level to make sure that people directly exercise their democratic rights" (Zheng, 1997). The Chinese leaders then observed with horror the introduction of Western-style democracy in Indonesia. Soon, Jiang was telling Party delegates that he did not favor elections above village level. His preference went to picking a whole new corps of young, professionally qualified, reformist and (politically) trustworthy cadres. Reform of the cadre system is reported as being the only move in political liberalization to be expected for the rest of the decade (Lam, 2001b). Nonetheless, when Sichuan province went ahead under its own authority in November 1998 in Nanjing township, the elections were eventually reported in the national press in 2001. Beijing too gave approval for Guandong province to hold direct township elections. Both Presidents Clinton and Bush have spoken out in China, and in the presence of the Chinese leadership, in favor of religious freedoms and free elections. The signal is clear enough: the Chinese leadership is not opposed in principle so much as to the circumstances and conditions in which these freedoms are exercised in China.

Towards a consolidated democracy "China-style"

Where, then, are the detonators of regime change in China? In the case of authoritarian dictatorships, when the leader dies so does the regime. In China, the party-state lives. Therefore there have to be other detonators of regime change: these may range from defeat in war, to military coups, failure to suppress organized opposition, or the formation within the regime of a powerful group ready to negotiate with an organized opposition.

None of these detonators has played a part in China. As we saw in Chapter 2, the regime has been careful to avoid major military conflicts, especially after the bloody nose it received in its war against Vietnam in 1979. The armed forces are just another expression for the party-state, and they remain under strong political control. The regime brooks no extra-regime opposition. In Taiwan, events took a different course in the 1990s, when a series of constitutional reforms led to the establishment of a mixed presidential-parliamentary system. In Hong Kong, over which China resumed sovereignty in June 1997, and despite a return to executive rule, the democratic reforms introduced by the UK had taken root. Talk of regime change was therefore in the air. But by December 1998, Jiang Zemin (1998) referred tentatively to something called "China-style democracy". What that implied is that the reformers in the regime would have to disprove the contention that the bottleneck to institutional transformation was political reform; they would have to demonstrate that the regime was capable of transforming itself into a legitimate manager of a China-style state under law. The regime has to show that it can hold the political fort while all is flux round about.

Now in the pretransition phase, the proximate condition for breakdown of the old order is that the incumbent power is unable to resolve a growing list of problems. In contemporary China, three key related problems are the present trend to an open society, freer labor markets and partial representation. They are not susceptible to quick fixes, and they can be addressed only through further reforms. Sooner, rather than later, this involves reformers in a competitive rush to build up their power bases against their opponents in the regime. One way to do this is to woo China's various opposition groups. Eventually, China's political system becomes democratized through the holding of general elections, the drawing up of a constitution, and the consolidation of the reforms that the country's present rulers have initiated. For this to happen peacefully, a defining moment would come when the leadership announces the introduction of new norms governing future political development. As I argue in the last chapter, there is every reason to believe that the body language of the regime indicates movement in that direction. For the moment, this is not practical politics. If it were, then there would be two contending coalitions, one initially led by hardliners in the regime against any change, and softliners who argue the case for a dialog with moderate opponents (O'Donnell and Schmitter, 1986). For the moment, China is a mature post-totalitarian regime, and the first concern of Party members is to secure their positions, enjoy their wealth, avoid upsets, and place some unspecified limits on the leadership. Making life agreeable for fellow citizens while wielding a big stick appears a reasonable formula.

The conclusion is paradoxical: viewed through political lenses, China's near future looks particularly unclear. It is by no means clear that the monopoly party-state can introduce a rule of law. But measured in relation to an ideal state of "consolidated democracy", the future is not entirely so. In fact, we know more about China's future than we give ourselves credit for. Let's ask ourselves the factors about China that we know to be in the pipeline, as it were, and then we can list the key uncertainties. The uncertainties lie in the imponderables, such as the behavior of randy Chinese males, the possible emergence of Mao-type figures from the back of beyond, the revolutionary material lying around in China for radical political leaders to exploit, or the personal rivalries and failings of the political leadership.

The two – what is in the pipeline, and the imponderables – together are the central components of credible scenarios.[1]

There is a lengthening list of things that are in China's political pipeline. We know the tasks confronting China if it is to become a consolidated democracy, and how far the regime is from that. We know that the party's ideology is a barrier, but one that is not insurmountable. We have evidence that widespread poverty, a mass peasantry, and a traditional political culture are not ideal materials to create a well-functioning constitutional democracy, even China-style. We know that the Chinese people are scared stiff of a return to the tragedies of the previous two centuries. We know that the party-state is only too well aware of the narrow way, and the many dangers, that lie ahead. We know that our four elements of the world's transformation – US pre-eminence, global markets, the Zeitgeist of market-democracy, and the internationalisation of production – bind China irreversibly into the global system. We know that the regime wants to join the lead group of powers in the world, and that the necessary but not sufficient condition for membership is creating a state under the rule of law. We know that the Party's prime legitimation of its hold on power is that it is the sole guide available to chart China's road to prosperity. We know that the party-state is not keen on experimenting with utopias, and that it prefers to feel its way into an uncertain future. We know that this has entailed, and will continue to entail, moving away from the command to the market economy, to deepening interdependence and away from autarky. We know that this creates major tensions in the rural-urban balance to be struck by the regime. We know, therefore, that while the political system changes little in appearance, a constant flow of legal and of economic policy measures are being implemented. Incrementally, we also know that these imply extensive changes in the political system. We need no reminding that political leaders are liable to moral failings, and that this is something that China truly shares with the rest of the world. We can only state as a probability the future timing or content of such measures, as each one is the outcome of political negotiations among the changing kaleidoscope of factions. Not least, we can only

---

[1] See Chapter 6 in Jonathan Story, The Frontiers of Fortune, especially the discussion of Pierre Wack's Shell scenario method.

guess at the time such reforms will take to implement before China becomes a consolidated democracy. But we know that the regime's monopoly powers are shrinking fast, as the plural reality of China bursts into view, and that a frightened regime is therefore in danger of dithering between a policy of no rush or accelerated reform.

The present leadership deploys the future as a resource to locate problems too knotty to deal with now; the Party's shrinking political monopoly suggests that reforms should be speeded up. That is where the reformers' efforts to supplement their domestic power base through alliances abroad come into the picture. The reformers' main policy here is to join the WTO and to import all the regulatory baggage to China from the developed world. Not surprisingly, serious differences have opened up between economic nationalists and economic liberals (Wang, 2000). The former wish to protect domestic firms, to guide foreign investment to fit national needs, and to promote national ownership, whereas the latter seek to promote China as a platform for efficient production. A central question for the regime's future is whether policy can continue to be fashioned through mutual trade-offs between the two broad coalitions, or whether one coalition emerges victorious

> The Party's shrinking political monopoly suggests that reforms should be speeded up

over the other. The very fact that the regime has to maintain such a balance indicates that China's party-state cannot keep to the status quo. It has to continue to move towards laying the institutional foundations of a constitutional order if it is to keep the reformers satisfied.

In short, we know what we know and we know what we don't know about China's future, which is decidedly an improvement over knowing nothing. In particular, we know that public opinion is the ghost at the party-state's banquet, and that it would not be wise for the leadership to take the Chinese people's acquiescence in their rule for granted. What we know above all is that the leading edge of reform is with regard to economic policy institutions, and that this is in effect transforming the Chinese polity. There is no turning back. WTO membership is the battering ram of the reformers to accelerate domestic changes.

References

Anita Chan and Robert E. Senser, 1997, "China's troubled workers", *Foreign Affairs*, 76(2), pp. 104–17.

Jie Chen, Yang Zhong and Jan William Hillard, 1997, "The level and sources of popular support for China's current political regime", *Communist and Post-Communist Studies*, 30(1), pp. 45–64.

China Daily, 1999, March 16.

Jack A. Goldstone, 1995, "The coming Chinese collapse", *Foreign Policy*, 99, pp. 355–64.

Sebastian Hellman and Sarah Kirchberger, 2000, "The Chinese Nomenklatura in transition", *China Analysis*, 1.

Valerie M. Hudson and Andrea den Boer, 2002, "A surplus of men, a deficit of peace: security and sex ratios in Asia}s largest states", *International Security*, 26(4), pp. 5 –38.

Samuel P. Huntington, 1968, *Political Order in Changing Societies*, New Haven, Yale University Press.

Robert O. Keohane and Joseph S. Nye, 1998, "Power and interdependence in the information age", *Foreign Affairs*, 77(5), pp. 81–94.

Z. Kevuan, 2000, "Towards the rule of law in China: experiences in the last two decades", *China Report*, 36(4), pp. 491–509.

Willy Wo-lap Lam, 2001a, "Reforming political structure in China: which road to take", *China Brief*, 109(2), pp. 256–9.

Willy Wo-lap Lam, 2001b, "China's cadres play 'Survivor'", April 17, www.cnn.com

Diana Lary, 1997, "Regions and nation: the present situation in china in historical context", *Pacific Affairs*, 70(2).

Juan Linz and Alfred Stepan, 1996, *Problems of Democratic Transition and Consolidation: Southern Europe, South America and Post-Communist Europe*, Baltimore, Johns Hopkins University Press.

Ju-Ao-Mei, 1992, "China and the rule of law", *Pacific Affairs*, 5(10), pp. 863–72.

Barrington Moore, Jr, 1972, *Social Origins of Dictatorship and Democracy: Lord and Peasant in the Making of the Modern World*, Boston, MA, Beacon Press.

Andrew J. Nathan, 1997, *China's Transition*, New York, Columbia University Press, p. 26.

Barry Naughton, 1995, *Growing Out of the Plan*, Cambridge, Cambridge University Press.

New York Times, 2001, "Companies compete to provide Saudi Internet veil", *New York Times*, November 19.

G. O'Donnell and P. Schmitter, 1986, *Transition from Authoritarian Rule: Tentative Conclusions*.

Mancur Olson, Jr, 1963, "Growth as a destabilizing force", *Journal of Economic History*, XXIII.

Minxin Pei, 1998, "Is China democratizing?", *Foreign Affairs*, 77(1), pp. 68–82.

Li Shixlong, Xiqui Fu, 2002, Religion and National Security in China: Secret Documents from China's Security Sector, February 11, www.freedomhouse.org

Joseph Stiglitz, 1998, "Second-generation strategies for reform for China", address given at Beijing University, Beijing, China, July 20. www.worldbank.org/html/extdr/extme/jssp072098.htm

Jonathan Story, 1997, "Deng's legacy: China online", INSEAD, Fontainebleau, France.

Jonathan Unger and Anita Chan, 1995, "China, corporatism, and the east Asian model", *Australian Journal of Chinese Affairs*, 33, pp. 29–53.

Robert Wade, 1990, *Governing the Market: Economic Theory and the Role of Government in East Asian Industrialisation*, Princeton, Princeton University Press.

Yong Wang, 2000, "WTO: China's domestic WTO debate", *China Business Review*, 27(1).

George Will, 1997, "China's turn", *Washington Post*, April 17.

Deng Xiaoping, 1991, "The necessity of upholding the four cardinal principles in the drive for the Four Modernisations", in *Major Documents of the People's Republic of China*, Beijing, Foreign Language Press, p. 49.

Fareed Zakaria, 1997, "The rise of illiberal democracy", *Foreign Affairs*, November/December, pp. 22–43.

Jiang Zemin, 1998, "Speech at the conference commemorating the Third Plenum of the Eleventh Congress of the CCP", *People's Daily*, 19 December.

Dingxin Zhao, 2001, "China's prolonged stability and political future: same political system, different policies and methods", *Journal of Contemporary China*, 10(28), pp. 427–44.

Yongian Zheng, 1994, "Development and democracy: are they compatible in China?", *Political Science Quarterly*, 109, pp. 256–9.

Yongian Zheng, 1997, "Power and agenda: Jiang Zemin's new political initiatives at the CCP's fifteenth congress", *Issues and Studies*, 33(11), pp. 35–7.

6

Applying the Dracula principle: China joins the WTO

IN HIS SPEECH to the NPC on March 5, 2002, Zhu Rongji stated that the country was "facing new difficulties and severe challenges". In a two-hour speech ranging over the last four years, he ran through a long list of problems faced by China, from corruption to unemployment and 'deep-seated' difficulties in the economy. He also repeated what he had often said before: that WTO entry would pose a severe challenge to many of China's less competitive industries. Negotiating accession proved one of the premier's prime achievements in four years in office, and one that created a good deal of anxiety in China and around the world. In China, pessimists fear that agriculture and industry will suffer from the competition, creating serious social strains. China, they claim, will play wrecker to the WTO. My interpretation begs to differ: China's entry to the WTO in 2002 helps underpin its reputation as a reliable partner, and embarks China on a process of regime change. That includes China's business system. What stretches ahead of the CCP is the introduction of norms, rules and standards elaborated by the rich countries of the West over the past half-century.

Let's start by looking at why China's request to join the world trade club took so long, the implications for the regime of joining an interdependent world, the caravan of forces that unblocked the talks in 1997–8, China's new trade regime, and why China is much more likely to become a pillar than a wrecker of international society. We'll visit China's business system in detail in the next chapter.

The long march to respectability

Negotiations on China's accession opened in 1986, and then dragged on interminably. As Premier Zhu Rongji quipped, "My hairs have turned gray waiting for the outcome." Why did negotiations last such a long time? Many factors contributed, such as the mechanics of the negotiation process, the expansion of membership, an ever-more ambitious global trade agenda, and the demands for far greater policy transparency placed on candidates. The main issue was that China's Communists were not *salonfähig*, as they say in polite Viennese society. Let's examine each in turn.

Accession involves two sets of negotiations that run in parallel. The first set of negotiations is conducted on a multilateral basis between the applicant and members in a working party. This is followed by a detailed review of what has to be done for the applicant to bring practice into line with WTO requirements. The second set of negotiations is conducted bilaterally between the applicant and the WTO members who wish to negotiate. The results of these bilateral negotiations are applied to all members under the most favored nation (MFN) principle. Add to this the clashing trade policies of the great trading powers, an expanding membership, and a more demanding trade policy agenda and we account for at least half of the long delay before bringing China into the world trade club.

The WTO's ancestor, the GATT, started as an accord among the main industrialized states. With each successive round, membership has become more inclusive. Initially, twenty-three of the fifty-one states in the global system signed up. During the cold war, membership of the GATT was limited to countries falling within the Western spheres of influence. Castro's Cuba was one exception, but that was because Cuba as a founder of the GATT never made the mistake, like China in 1949, of leaving after the revolution of 1959. By the time of the Soviet Union's collapse, and the conversion of developing countries to more open market policies, the 128 signatories from the GATT in effect accounted for 90% of world trade. Since then, accession proved arduous and slow. The list of those who joined reads like the Pied Piper's lost children: Bulgaria, Ecuador, Estonia, Kyrgyzstan, Latvia, Mongolia, Panama, Romania and Oman. Thirty-three others applied, which may be listed in three categories: the politically important states of China, Taiwan, Russia and Saudi Arabia; the many transition countries from the old Soviet empire; and the rest, including Algeria. China was not alone in being invited to dust its feet on the club's threshold, while the members went about their business inside the walls.

A more ambitious global trade agenda absorbs quantities of bureaucratic expertise and simultaneously demands far greater policy transparency, along the lines of the Dracula principle: problems disappear when light is shed on them. In the shorter term, China experiences things the other way round: the more light is shed on sensitive areas of public policy, such as procurement, financial services, and copyright and patent law, the more problems there are to deal with. At least China will be able to use the WTO's greatly reinforced dispute settlements procedure and an appeals process against the world's trade powers, and not just endure the ignominy of being last in PriceWaterhouseCoopers' "opacity index" (www.opacityindex.com). This index claims to enable governments and investors to identify the incremental borrowing costs imposed by opacity in law, economic policy, corporate reporting, corruption and government regulation. China is number thirty-five out of thirty-five, occupying the dungeon a stairwell down on Russia. So what can we anticipate when light is shed on China's political, market and business practices as it emerges via WTO accession from PriceWaterhouseCoopers' dungeon? Let us see what we can glean from the booming industry of transitologists.

Transitology and the roller coaster of US-Chinese relations

Practitioners of transitology ask two initial questions: (1) What drives political and economic regimes to change from one type to another? By class war, say the world's Marxists; by mounting the progressive staircase of history, say Western modernizers. And (2) How do they go about managing/not managing transition? China's conservative, cohesion-oriented Communists invoke time as a necessary, but not sufficient, ally in steering China towards a future as a full member of the world trade system. They feel comfortable the more the future extends towards infinity. China's negotiating partners in the WTO, and the USA in particular, are keen to bring the future forwards. They want China to open its markets as soon as possible.

Now in the longer-term perspective, the mood in the music of US-Chinese relations has been highly cyclical: the high point of February 1972 was only reached again in 1978; the early years of the Reagan presidency brought Chinese-US relations to a new low, revived by Reagan's 1984 visit. The next five years are seen in retrospect as to the relationship's halcyon days.

When China submitted its application in the GATT, the UK and China agreed to include Hong Kong. The UK, on China's accord, announced that Hong Kong was a separate customs territory under the GATT, a status short of statehood. Taiwan requested a similar status in order to avoid tensions with the mainland. Meanwhile, China participated in the Uruguay Round as an observer, in other words as an informal participant. With such favorable political winds blowing, China's own economic reforms opened a vista on the country's eventual reunification. If all Chinese territories came to apply similar rules, powerful forces would be set in train promoting convergence on shared norms of market-democracy.

Politics pricked the dream of convergence. The events of June 4 put paid to any hopes, however exaggerated, of early accession. The GATT talks were broken off. Beijing tried to shore up its relations with the Bush administration by cooperation in the Gulf War, but this Chinese-US rapprochement was complicated greatly by Taiwan's bid for accession to the GATT in 1990. The fear in Beijing was that the Western powers, including Japan, might be tempted to bring Taiwan into the WTO and keep China out.

Meanwhile, Canada had successfully championed the cause of the GATT's upgrading to become the WTO – a GATT with more judicial teeth. Here was an opportunity for reformers in the party-state to welcome resumption of the accession negotiations in February 1992. Reformers were helped along, too, by Deng's southern tour, where he enunciated the idea that it was not only a capitalist country that could develop a market economy. The fourteenth Party Congress in October duly committed China to "faster and bolder" economic reforms in the direction of a "socialist market economy", involving price deregulation, the marketization of state enterprises, and the promotion of foreign direct investment. That month, China's leadership signed a memorandum of understanding with the outgoing Bush administration to accelerate market opening. China also used its allies in the GATT to ensure that the Taiwan working party was formed on the principle that "all contracting parties acknowledge the view that there is only one China", and that "Chinese Taipei, as a separate customs union, should not accede to the GATT before the People's Republic of China". China's currency, the yuan, was devalued by about 60%, prompting a rapid surge in the trade surplus with the USA, the EU and Japan.

The incoming Clinton administration was not inclined to treat China with kid gloves. Congress was irate over China's treatment of the students, and China's exports with the USA were growing apace. The mood endured over Clinton's first term, when the administration placed China in its human-rights doghouse, opposed its bid to host the Olympics 2000, criticized China over Tibet, and kept high-level contacts to a minimum. Eventually, Congress gave the green light to the WTO, which opened for business on January 1, 1995.

This provided a further challenge to China's trade diplomats. China had signed the Uruguay Round, pledging to abide by international rules, and pushed hard to join the WTO. But Beijing's motives were clearly mixed: on the one hand, it wanted the prestige of joining the WTO as a founding member; on the other hand, it wanted to join in order to slow down future WTO discussions about opening up service markets.

Joining the WTO to block its functioning was scarcely a policy stance designed to win friends in Washington, Brussels or Tokyo. China, the US trade negotiators insisted, was in a stage of "takeoff" and had to open its doors like a developed country. It was running a large trade surplus, its exports had a high value-added content, and its market institutions were opaque. China, US trade negotiators were saying, is not yet a market economy. It retains many features of a command economy, which means that Chinese exports on world markets are sold at prices below cost – the definition of dumping.

If China's true per capita income was $380, Washington suggested, then how come Chinese people lived on average to 70 years as if they were enjoying per capita incomes of $2,000 plus? Larry Summers, the then chief economist at the World Bank and later a star of the Clinton administration, flatteringly described China as overtaking the USA as the world's number-one economy some time between 2003 and 2014. The statement was recorded in a clarion call by *The Economist's* senior Asian correspondent, Jim Rohwer, in a special sixteen-page survey, "The Titan stirs": "China is already the world's third – or fourth – biggest economy, behind only America, Japan and maybe Germany. The official figures belie this ... The official figures about China are gibberish." On May 10, 1993, *Time* ran a thirty-two-page story entitled "The next superpower". At the end of the year, William Overholt (1993), then managing director of the Banker's Trust in Hong Kong, and editor of a biannual report *Global Assessment*, for which I was writing, launched his book *China: The Next Economic Superpower* on the world. The prospect of missing out on a Chinese El Dorado touched off a flood of inward investment (see Figure 8.1 in Chapter 8). The flattery also had a more prosaic effect, whether intended or not: China, the USA insisted, had to open its door wide like a developed country.

US and EU requests China be a market democracy

Here was the crux of the US position: unless China's domestic system was fundamentally reformed, then the USA would face a giant Japan. China, the US leitmotiv ran, was known to be learning as fast as possible from the Asian developmental states how best to "protect in and export out". It should not be allowed to become another, much bigger Japan. If equality was the new norm for voting in the WTO, then that implied equality of conditions for all on a global, level playing field. China, the USA insisted, would have to undertake all the

> China was known to be learning as fast as possible from the Asian developmental states how best to "protect in and export out"

duties of a member state, including full convertibility of the yuan, the end of import controls and export subsidies, and the unwinding of internal barriers to trade. As long as China could not, or did not, offer such conditions, then it had to expect the USA to use the WTO's legal loopholes to impose import constraints on China's exports. In plain language, the USA was telling China to become a market-democracy as fast as possible, or to continue to dust its feet on the threshold of the world organization.

China, US diplomats kept repeating, had to be treated as a developed country. After all, China is large: it leads the world's output league tables in steel, coal, fertilizers, TV sets and bicycles; overseas Chinese investors use it as an export platform for lower-value-added operations; its trade surplus continues to rise in both capital- and labor-intensive areas.

China's WTO negotiators disagreed, and insisted that it join as a developing country. The country is very poor, nearly as poor as some of the poorest territories in the world. Most of the forty-eight poorest countries in the world are located in sub-Saharan Africa, with a per capita income just 10% of the world average compared with China's 15%. Both China and India belong to the World Bank and the IMF, which consider them to be developing countries. Winning prolonged transition periods in the WTO accession negotiations held two advantages: a status of a developing country ensured China the right to continue industry protection, and it signaled that there was no alternative form of government in China for a long period ahead.

China's negotiators soft-pedaled the industry protection argument because their defense in negotiations of various protectionist positions became untenable, not because China required shorter transition periods to win friends (Yongtu, 2000). It became untenable when Chinese negotiators discovered that the high nominal tariff rates inherited from the command economy were not being enforced. They were informed of the gap between nominal and actual tariff rates on New Zealand mutton by New Zealand's negotiators. The mutton was entering the China market at zero rate. Another example of how ineffective China's protectionist devices are is illustrated by the case of the PLA's Tiancheng Group. Zhu Rongji, according to US intelligence sources, accused the Group at a July 1998 anti-smuggling conference of avoiding payment of fifty million renminbi in import and sales taxes on a purchase of partially processed iron ore from Australia. "Every time our customs officials tried to snare these bastards", Zhu Rongji was reported as saying, "some powerful military person appeared to speak on their behalf'" (Lawrence, 1999). The top brass was not amused, and Jiang Zemin appeared at the conference four days later to confirm that "some units and individuals" in the PLA were smuggling. In other words, in a rapidly marketizing country such as China, high formal barriers to market entry create incentives for entrepreneurs to get around them.

So much for the market aspect of transition. Its political meaning for China proved more important. "Transition" referred to a new category of states, defined in the jargon of the international institutions as "transition economies", i.e. transiting from the planned to the market economy, from dictatorship to democracy. The word's political career originated in southern Europe in 1974–5 and then spread as one dictatorship after another succumbed to a contagion of market-democracy around the world. Suitably enough, it was that great factory of intellectual fudge, the European Commission (1995), that slipped the "t" word into its March 1995 position on EU policy towards China. In the case of China, its value lay in its malleability: everyone could read into "transition" whatever they wanted. The concept infiltrated the mid-1990s debate in the USA on whether to contain or to engage China, entered Australian discourse, and then colored Chinese mainland and Taiwan political language.

The transition formula is so popular because it postpones the moment of decision for everybody when China moves to being a mature socialist market economy or a consolidated market democracy. It enables the USA to do business with China now and leave democracy to evolve in China some time later; the French and Germans may compete on Chinese markets in return for China taking steps towards regime transformation; Premier Zhu Rongji could tell a US audience to "not be too impatient" regarding human rights in China, because peoples with different levels of income had different needs, therefore different conceptions of what constituted human rights (CNN, 1999). In the longer term, he was saying, we'll all converge on greater wealth and political norms. In short, Chinese leaders hint, eliptically, that the price of joining the world trade club is for China to democratize eventually and of course China-style. The "t" word allows all participants in the process of China's irreversible inclusion in the global system to use the future as a place to locate present disagreement.

China's interdependence and the
challenge to the party-state

China's accession negotiations provide an example of how diplomacy in an interdependent world economy is a twelve-way game (see Putnam (1988) on two-way games and Story (1988) on multiple levels). Public policy linkages in any bilateral negotiation are depicted in Figure 6.1. It is worth noting that all of these linkages are two-ways streets, however unequal the relationships may be. The two-ways are illustrated by the arrows pointing both directions. The two circles represent the Chinese polity and the US polity. The density of their interactions is assessed through six pairs of relationships: transnational and diplomatic relations are horizontal; domestic relations of authority and consent are vertical; and oblique relations trace influence attempts of public officials or lobbies from one country to effect policy or dispositions in the other country. Third parties are always concerned by ever more intense bilateral relations, even when their interests

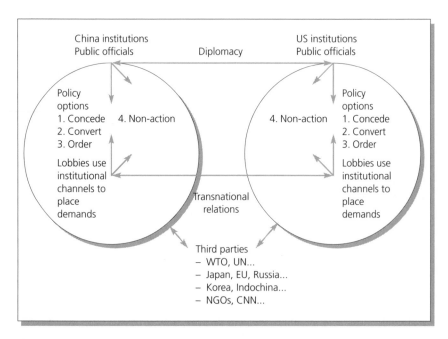

Figure 6.1 ◆ Twelve public-policy linkages in a bilateral relationship

may be covered by the extension of market access accords to everyone through the MFN clause. Let's look first at the China polity and then at the US polity as a prelude to presenting the diplomacy between them.

Chinese domestic politics and the WTO negotiations

Consider transnational relations, recording the growth in trade and exchanges between China and the USA. In 1978, China's trade to GDP ratio was 10%; this rose to 30% by the turn of the millennium. US imports from China grew during the 1990s at 21% per annum, rising from 2.8% of total imports in 1990 to 7.4% by the end of the decade. The USA absorbed 21% of China exports then, compared with 16% accounted for by the EU and 16% accounted for by Japan. Foreign direct investment into China rose from nearly zero to $40 billion in 1999, equivalent to 4% GNP. Fifty to sixty per cent of this overseas investment came from the Asia-Pacific region, especially through Hong Kong. An unknown fraction of this Hong Kong money is attributable to "round-tripping" by state enterprise managers, who have been siphoning money offshore and then bringing it back to the mainland for investment in the special economic zones, where the regulatory environment is a light touch. Even so, China has had a large slice of cross-border business flows to developing countries: up to 40% of total foreign direct investment flows, 10% of lending by banks, and one-third of imports into lower- and middle-income countries in the Asia-Pacific region, representing 45% of total Japanese imports.

> China has a long way to go before replacing Japan as Asia's prime economy

China is a rising power in Asia and this worries its neighbors, especially India and Japan. But China has a long way to go before replacing Japan as Asia's prime economy.

Domestic relations of authority and consent are illustrated on the vertical plane. Every country has its own institutional channels to relay demands from local lobbies to central government, and to communicate decisions from the center to the provinces. These decisions can be classified in four ways: the central government *concedes* to local or to lobby demands, seeks to *convert* local authorities or lobbies to central government preferences (through side payments, etc.), or *orders compliance* accompanied by effective sanctions. The fourth involves *non-action*, involving a prolonged period of inaction by public officials for any number of reasons, ranging from reluctance to confront entrenched lobbies through to a decision to postpone action until the time is right.

In China's bid to enter the WTO, all four types of decision have co-existed. Non-action was Li Peng's preference during his long premiership from 1987 to 1998. Often identified as a leader of the heavy-industry brigade, he was in no hurry to negotiate. A committee had been set up in 1986 to coordinate positions among the varied ministries and agencies affected by the prospect of having to comply to international trade norms (Wang, 2000). It was never able to overcome opposition. All the major ministries and agencies owned their own corporations, made up the rules of the game as they went along, and acted as their own referees. They were expert at endless procrastination, eager to postpone decisions, and innovative at placing exhorbitant demands. Their overlapping responsibilities for tariffs, quotas, production and issues of market access brought them into competition with one another, while many of the major industrial and sectoral ministries saw little opportunity and much danger in signing up to international trade agreements. In the trade arena, over forty ministries, commissions and agencies shared responsibility for

> The key issue for the USA is whether China's central government can implement its WTO commitments

SOEs, industrial policy and safety regulations. Local government officials included one-time reformers, entrepreneurial officials and ideological opponents, who wished to protect local industries, particularly in the huge, older SOEs of northeast China.

The key issue for the USA is whether China's central government can implement its WTO commitments. Much of the drive for this has come from Congress, which used the renewal of China's MFN status as an opportunity to attack President Clinton's China policy on issues ranging from export dumping to human rights. Here was a prime reason for China acceding to the WTO as fast as possible: once a member, China would not appear on annual trial in the US Congress. But the price would be to ditch the party-state's policy style of consensus decision-making, where "no one [is left] worse off than before" (Shirk, 1993). As China's chief negotiator for GATT, then for the WTO, has stated: "The difficult process of China's joining the WTO is in many ways a real reflection of the difficult process by which China has been transforming itself from being a country with a planned economy into a country under a market economic system" (Yongtu, 2000). The US move in the mid-1990s to engage with China only strengthens the trend (see Box 6.1).

US, European and Japanese corporations also urged the regime to accelerate reforms. The presence of approximately 45,000 factories, branches and offices on the mainland, according to Wang (2000), provoked a rise in economic nationalism at all levels of society, from economists to government officials, the media elite, entrepreneurs and common citizens. Despite its conservatism, this economic nationalism does not support simply closing the nation's door to foreign investment. Rather, it advocates economic independence and the idea that the Chinese must be the masters of their own economy. In general, economic nationalists believe that China must encourage domestic investment and indigenous economic development because the goal of most foreign investors is to profit from, not strengthen, China's developing economy. Economic liberals, on the other hand, believe that foreign investment may be the best and quickest way to develop the Chinese economy and strengthen the country as a whole. Proponents of this view are also found at all levels of society.

Box 6.1 US domestic politics over China

The US coalition for China's inclusion argued that *engagement* favored regime evolution, provided access to an inexhaustible supply of labor, supplied a platform for exports, and opened China once again to missionary activities. The coalition for *confrontation* expressed concern about the threat of China to the USA and to Taiwan; about China's religious and pro-abortion policies; and that China's accession to the WTO would induce a worldwide "race to the bottom", in both wage scales and workers' rights. Human rights activists and environmental groups were also opposed, on account of China's record.

Until 1997, the party-state leant in favor of consensus between the two strands of economic policy thinking. The fifteenth Party Congress declared certain strategic sectors off-limits to foreign investors, a position refined in the *Catalog Guiding Foreign Investment in Industry*. The catalog indicates where investments should be channeled: into encouraged sectors, for high-tech or in less-developed regions, and away from restricted sectors, where approval is required, often both provincially and nationally. A third category prohibited foreign investment in services and internal trade, including distribution. Most importantly, the government began to encourage mergers and acquisitions among SOEs in all industries to improve economics of scale, as well as to create competition in industries, such as telecommunications, which were virtual monopolies. Victory, in other words, went to the party-state's consensus decision-making style. The series of domestic and international factors that came together in the years 1996–8 made this status quo unsustainable.

The turning point of 1997–8

A caravan of forces converged on Chinese party-state politics in 1997–8. Foremost among these was the agenda of Greater China. Taiwan was and is the sole exception to the general rule of the world's chanceries' infatuation with the "t" word as far as China is concerned. Taiwan yearns for certainty, not fudge. So it turns the argument about transition to its own purposes, suggesting that reunification has to wait until mainland China becomes a democracy and as prosperous as Taiwan. This is fine with the Communist party-state because it postpones democratization on the mainland to an indefinite point in the future. It is the interim period that produces cross-Straits tensions: Taiwan seeks to end its de facto status as an appendage of the mainland with regard to international organizations. In 1993, the Taipei government opened a campaign to upgrade the island's profile as an inter-national player. There were two main reasons for this shift (Tucker, 2000):

◆ Taiwan found itself a hostage to US–Chinese trade battles. The USA refused China developing country status because of its high level of

manufacturing exports. Much of this flowed from Taiwanese investments on the mainland – by the turn of the century, numbering 43,000
projects and worth about $44 billion. Because direct business contact
with the mainland was unlawful – a position that has been changing
rapidly since both mainland and Taiwan are in the WTO – these exports
derived in large part from assembly operations mounted via Hong Kong
by Taiwanese businesses. Matters were made worse by reports that
Taiwan businesses on the mainland were engaged in intellectual
property theft.

◆ The June 1989 tragedy on Tiananmen Square gave a powerful impetus
to an active Taiwan democracy movement, which had been taking shape
since the mid-1970s. A prime political demand was an end to the ruling
Kuomintang's reunification policy. This inflamed opinion in the
mainland party-state, which broke off relations with Taiwan in June
1995, and then conducted military exercises and missile-firing tests off
the Taiwan coast at the time of the general elections there in March
1996. Mainland threats prompted the USA to deploy two aircraft
carriers in the Taiwan Straits.

Both the USA and mainland China drew back from the precipice of confrontation, and by October 1997 the conditions were ripe enough for
Clinton to set the tone (White House, 1997). Emphasizing the benefits for
the USA of working closely with China in confronting the many challenges
facing the countries of the Asia-Pacific, the President insisted that China was
being drawn into "the institutions and arrangements that are setting the
ground rules for the twenty-first century – the security partnerships, the
open trade arrangements, the arms control regime, the multinational coalitions against terrorism, crime and drugs, the commitments to preserve the
environment and to uphold human rights … This is our best hope, to secure
our own interest and values and to advance China's in the historic transformation that began 25 years ago, when China reopened to the world." A
pragmatic policy of engagement, Clinton concluded, "of expanding our
areas of co-operation with China while confronting our differences openly
and respectfully" is much better than a policy of confrontation, predicated
on the belief that China's institutions do not evolve. Seeking to confront

and contain China before it becomes too strong is "unworkable, counter-productive, and potentially dangerous".

The permissive conditions for this updating of the engagement policy, initiated with President Nixon's visit in 1972 and the end to the US trade embargo, may be grouped in terms of significant changes in regime personnel, in Greater China affairs, in China's geopolitical neighborhood, in the China policies of the major trading powers, and in a very altered outlook for the Asia-Pacific economy:

♦ Paramount leader Deng Xiaoping died in February 1997, at the age of 92, followed by a smooth handover in power to the new leadership. In September, the fifteenth Party Congress confirmed the party-state's commitment to market reform. In March 1998, Premier Li Peng, who had openly opposed WTO accession talks, was replaced by Zhu Rongji, the former mayor of Shanghai. Zhu Rongji considered globalization to be unstoppable, and that China had either to join or get left behind. The new premier accelerated the pace of reforms, notably with regard to the administration – he cut central government personnel by 50% in a few months – housing and education, banks, subsidies, and state enterprises. This was all in line with China's commitment to WTO principles.

♦ On June 30, 1997, Hong Kong reverted to Chinese sovereignty, providing a window on the South China Seas, a major port, a monetary authority with $60 billion in reserves, a highly educated population, and a sophisticated governance structure. Hong Kong was already a participant in the WTO, operating as a free port with very high standards of administration, a predictable legal system, guaranteed property rights, and a civil society enjoying free flow of information and per capita incomes thirty times that of the mainland. Over two-thirds of mainland exports to Hong Kong represented outward processing arrangements often run by Taiwanese businesses and going to US markets, where Hong Kong enjoyed large trade surpluses. In February 1998, the USA concluded the trade accord with the WTO on Taiwan's eventual entry. Greater China's unity seemed tantalizingly close, but also still distant as a prospect.

♦ Taiwan's concerns at being left adrift in the wake of mainland–US relations prompted a speeding up of bilateral negotiations with the USA to pave the way for WTO entry. After seventeen rounds, the talks were concluded in February 1998. In June, President Clinton visited the mainland for a ten-day presidential trip. There, he delighted the leadership with his "Three Noes" statement: no to Taiwanese independence; no to One China, One Taiwan; no Taiwanese entry to international organizations where statehood is required for membership. Taiwanese eyes were not smiling. US "engagement" with China is clearly conducted on the assumption that the Greater China of mainland+Taiwan+Hong Kong+overseas Chinese in the Asia-Pacific is already a virtual reality. With Macao back under Chinese sovereignty in 1999, Greater China disposes of four seats in the WTO – but we jump ahead. Back to our turning point of the second Clinton administration.

◆ The geostrategic environment of China took a sudden lurch for the worse in the course of 1998. In May, the Indian and Pakistani governments exploded their nuclear devices, while in August, North Korea launched its ballistic missile, the Taepo Dong 1, over Japan. This dealt a devastating blow to arms-control policies, prompted the USA to bring forward preparations on missile defense, and accentuated the attraction to the Clinton administration of China as an indispensable partner for the USA as manager-in-chief of Asia-Pacific affairs.

◆ In September 1997, when Japan's Prime Minister Hashimoto visited China, the two sides reached the China–Japan bilateral accord in the WTO negotiations on market access for goods. The European Commission (1998) outlined its strategy to engage with China in order to accelerate China's "transition to an open society based on the rule of law and the respect for human rights". The one exception among the rich trading powers was the USA, with whom no progress was recorded on China's WTO bid between Jiang Zemin's October 1997 visit to Washington, DC and Clinton's visit to China in June 1998. Nonetheless, the climate of US-Chinese relations was favorable. All rich countries were now embarked on a China engagement policy.

◆ The Asian financial crash began in June 1997 in Thailand, spread to Taiwan, Korea and Indonesia, and then spread around the world and back. China experienced a slowdown in growth, a fall-off in inward investment, and a decline in exports. This indicated clearly that the world market was China's main motor for growth, and that the heart of that motor was ticking in the USA and the EU. In January 1998, at the height of the 1997–8 Asian-Pacific financial crash, President Clinton proposed a new round of global trade negotiations. The EU and Japan chimed in, as did thirteen medium-sized countries with a similar proposal in a joint statement, signed that year in Hong Kong.

◆ Both the European Commission and the Clinton administration took the lead in the 1990s on liberalization of telecommunications and financial services. Both were keen to involve the Asian states. The major break-throughs occurred in the course of 1997: sixty-nine countries signed up to an agreement guaranteeing market access to international telecommunications suppliers on a non-discriminatory basis. In March, forty countries signed an Information Technology Agreement. Both agreements covered 90% of global trade. Then in December – at the height of the Asian financial crash – seventy countries agreed to liberalize financial services. The hardware and the software for the world's communications and payments infrastructure are being laid hand in hand.

For China, the slowdown in domestic demand had to be compensated for by making inward investment attractive, and by maximizing external sources of revenue. This meant grasping the opportunity provided by the grand-scale adjustment going on in the world's industrial structure, China's WTO negotiator, Long Yongtu (2000a) argued to the party cadres. China had to deepen its already close relationships with the world's multinational corporations. There was no evading the difficulties, he argued, arising from the fact that the inherited state structure was incompatible with WTO mem-bership: "A very major problem … is that every department is not only itself the appointed referee, but also a player in the game, and also the same people who make up the rules of the game." (Long Yongtu, 2000b)

We can understand the forces at work and the diplomatic demands placed on China by the USA and others by referring to Figure 6.1. Over time, demands conveyed by the industrial powers on China may be granted or ignored; if they are ignored for too long, China loses *credibility* in the eyes of others, unless it is prepared to go some way to bring its actions into line with its rhetoric. In other words, China was challenged in 1998 to make its actions consistent with the spirit of WTO accession. A reputation for consistent inconsistency (the analogy of the eternally repentant drunkard) is shaken off with great difficulty. Building a stock of credibility takes time, during which the *legitimacy* of the new policy may be challenged by domestic groups who benefited by the previous consensus or non-action policies. Legitimacy of policy is expressed in terms of perceived benefits and costs, now and in the future, among citizens. This is the party-state's Achilles heel: when it moves to adapt the market-adjustment policies required of WTO members, it has to be prepared to allocate benefits and costs around the population. The losers are bound to ask the question: By what right do you, the party-state, not protect me? Answering "Because we came to power in 1949" is clearly not enough.

With Zhu Rongji's appointment as premier in March 1998, economic liberals won a major battle as the new government proceded to accentuate the drive to attract foreign direct investment to China, and to involve China more deeply in global networks (Story and Crawford, 2000). For Zhu Rongji, this meant that there had to be visible evidence to US observers of market-opening actions in China. Hence, the premier's two-dimensional strategy: WTO-consistent reforms of the party-state had to be accompanied by a package of concessions by China, which Clinton could accept to shore up support for the deal in the USA. That package had to be implementable in China if it was to be credible in the USA, and vice versa. Proponents and opponents of China in the WTO on both sides of the Pacific reached out in mutual support. This feature of China's WTO entry saga is extremely significant: interdependence makes domestic structures, policies and performance the substance of international diplomacy. In fact, it breaches the principle still adhered to in the Asia-Pacific of non-interference in the domestic affairs of other states.

The negotiations

The history of the negotiations may be briefly sketched (see Box 6.2). The Chinese leadership's renewed bid to join the WTO through bilateral negotiations with the USA started well enough in 1998 with a routine exchange of

Box 6.2 Overview of China's economic reforms and WTO negotiations

- 1978: Deng Xiaoping launches China's Open Door Policy. First reforms take place in agriculture, as individual households are allowed to work land for up to fifteen years. Only twelve trading companies are entitled to engage in foreign trade; this number is gradually expanded.

- 1980: China becomes a member of the IMF.

- 1980s: Government allows the collectively owned township and village entreprises to operate outside the central plan.

- 1986: China applies to join the GATT, the predecessor of the WTO.

- 1989: Work in the GATT Working Group is suspended for two years following Tiananmen.

- 1993: China eliminates its dual exchange rate.

- 1994: China makes a first effort to conclude its GATT negotiations.

- 1995: The WTO is established and the Uruguay Round commitments enter into force for WTO members, widening the scope of GATT rules to include new or increased market access and other commitments in goods, agriculture, textiles, services, and intellectual property rights. The WTO has a binding dispute settlement system for the first time.

- End of 1995: China accepts full convertibility for current account transactions (Article VIII Membership of the IMF).

- 1996: In order to inject new momentum into the negotiations, the EU proposes that China may have transition periods to implement certain WTO obligations after WTO accession. This is accepted by WTO members.

- 1997: China agrees to phase out its trading monopoly and to grant full trading rights to all Chinese and foreign individuals and companies within three years of accession. China agrees to implement fully the WTO TRIPs agreement upon accession.

- 1997: China's Party Congress initiates a new phase of the reform process by announcing an overall restructuring of the state enterprise sector, including elements of privatization. (The sector employs well over 120 million people and accounts for 30% of GDP, down from 70% fifteen years earlier.)

◆ 1998: China submits new tariff and services offers.

◆ 1999: Significant progress made across all fields of the negotiation (agriculture, goods, services, rules), including in bilateral negotiations with the USA, the EU and other partners.

◆ November 1999: China concludes bilateral market access agreement with the USA. Most market-opening commitments will be implemented by the year 2005.

◆ May 19, 2000: China concludes bilateral market access agreement with the EU. Most market-opening commitments will be implemented by the year 2005.

◆ May 24, 2000: The US House of Representatives supports PNTR for China (September 2000: Senate approves bill).

◆ June 2000: WTO Working Party drafts China's Protocol of Accession.

◆ November 2001: China becomes a WTO member.

Source: European Union. http:// europa.eu.int/comm./trade/bilateral/china/chr.htm

letters, nearly died over a serious April 1999 negotiation breakdown, then resumed in late summer to yield the US-Chinese accession agreement in November, only to be upstaged in December when a red–green lobby of advanced industrial country unionists, environmentalists and antiglobalizers brought the WTO meeting in Seattle to a standstill. In the USA, the accession agreement went before Congress in the course of 2000. Then, just before the House vote in May 2000 on the extension of permanent trade status to China, the EU foreign ministers backed the Commission's proposed package for China's entry talks. As Trade Commissioner Lamy said: "The US got 80% of what we wanted. Now the US will get, on top of what they got, what we get" (see Table 6.1). Trade relations between China and Japan deteriorated as Japan slammed on tariffs on stone leek, mushroom and rush imports from China, and China retaliated with 100% tariffs on a clutch of Japanese manufactures. But the tailends of business to bring China into the WTO were wrapped up quickly following the terror attacks of September 11 on the Twin Towers and the Pentagon, when China offered to cooperate with the USA in the war on terrorism. China was duly ushered

Table 6.1 ◆ US-Chinese and EU-Chinese market-access agreements

Tariff concessions	US-Chinese agreement	EU-Chinese agreement
Goods		
Industrial goods	In 1997, average tariff 24.6% to fall to 9.4% by 2005. Most cuts by 2003.	On 150 specific goods, average tariff to fall from 18.6% to 10.6%. Special categories from 25–35% to 10–5%.
Information technology	By 2005, average tariff to fall from 13.3% to 0 for all ITC products.	
Autos and auto parts	By 2006, average tariff down from 80–100% to 25%. Parts to 10%.	
Textiles	Keep safeguard to December 31, 2008, after "expiry" of WTO Agreement.	China's tariff = EU's on China's exports.
Agricultural products	By January 1, 2004, average tariffs to 17%. On priority items, from 31.5% to 14.5% by 2004. Wine 65% to 20%.	All spirits: 65% to 10%. Wine: 65% to 14%. Butter: 30% to 10%. Olives: 25% to 10%.
Quotas	Quotas out in five years. By 2002–5, on top US priorities. Auto quotas out by 2005. Import 20 films p.a.	Fertilizer, rape oil NPK: quota improved.
Services		
Telecommunications	Beijing–Shanghai–Guangzhou corridor to open on accession in all sectors. End restrictions on paging. Mobile/cellular in five years; domestic wireline services in six years; value-added services in two years.	Opening of Beijing–Shanghai–Guangzhou intercity market. Opening of domestic-leased circuit services. More competition in international corporate communications.
Insurance	In five years, group, health and pension – about 85% of total premiums – to be opened. All geographic limitations ended in three years. Large-scale risks opened. Licenses to be awarded on basis of prudential criteria.	In two years, business scope expanded to life and all non-life activities, except for statutory insurance. Opening of Shenzhen, Foshan. Brokers to undertake large-scale commercial risk, reinsurance.
Banking	Full access for US banks in five years. In two years, local-currency business with Chinese enterprises. With individuals in five years.	Zhuhai banks' accelerated access to local-currency market. Credit market opened for trucks, tractors and motorcycles.

Table 6.1 ◆ (continued)

Tariff concessions	US-Chinese agreement	EU-Chinese agreement
	All geographic and customer restrictions removed in five years. National treatment for foreign banks in designated areas.	
Tourism	Hotels and travel services allowed unrestricted access, including to government resorts.	Scope of travel agency services extended to allow corporate travel services.
Audiovisual	Video/sound recordings to be distributed by foreign enterprises.	
Legal	Foreign majority control except for practicing of Chinese law.	Authorization to provide services in Chinese law.
Accountancy	End mandatory localization requirement.	No local partner required for accounting, taxation or management consultancy services.
Architectural, market research		Cross-border services. Relaxation of current controls on confidentiality of research.

Investment-related measures

Motor vehicles	Auto financing by foreign non-banks, regarding import, distribution, sales, maintenance, repairs.	Product range determined freely in two years. Provinces to authorize investments to $150 million (currently $30 million). Wholly foreign-owned enterprises allowed in engine manufacturing.
Telecommunications	Value-added and paging services investment: 49% foreign ownership in the first year of accession; 50% in the second year. Mobile services: 49% in five years. International and domestic mobile services: 49% in six years.	Foreign investment in local mobile operators: Upon accession: up to 25%. Within one year of accession: up to 35%. Within three years of accession: 49%. Settlement of UNICOM claims.

Table 6.1 ◆ (continued)

Tariff concessions	US-Chinese agreement	EU-Chinese agreement
Insurance	50% ownership for life insurance. On accession, reinsurance open, also non-life, branching or 51% ownership; formation of wholly foreign-owned subsidiaries in two years.	Fifty-fifty equity joint-venture insurers. Seven new licenses to begranted (five life, two non-life). Plus two companies to open in a second city. In five years, all restrictions removed on brokers.
Distribution and auxiliary services	Over three years, distribution rights provided. All restrictions on provision of services auxiliary to distribution phased out over three to four years.	Large retailers (at least 20,000 m² or more than thirty outlets) no longer limited to 50% equity participation.
Tourism	In three years, hotel operators allowed to set up 100% foreign-owned hotels.	Capital requirements to reduce to parity with local firms. Minimum annual turnover required to qualify as foreign investor reduced by 20% to $40 million.
Construction		Foreign majority in equity joint ventures. In three years, foreign companies to get to carry out projects.
Audiovisual	49% foreign participation in joint ventures.	

General WTO principles/agreements

National treatment		National treatment principle to apply to pharmaceuticals pricing, retail of imported cigarettes, spirits.
State trading	Private trade in agriculture. New rights to import and distribute.	Silk, crude/processed oil, fertilizers export sector to be opened to private traders.
Sanitary and phytosanitary measures	China to eliminate barriers not based on scientific evidence.	
Export subsidies	Eliminate on agricultural products.	Eliminate on industrial goods, on offset requirement in civil aircraft sector.

Source: Daniel Arthur Laprès

in as a member at the Qatar meeting of the WTO in November 2001. During the course of negotiations, four lessons may be learnt about China and world diplomacy.

First, Chinese-US relations on trade-related issues are high-risk for the respective leaderships. Consider the Clinton–Zhu Rongji summit in April 1999, when the premier proposed a number of key concessions, drawn up in secret and advanced with the support of the party-state leadership. Zhu Rongji's goal reportedly was to present his domestic opponents with a *fait accompli*. But Clinton insisted on adequate protection for US labor unions and vulnerable industries, and thereby ditched China's Premier. That helped Clinton's reputation as a tough guy, but the incident nearly brought down Zhu Rongji. Motto of the story: the risk for Chinese and US leaders is that they have to enter trade deals seen as treacherous by some on their own sides, while hanging tough with regard to the other's demands, thereby making a deal difficult to conclude and to sell to domestic audiences other than as a victory.

Second, trade relations cannot be segregated neatly from other turbulent dimensions of US or Chinese politics. After Clinton had ditched Zhu Rongji came the NATO bombing of the Chinese embassy in Belgrade. Zhu was denounced as a traitor for negotiating with the USA; organized protestors in Beijing picketed the US embassy; Zhu was shorn of his portfolio for state-owned enterprise reform and foreign direct investment, and his pending resignation was rumored. However, by mid-October of that year, Zhu Rongji resurfaced. The top leadership, it was reported, had achieved a consensus that WTO accession was critical to China's economic development. Motto of the story: Chinese negotiators need 100% home backing to negotiate effectively with the USA.

Third, it was not easy for Republicans and business groups to form a vital center in favor of Clinton's China policy. On the left, a majority in the Democrats sided with organized labor as well as human rights and environmental advocates, most of whom opposed China's accession to the WTO. But the African-American caucus split when the trade unions in the USA's biggest trade union, AFL-CIO, opposed trade-opening bills for sub-Saharan

Africa and the Caribbean. In May 2000, the House voted by 237 to 197 for permanent normal trading relations (PNTR) with China. In October, PNTR passed the Senate eighty-three to fifteen. The US-Chinese bilateral WTO agreement was initialled on November 15, 1999. Motto: pluralist politics in the world's leading power tie Chinese affairs into US policies on world affairs. Conversely, as China's economy grows in importance, so politics within China will tie US or EU affairs into Chinese policies on world affairs.

Fourth, China is the bane of the antiglobalizer warriors, who won their spurs at the battle of Seattle in December 1999. John Sweeney, President of the AFL-CIO, denounced the China–WTO accord as "disgusting" and immediately began to mobilize trade-union opposition. To gain the support of the AFL-CIO, Clinton promised to include a working group in the WTO negotiating agenda to study the relationship between labor standards, environmental conditions and trade. This would, Clinton hoped, solidify support for the so-called "Washington consensus", the global coalition of corporate and government elites favoring open markets and put together by the USA. The tactic backfired. Developing countries rejected Clinton's labor and environmental proposals, while advanced industrial countries resisted developing-country requests for longer transition periods before completing their market opening. Meanwhile, 40,000 anti-WTO protestors took to the streets in Seattle and essentially shut down the WTO meeting. Motto of the story: China is pro-trade and wants to join the world's lead powers; rich country radicals are anti-trade and want to keep China out. Were he alive, Mao would have to change sides.

Wrecker or pillar of the WTO?

The US-Chinese WTO accord constitutes a massive program of economic system reform. Such is the judgment of Richard Cooper, a well-known US international economic policy guru, speaking at the China Development Forum in Beijing as the finishing touches were being put to the agreement. Premier Zhu Rongji has given a similar candid assessment of the odds facing his country's accession to the WTO: "Everybody is happy about the accession",

he said at a regional meeting. "But I am not that elated because I am worried
... Membership raises many questions, it may well be that disadvantages may
outweigh the advantages if problems are not handled well." A glance at the
content of China's new trade regime bears out such informed opinion:

◆ *Services:* Most of the negotiations with China and its trade partners were
  about the opening up of China's service sector. This was the broad sector
  ranging from telecommunications to banking, insurance and films where
  US firms dominated internationally. Services were still under extensive
  state control. A constant theme in negotiations turned around the
  continued effectiveness of investment barriers to foreign business,
  despite the fact that China had signed on to the Uruguay Round
  provisions. Barriers were geographic in scope, or as often as not
  limitations on foreign ownership. Foreign banks could conduct business
  in the local currency, and geographic restrictions were reduced. In
  investment banking, foreign firms were able to hold up to 49% in
  brokerage firms after three years following China's accession to the
  WTO (see Table 6.1). By contrast, foreign insurance firms were to be
  allowed 50% in joint ventures dealing with life insurance and 51% in
  non-life business. In telecommunications, because China was party to
  the Information Technology Agreement, all tariffs on computers,
  telecommunications equipment and other high-tech products would be
  eliminated. Ownership was the most contentious issue: eventually,
  foreign companies were granted a maximum 49% stake in a joint
  venture, rising to 50% within two years of China's entry. In the area of
  distribution, the government retains the right to restrict business,
  although full trading rights were to be granted within three years.
  In short, China's non-traded services sector is opening to foreign
  competition – how far remains to be seen.

◆ *Intellectual property rights:* China is one of the world's prime sinners with
  regard to intellectual property rights. Plants making counterfeit products
  are shut down by the authorities, only for the same owners to open for
  business somewhere else. In the broader scope of things, China is an
  avid consumer of Western technologies. When the USA revived
  economic sanctions on high-tech exports to China after the Tiananmen

incidents, the government looked to alternative suppliers. European and
Japanese suppliers jumped into the market. Another running saga was
the production of counterfeit compact discs: eventually, China and the
USA reached an accord in June 1996 to close up to thirty factories in
southern China, twelve of which were underground. The Chinese
government, aware that foreign investors need some assurance about
their property rights, has regularly sought to improve procedures –
difficult to accomplish when many counterfeiter operations were under
command of the PLA. Given the difficulties, China faces a 2005 deadline
for compliance.

◆ *Environment:* China has opposed efforts by the rich countries to
introduce environmental and workplace standards that could serve to
drive up local costs. Nonetheless, government attitudes have evolved
from outright opposition to a more selective cooperation. The reason is
simple. China's environmental problems are growing: for instance, urban
pollution is estimated as killing about 180,000 people per annum; 10%
of the land area of southern China suffers from acid rain; and the water
level under Beijing has fallen to untenable levels, due to heavy exploita-
tion for urban, industrial and farm usage (World Bank, 1997). Efforts
have been made to tighten up controls on air pollution, water
purification and acid rain, and the government has kept an eye on
foreign investments that aim to shift high-polluting industries from the
rich countries to China. Overall, as Li Peng, the former Prime Minister
noted, "China has not only to provide people with riches and material
products, but also gradually to improve the quality of life, and
environment as an important part of the quality of life."

◆ *Competition policy:* An effective competition policy can only operate in a
market economy where respect for property rights is assured through the
law. China is not yet a market economy, and property rights are not
assured. Consequently, throughout the negotiations, China's trade
partners were far from convinced that the central government would be
able to live up to its commitments. The US administration went out of
its way to sell China's entry to the WTO on the grounds that, once in,
China would be under the surveillance of other members as well as the

WTO itself. A new Commerce Department under-secretary post has been created to monitor China's trade commitments, along with a joint Congress-Executive human rights commission to monitor China's human rights record. Furthermore, the Chinese negotiators gave in to American demands for import surge protection for twelve years as well as the implementation of an anti-dumping regime to last fifteen years. The EU negotiated similar terms – hardly a ringing statement of confidence about China's future as a major world economy. As all signatories realized, enforcement depends on the center's ability to get provincial and city governments to toe the WTO line. This is far from assured.

◆ *Workers' and human rights:* Clinton adopted engagement as the best way to counter the arguments of China, Singapore and Malaysia in the early 1990s that Asian particularities prescribed a special reading of human rights. As we have already mentioned, the Chinese government's approach is to state that the people's most basic human rights are to food, shelter and clothing, and that only after levels of education and prosperity have been spread widely should citizens' rights be extended to electoral participation. In fact, China found extensive support for its views in the UN Human Rights Commission, from Russia, Japan, Australia, Canada, Switzerland and EU states, as well as from others in Africa and Asia. At root of the party-state's hostility to Western human rights activism lies the defense of its monopoly powers over the representation of workers and peasants. Clinton by contrast reached an agreement with the US apparel industry – including such household names as Nike, Reebok, Phillips and Van Heusen – to reduce the operations of sweatshops in China: the agreement included a ban on children under fifteen working, prohibition of forced labor, a maximum sixty-hour week, a ban on assault and harassment, and – anathema to the party-state – the rights of workers to join free trade unions.

◆ *Protection:* Tariffs are to fall from 17% in 1997 to 10.5% by 2005. China has made commitments to WTO partners. Major commitments are to reduce weighted-average nominal tariffs from 11.1% end-2001 to about 6.9% in five years after China's WTO entry and to abolish most non-tariff barriers by 2006. The most sensitive of all areas are China's food markets, on which the livelihoods of over 900 million people depend. In automobiles, quotas are to be eliminated and tariffs reduced from 80–100% to 25% by 2005. Tariffs on auto parts are to fall to 10%. In textiles, China stands to gain as the world's largest garment textile fiber producer and exporter. The textile industry represents 15% of industrial output, employs 10% of the workforce and accounts for just under one-third of total exports. Under the world's existing textile regime, China is limited to a 17% share of the world market for garments. Despite pledges to bring the whole sector under WTO rules by 2005, the USA is to keep its safeguards in place against rapid surges in exports from China until 2008, while the EU policy to China textile imports is one of reciprocity – as may be seen in Table 6.1. Overall, China's new trade regime by 2010 will be much more open than it has ever been.

Whether China meets these commitments within the transition periods of about five years is a general concern for China's trade partners. In part, China's future trade policy will be a function of how well-organized sectoral policy communities are. Figure 6.2 presents the existing degree of protection at home and abroad on the horizontal plane, and the combined impact of ongoing marketization policies, WTO entry and the expected sharpening of competition on the vertical plane. Textiles, where China's competitive advantage is great, is likely to benefit, while China's electronic industries – already open wide to international competition – will not find that its competitive environment changes much. Agriculture and financial services, on the other hand, will find competition much tougher. Those sectors that are affected most adversely are likely to be most strident in asking for protection. So which way is Beijing likely to move? Will it be a China with a gripe and a protectionist chip on its shoulder? Or will it be a cheerful China open to world markets?

China as a wrecker

Accession to the WTO means that China has to establish a reliable dispute-settlement mechanism, which implies greater uniformity of standards and transparency in the political process whereby laws are made, implemented and appealed. Traditionally, China's is a rule-by-law state,

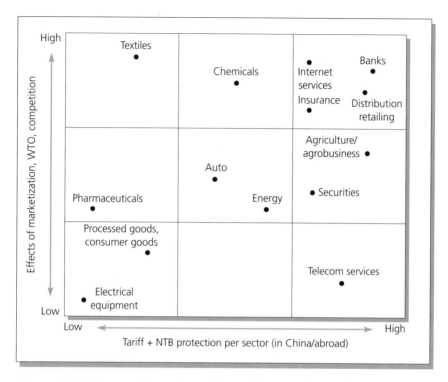

Figure 6.2 ◆ Expected impact on China of its accession to the WTO

Source: McKinsey Quarterly, http://www.mckinseyquarterly.com/ and China Business Council,
http://www.uschina.org.public/wto/

contrasted to rule-of-law civil societies, which require an independent
judiciary to challenge decisions of the state and local governments. Hence
the Chinese custom of *guanxi*, whereby family and other trusted relationships are valued far more than written contracts. In political terms, this is
expressed in tight-knit policy communities, which help to fragment the
Chinese economy along functional or geographic lines, making the China-
wide conduct of business more difficult and complex. All too often the
center has to concede to provincial lobbies, as the last generation of
regional reformers becomes entrenched in office and impose their decisions on companies that operate within their jurisdictions. In other words,
China's traditional, top-down, rule-by-law policy generates ineffective
central government: provincial power is essentially arbitrary and opaque,
and contracts are only loosely enforceable.

Much of the WTO reform program depends on whether Beijing succeeds in centralizing new powers that enable it to outflank the resistance of local interests. Those new powers would have to include taxation, finance, law and law enforcement, as well as traditional areas such as defense and money. Meanwhile, problems in implementing commitments, it is feared, will undermine China's credibility internationally. This is what many WTO members expect to happen, as judged by their refusal to drop safeguards such as anti-dumping measures against a country many quietly judge still to be run as a non-market economy. Domestic protectionism in China is thus likely to justify continued protectionism among the rich countries, providing Chinese diplomacy with an incentive to take the lead as advocate of developing countries. Far from being a champion of open markets, China in such conditions plays the wrecker in competition and sometimes in cooperation with India, the other very large and population-rich country in the WTO. China, with India, tilts the balance heavily in favor of poorer countries, as each state has one vote.

China, the pessimists say, will turn out to be a wrecker, casting its vote with protectionist forces and weakening international cooperation, the ways of which it has little experience. Already open to charges that it is undemocratic, China's accession does the organization no favors. Its officials are unelected, like the WTO's, and China defends sovereignty as a principle of its diplomacy. If China fails to implement its commitments, then the WTO can give the green light to injured parties to impose trade restrictions. To avoid this, China will use its freedom to settle disputes outside the WTO through bilateral negotiations or in the context of regional fora. This only reinforces the trend to exclusive deals between the big trading powers, thereby undermining the WTO's credibility. In short, China's entry makes it more likely that the organization is impaled on its dilemma: if its decisions bite, then the organization risks being accused of exceeding its legitimate mandate; if it does too little, it risks losing credibility in the eyes of governments and businesses dependent on global markets.

A cheerful China

The opposite view holds that China has everything to gain by playing in the court of the great trading powers as a constructive partner. When China took up its seat in the UN in the early 1970s, similar concerns about China as a wrecker had been expressed. But China, it turned out proved, a responsible member of the UN and of its agencies. Furthermore, China has little incentive to become another Japan when circumstances over fifty years after the end of World War II are so different. Japan's business system built up in the 1950s and geared to 'export out, protect in' has little to recommend it as a model for China in the twenty-first century. Greater China ambitions are best fulfilled for China within the WTO, as illustrated by China's entry ahead of Taiwan in 2001. And when China came out in general support for the US war on terrorism, the USA waived China through, rapidly lowering the last barriers to China's joining the world trade club. Entry of mainland China alongside Taiwan leaves open the prospect of evolution in China's "sort-of-Communist" polity, to paraphrase Ronald Reagan, and also buys time during which *santong* (the three direct links of trade, post and travel) and *siliu* (the four exchanges – academic, cultural, economic and athletic) are encouraged. These two are the first steps, according to Beijing, along the way to implement the formula of one country, two systems.

China is fast becoming a trade power in its own right. Comparing the trade regime of 2010 with that of 1978 is like comparing night and day. In 1978, China was an impoverished country cut off from the rest of the world. By 2010, it will have long since joined the lead group of world trade powers. China ranks in the world hierarchy after the EU, the USA, Japan and Canada at the turn of the millennium. By 2010, mainland China in all likelihood will have nudged Canada into fourth place and will be racing to overtake Japan in third. A ranking summing up the commerce of the mainland, Taiwan and Hong Kong – and including only the latter's exports of local output, not through-trade from China or elsewhere – already places Greater China fourth in the world hierarchy. China ranked third as recipient of inward investment, after the USA and the UK moved up to number one. Such a China is clearly going to demand a major say in the setting of world trade rules – indeed, as argued in Chapter 2, China's prime foreign policy objective is prestige and recognition of its weight in world affairs by the powers that be. As long as that is forthcoming, China will do everything to shore up its credibility as a reliable trade partner. In brief, China will turn out to be a team player, a pillar of international society.

In 2001, China's *annus mirabilis*, China had gone a long way to fulfill its ambitions: WTO accession, Beijing chosen to host the 2008 Olympic Games, the APEC Summit held in Shanghai, and the national football team in the World Cup for the first time. China's regime, for long a political pariah, has become *salonfähig* – socially presentable in high international society. A practical benefit is that China will now be writing the laws on international trade together with the lead powers, rather than having the rules written for it on the outside. China wants special relations with the powers that be and the ability to quote equality of rights in international instances.

China has little interest in invoking the hackneyed argument of the world's legion of *bien-pensants* from the 1960s, who suggested with their habitual enthusiasm that countries of unequal development should be treated unequally. What they meant, of course, is that developing countries should be given special privileges. The reverse happened for the many states not enjoying special relationships with the world's trading giants. Losing the battle over its definition as a developing country is therefore a blessing in disguise: China's negotiators will not be in a begging posture when the world's textile regime comes under WTO rules by 2005. On the contrary, China's membership in the WTO will help to train the spotlight on rich countries' protectionist policies, as an alternative to Western focus on China's shortcomings in human rights. In effect, it delivers developing countries the moral high ground on a plate: global trade will boom or shrink for many years yet, depending on whether the rich countries comply with their commitments in the WTO. That, rather than developing countries' import substitution policies of yesteryear, is the main threat on the way to shared global prosperity in the post-cold-war world.

> The transformation of China's business system is the key to its insertion into world trade

The conclusion is simple: the rich Western powers that still set the tone on global trade policy have a choice between putting up the barriers against China, as the antiglobalization forces at work in their societies want, or welcoming it into the WTO as a pillar of the global system and agreeing on a gradualist policy of transition to a fully fledged market-democracy. The transformation of China's business system is the key to its insertion, satisfactory or otherwise, into world trade. China is embarked on regime change to constitutional governance.

References

CNN, 1999, "President Clinton and Chinese Premier Zhu Rongji hold press conference", April 8, Transcript 99040809V54.

European Commission, 1995, "A long term policy for China Europe relations", http://www.ecd.org.cn/new/n3.03.htm

European Commission, 1998, "The EU and China: building a comprehensive partnership with China", http://europa.eu.int/comm/external_relations/china/com_98/com98_0.htm

Susan Lawrence, 1999, "Bitter harvest", *Far Eastern Economic Review*, 162(17), pp. 22–7.

William Overholt, 1993, *China: The Next Economic Superpower*, London, Weidenfeld and Nicholson.

Robert D. Putnam, 1988, "Diplomacy and domestic politics: the logic of two level games", *International Organization*, 42(3), pp. 427–60.

Susan Shirk, 1993, *The Political Logic of Economic Reform in China*, Berkeley, CA, University of California Press, p. 334.

State Council of the People's Republic of China, Catalog Guiding Foreign Investment in Industry, Order No. 21 of the State Development Planning Commission, State Economic Trade Commission and Ministry of Foreign Trade and Economic Cooperation of the People's Republic of China.

Jonathan Story, 1988, "The launching of the EMS: an analysis of change in foreign policy", *Political Studies*, XXXVI, pp. 397–412.

Jonathan Story and Robert Crawford, 2000, "Y2K: the bug that failed to bite", INSEAD case study. INSTEAD, Fontainebleau, France.

Nancy Bernkopf Tucker, 2000, "The Taiwan factor in the vote on PNTR for China and T's WTO accession", *NBR*, 11(2), pp. 5–18.

Yong Wang, 2000, "China's domestic WTO debate", *China Business Review*, 27(1), pp. 54–62.

White House, Office of the Press Secretary [of the USA], 1997, "Remarks by the President in address on China and the National Interest", *Voice of America*, Washington, DC, October 24.

World Bank, 1997, *China 2020: China's Environment in the New Century*, Washington, DC, World Bank, pp. 2–3.

Long Yongtu, 2000b, "On the question of our joining the World Trade Organization", *The Chinese Economy*, 33(1), pp. 15, 28, 49, 53–76.

Long Yongtu, 2000a, "On the question of Economic Globalization", *The Chinese Economy*, 33(1), pp. 53–76.

7

Keeping it in the family: corporate reform in China

THE COMMUNIST PARTY-STATE of China is like a chimera – the fire-breathing giant of Greek saga, with the head of a lion, the middle body of a goat, and the tail of a snake or dragon. The Party's head is still Marxist-Maoist-Leninist, its middle body is one large political market for preferences, and its tail is composed of gung-ho companies open to the full gale of global competition. It breathes fire through its ears and exudes sweet capitalist sounds through its nostrils. It breaks wind from orifices located around its middle body, while its tail wags furiously twenty-four hours a day. Adapting Paul Valéry's lapidary statement on individuals, China is like other nations of the world that distinguish themselves by what they show and are similar in what they hide. What makes them similar are their little secrets – the ambitions of individuals, the preferences of elites, the back-room deals or the legacies they confront. What makes them different is the front they present to the world. We'll start by introducing the concept of a business system; then we will present four key conditioning factors of cor-porate governance in China, proceed to corporate reform since 1998, and end on the development of China's capital markets. In the next chapter, we'll discuss the broader impact on foreign business prospects as China beds into the global system.

China's business system

China, as much as any other country, has had to adapt its business system to the expansion of world financial markets, underpinned by the explosion in communications technologies. Developing countries have been encouraged to open up their financial markets and go online. Naturally, the promised benefits have been conditional on developing countries meeting the ever-higher standards offered by investors in the rich markets of industrialized countries. Many failed to do so. Currencies tanked as dodgy banking systems folded. Between 1977 and 1995, sixty-nine countries faced banking crises so severe that their banks (and local middle classes) were bled dry. Then came the Asian financial crash, starting in June 1997. In September, the CCP's fifteenth Party Congress declared state-owned enterprise reform a priority; in November 1997, financial market reform was launched at a National Affairs Conference, attended by most of China's high-ranking officials. Further reforms of China's business system were an urgent necessity.

The term "national business system" has been coined by Richard Whitley (1999) to describe specific patterns of economic coordination and control in market economies. Each business system has three components:

◆ First come the *state institutions* that govern access to labor and capital. In China, the term "state institutions" refers to the public bureaucracy at central, provincial, local, city and autonomy levels; their overall cohesion, prestige and autonomy relative to other forces; and their posture towards sharing business risks and to regulating markets.

◆ Second comes the type of business system issuing from *coordination of economic activities* between stakeholders. The focus is here very much on owner/managerial coordination, non-ownership coordination such as technological alliances, and employer–employee relations. This yields a spectrum of types from loose coordination among firms, as in the UK, through local coordination of firms, as in northern Italy, to sectoral-based coordination, such as steels or chemicals, to highly hierarchical and authoritive structure of business interest representation where membership of firms is obligatory, such as is found in Germany and Austria. Then there is the business system type, best illustrated in the case of France, where the state is, or was, the focus of business interest collaboration. This is the type still most descriptive of China, although district, sectoral and hierarchical features are also present.

◆ Third comes the nature of firms, *which are "ownership-based units of decision-making and control"* (Whitley, 1999). Owners and their agents are authorized to control resources for private profit in competitive markets on account of the legitimacy conferred on them by the central status of property rights in capitalist societies. Two characteristics differentiate firms in different market economies: *governance* relates to the way firm policy is made and the constraints or discretion conferred on owners or managers by the financial, labor or political systems in which they operate; *capabilities* of firms refer to the organizational attributes of organizations that enable them to incorporate the skills and knowledge of their employees in the development of their products and services. This touches on the level of workforce skills, the development of collective competences, and innovation.

Let's apply this scheme to present four key elements that condition China's corporate reforms. One is how the party-state's institutions have dealt with business risk, particularly as seen through the evolution in public finances; another is the tight link between China's financial system and SOEs; the third is the party-state's provision of an urban safety net for workers; and the fourth is the level of trust in workforce and society towards public officials.

Party-state institutions' changing approach to business risk

The first element of the business system is how business risk has been treated by state institutions. In China, the approach to risk has obviously changed over time since the initial reforms of 1978 and two and more decades later. This can be illustrated by Figure 7.1, which traces political and market interaction as the business system changes. The main theme is that financial-market opening has embarked China on a process of marketization

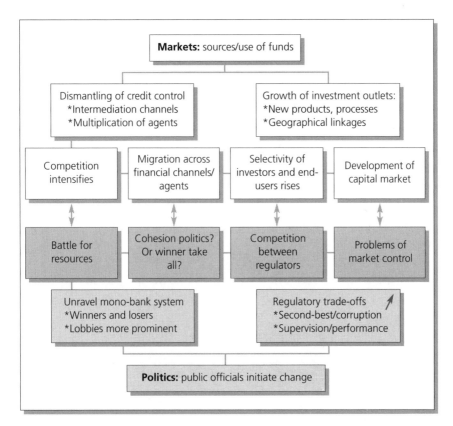

Figure 7.1 ◆ China's financial market opening

that could be reversed only at great cost: that is not the same as saying that China is moving to an economic society, which is one of the five conditions for stable democratic governance. Marketization can lead to the consolidation of a Japanese-type system, to an Anglo-American shareholder economy, to a Russian-type mafia state, or, worse, to a Zaire–Congo disaster. These alternatives are ever present, and eventual success will depend, as I argue in this chapter, on the CCP abandoning its privileged position.

In 1978–9, Chinese *public officials initiated change* in that they began to move away from the mono-bank system, according to which the People's Bank of China (PBoC) was the main national and sole commercial bank. The PBoC was sole repository of deposits and the sole lender. Long-term investment funds were channeled through the budget: all investment projects were budgetary grants, managed through the People's Bank of Construction. The Bank of China specialized in foreign exchange transactions. Total household savings were 6% of a small GNP. In 1998, *credit control was dismantled*: bank lending had replaced budgetary credits as the dominant form of external funding for enterprises. The number of *intermediation channels* between savers and borrowers had *multiplied*, along with the growth in the number of financial market agents. Four large specialized banks – for agriculture, industry, infrastructure and foreign trade – were spun off from the PBoC in 1983–4. The PBoC was granted the functions of a central bank a year later, but credit allocation remained under strong central and local government influence. The big banks spawned investment trusts, as did local governments, in order to avoid credit limits on loans to enterprises. Overall, there were six universal banks, including China International Trust (CITIC), a few smaller regional development banks, more than 50,000 rural cooperatives, and about 4,300 urban cooperatives. The big four controlled 85% of total bank assets. The rest of the banking system consisted of non-bank financial institutions, plus three policy banks specializing in financing "development"; they were also spin-offs from the big banks. With total assets of US$1,150 billion at the end of 1998 (120% of that year's GDP), the big four remained the pillar of China's financial system (Harding, 1999).

As *investment outlets* expanded, the government kept tight control, seeking to limit disintermediation between different *localities* or between financial *products*. It used the banking oligopoly to transfer resources from the rich coastal provinces to the poorer, rural areas inland. Local governments and SOEs received preferential treatment in interest rates and via bureaucratic fiat. At the end of 1998, an estimated 90% of all Chinese banking system loans went to SOEs, which left only 10% for the commercial sector of the economy (Moody's Investors Service, 1999). But *competition intensified* among financial institutions for China's household savings, and cash-hungry organizations probed the systems for loopholes and exemptions. As we shall see, they ended up turning to the security markets, which were reopened in Shanghai and Shenzhen in the early 1990s. *Development of the capital market* was a key feature of the 1990s.

The CCP is "the party of public finances"

The second key element to condition China's corporate reforms is the central role of the CCP – alias the *Gongchan Dang*, "the party of public assets". Before the reform policy, there were only a few mass organizations, such as Communist Youth and the Women's League, designed to channel enthusiasm under Party leadership. By the 1990s, there were 1,810 national associations approved and registered by the state and another 200,000 at provincial and local levels (Xinhua News Agency, 1995). Each local government has its own associational empire. This system has a number of key features: associations are registered and controlled by state authorities; they are granted monopoly status, so competition between them is limited; and party secretaries often take the chair. Then there are the SOEs, where director positions are chosen through the Party's *nomenklatura* list. Lobbying, as in France, focuses on ministries and agencies with regulatory authority over organizations. As in France, big organizations are the most *prominent lobbyists* with central government, while smaller firms reach for support more from local governments. Firms are influenced by the regular flood of state initiatives relating to the financial system, taxation, accounting norms, standards, procurement, and a host of other factors. While all this is common knowledge, lobbying nonetheless remains secretive – participation of Party, state and military officials in lucrative business is the norm. In short, the past and present state of flux in China's marketization process is such that business is embedded in China's extensive political market for influence. This is particularly the case for private business, which can thrive only with the say-so of officialdom.

Box 7.1 Zhang Hongwei on politics and business

Zhang Hongwei, founder of the Orient Group, the first private company to be allowed to list its shares, explains: "You have to take part in politics because politics and business are interrelated. The non-state-owned sector has to be represented in the political arena. In China, doing business is different from doing business in other places; you only spend 30% of your effort on business. The other 70% is spent on dealing with all kinds of inter-personal relationships" (Reuters, 1994).

By 1998, SOEs were a millstone about the party-state's neck – half lost money, all of them hoarded labor, and many operated with antiquated equipment. What to do? As the battle for resources sharpened, the party-state faced a harsh choice: the leadership either had to revert to financing SOE requirements through the printing press, or they had to sacrifice their prime constituency of urban labor on an altar of industrial adjustment. If the regime returned to the average annual inflation rates of 10% characteristic of the years 1978–94, then it would forego the quiet support of the vast mass of Chinese savers. If it sacrificed the industrial working class, then the party-state might lose its prime political base in the cities. The private sector, by contrast, was booming, accounting for 37% of total industrial output and providing 80% of new growth and 90% of new jobs in China (Oxford Analytica, 1997), but it received only 1% of bank loans. It was time to bring in private business from the cold.

The party-state turns away from the old social contract

The third key element to condition China's corporate reforms is the party-state's gradual abandonment of its key constituency, just as its control over the countryside has slackened since the dissolution of the rural communes in the early 1980s. *Cohesion politics* dictated support for the urban working class. In the mid-1990s, up to 80% of the active urban workforce was employed by SOEs owned by either central or local government. Across China, families were still registered by domicile, preventing migration from one region to another. Welfare, education, health and pensions were provided by the employer and never extended to the rural workforce. The result was growing discrepancies in incomes between the slower-growth areas of western China, or the rustbelt industrial centers of the northern provinces, and the fast-growing centers of southern and coastal China. Regional governments adopted a variety of initiatives, ranging from the creation of interregional labor coordination centers to authoritative restructuring of the local labor force to reduce overmanning. But such initiatives perpetuated China's fragmentation into local labor markets and provided a constant rationale for beggar-my-neighbor protectionist policies to safeguard local jobs. They also ensured that the 1986 bankruptcy law remained a dead letter, as local governments preferred to merge enterprises rather than put them out of business. Without a social security net, workers depended entirely on their enterprise for wage and welfare.

The decade of the 1990s demonstrated that maintaining social cohesion meant propping up inefficient SOEs at ever greater cost to the country. Clearly, such a policy was not sustainable. The tightening of financial controls by the center over loans to town and village enterprises slowed their capacity to absorb surplus labor from rural areas, where the "floating population" has been estimated to be as high as 120–175 million. Up to six million jobs were being lost in rural areas on an annual basis. With central government revenues shrinking fast, transfers were not available to compensate poorer regions. There was also a limit to how far the big four banks could pour household savings into loss-making enterprises just to pay for wages and stockpiles of unsold goods. Furthermore, the one-child policy was changing China's age profile: while 6% of the population was elderly in 1998, 11% of a larger population would be over sixty-five by the 2020s. In 1995, the Minister of Labor launched a pension scheme to be financed by payroll tax, but both enterprises and workers had incentives to evasion. The implication is that the present value of future pension obligations drives sovereign state debt from its official 20% GDP in 1998 to as high as 100% GDP (ADB, 1997). The only way for the state to finance such obligations was to privatize fast and to fudge on its commitments.

Public opinion and the party-state

The fourth element to condition China's corporate reforms is the level of trust towards public officials in workforce and society. The evidence suggests that the general public in mainland China has rather low expectations about government. The public may complain, and even blame officials for wrongdoing, but people do not withdraw their support (Shi, 2001). There is thus a stock of lethargy on which the regime can draw as it proceeds on its way. But the public is far from fatalist. For instance, private business and farmers have used the nascent legal system to protect themselves against local officials. In the case of Peijiawan village, 640 kilometers west of Beijing, farmers filed a class-action lawsuit against the local authority for levying $75,000 worth of excess fees. In 1998, the local court found in favor of the farmers (Johnson, 1999). Contrast this use of available institutions to redress wrongs with the petty tyranny practiced on the shop floor by management and union officials. In one state cotton mill near Zhengzhou, the capital of Henan, a green poster hung conspicuously from a large blackboard on the workshop wall, warning other workers against failing to implement their job descriptions to the letter: "A serious warning – 1,236 points will be docked from operator Wang Xiaofeng's wages this month due to her successive breaches of the operating instructions ... for example, she always failed to stand up at the right position prescribed in the instructions ..." (Zhao and Nichols, 1996). The inference here is that there are many workers who would dearly love to escape the CCP's paternalism.

Many of China's public officials no doubt use their position to get things done. If formal channels stand in the way, then the *second best solution* is preferable in the meantime to root-and-branch reform. Doing things through informal channels is better than inactivity. This may well have been the motive of Chen Xitong, who became mayor of Beijing in 1983. On his watch, Beijing's GDP shot up, inward investment soared, and tourism boomed. He was brought into the Politburo in 1992, but he fell foul of Jiang Zemin and was arrested in April 1995. Chen reportedly received gifts in the amount of $2.2 billion in exchange for construction permits. His son, Chen Xiaotong, and head of Beijing's New Century Hotel, was detained two days after his father's resignation. Chen was convicted on two crimes – bribery and embezzlement – and sentenced to twelve years in jail. While Chen Xitong's case is as much about political competition as about the boom in political markets for licenses and permits, the same cannot be said for the case of the State-General Anti-Corruption Buro, which was convicted in 1998 of diverting confiscated funds from crime activities to the benefit of its own members (*People's Daily*, 1999).

The regime is clearly aware that *corruption* is a gangrene from which it could perish. According to the US State Department (2002) record, the campaign against corruption, which began in earnest in 1996, yielded by 2000 a crop of 1,292 bent judges, 494 officers during that year, fifty-four of whom were criminally responsible for malfeasance, and 17,931 government officials guilty of corruption or of accepting bribes; during 2000, 1,450 court employees were punished for misconduct. Overall, 2,000 people have been executed as part of the campaign. The danger is not so much the blurred line between its anticorruption campaign and obscure battles for power within the party-state. It is simply that official corruption and organized crime converge to keep the gravy train running as long as possible, at the public's expense. Consider the construction industry – a perennial meeting place of powerful politicos and bent contractors. On April 1, 1999, at a county town south of the giant city of Chonqing, the local Rainbow Bridge collapsed, throwing scores of local residents and a team of armed policemen into the waters less than three years after opening (Ding, 2001).

This was just one of the many public works scandals brought to light in the post-Deng anticorruption drive. Typically, the project proposer holds the purse strings and also supervises the project. Builders and supervisors tend to come from the same locality. The normal kickback is 3–5% of the project, but officials are often tempted to subcontract up to three or four times to spread benefits and contacts as widely as possible. The result is that the final subcontractor uses poor materials, as in the case of the main dikes on the north side of Honghu Lake, Hubei province, which are vital to protect the greater Wuhan industrial area from floods. With only half of the original funds in hand, the private builder used bricks, broken tiles and tree roots instead of steel and concrete. Assuming a scam rate of 4–5% of total government projects for the years 1985–97 and kickbacks of another 5%, the total scam for the period has been calculated as equivalent to the country's educational budget for 1989–95. The Communist honeypot is too tasty for the sake of its guardians.

The new policy: corporate reforms

Without any doubt, the Asian financial crash of 1997–8 served as a wake-up call to China's leadership. It was not just that China's export markets were affected directly by the downturn in Asia-Pacific's growth. The worry was that China's business system, like those of its richer neighbors, was geared to expansion of output. Adapting to changing consumer tastes, technologies and competition came second. Not surprisingly, it shared all their problems: fragility of the banks, stockpiles of non-performing loans, inadequate regulatory oversight of financial flows, failed management, corporate indebtedness, and massive overcapacity in key industrial sectors. In Shanghai, the glittering new business center across the river in Pudong was littered with half-empty office towers.

> In Shanghai, the glittering new business center across the river in Pudong was littered with half-empty office towers

The Chinese leadership faced a number of challenges, requiring intricate negotiations and tradeoffs between the many groups and interests represented in the party-state. These included the surge in banks' non-performing loans to SOEs; the need to improve resource allocation, develop the internal market and create jobs; the growth of capital markets; and the need to foster an enterprise culture based on formal mechanisms of corporate governance both within firms and in their competitive environment. One key to increasing the party-state's *control over financial markets* was corporate reform.

In the 1998 package, reform was couched more in the Anglo-American language of shareholder value and customer responsiveness, than overtly modeled on the corporate structures of Japan and Korea as in the early 1990s. But simultaneously, the leadership was determined to keep control over the "commanding heights" of the economy. Keeping Chinese capitalism in the Communist family – that was and is reform's bottom line (see Figure 7.2).

New institutions

The ninth NPC in March 1998 announced major changes in state-corporate relations. The State Council, China's equivalent of the Council of Ministers, encouraged enterprises in key industries to consolidate in key groups – continuing a policy begun in 1994, when the Ministry of Foreign Trade and Industry urged the formation of "national champions", in preparation for China's entry to the WTO. The power of managing the SOEs, however, was taken away from the line ministries and given to a newly created Central

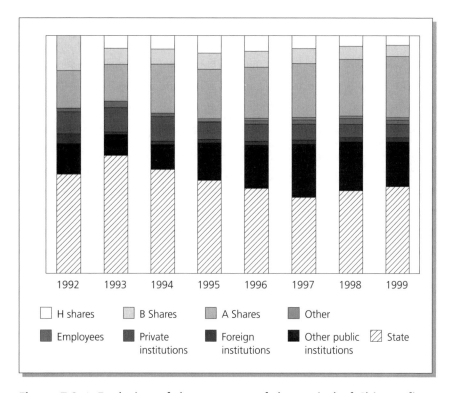

Figure 7.2 ◆ Evolution of the structure of the capital of Chinese firms listed on the stock exchange

Working Committee for Enterprises. The key function of this Party committee is to appoint senior management and to inspect their operations. A parallel state committee for state property is under the tutelage of the Ministry of Finance. The prime minister plays a central role in the committee's deliberations. Under this, State Asset Management Committees were set up to oversee state holding companies formed out of the old-line ministries. In other words, the party-state remains the ultimate owner of state assets, holds the overwhelming portion of shares, and directs the key personnel appointments.

Its prime ally in reform is the tremendous competitive pressures running through the markets. This can be seen by looking at four major types of corporate establishment in China: the large SOEs in relatively protected markets; the SOEs and collective enterprises in the competitive sectors, such as consumer electronics, foods and textiles and where price competition is fierce and barriers to market entry low; the smaller enterprises, often attached to local governments; and the booming private sector. Let's look at each in turn.

The large SOEs in protected markets

At the turn of the millennium, the central government runs 2,300 large SOEs. The policy is best described as *zhuada fangxiao*, to "grasp the large, and let go the small". The motives for the policy have been mixed. One is to raise SOE efficiency in the use of capital, and the other is to reach a size where SOEs are capable of taking on the multinationals in open competition. The two are not readily compatible. Ownership is firmly in party-state hands. The SOEs fall under the tutelage of the financial holdings companies. They operate, until WTO entry terms decree otherwise, in highly protected or regulated markets. The prior objective of China's political leadership since the early 1990s is to create national champions capable of taking on the multinationals on Chinese and world markets. Among the twenty-five industrial sectors in the 1995 industrial census, market shares of the top eight companies increased only marginally from an industry-wide average of 11.7% to 12.2%. The largest Chinese company, Daqing, an oil corporation, had only half the turnover of the smallest firm on the Fortune 500 (Huchet, 1999). As Wu Bangguo from the State Council put it:

> *America … relies on General Motors, Boeing, Dupont and a batch of other multinational companies. Japan relies on six large enterprise groups and Korea relies on ten large commercial enterprise holdings. In the same way now and in the next century our nation's position in the international economic order will be to a large extent determined by the position of our nation's large enterprises and groups" (Economic Daily, 1998).*

There are two buzzwords used to describe the party-state's use of Western tools to promote corporate transformation: *Corporatization* aims at clarifying property rights by converting Chinese SOEs into Western-type corporations. Also called transformation of ownership (*zhuanzhi*), the idea is to separate government functions from enterprise operations and allow for the introduction of governance mechanisms that establish accountability of management to the enterprise's owner (the state). This has prompted the elaboration of corporate law to provide a framework for companies becoming either limited liability or joint stock companies. *Diversification* refers to a gradual opening up of corporate capital to diverse, mainly institutional owners scattered about the party-state. This has been the prime rationale behind the development of the Shenzhen and Shanghai equity markets. The large SOEs constitute the 1,000 enterprises listed on the two markets. In these firms, the state in the form of many different organizations keeps 60–70% of "red-chip" shares, as they are appropriately called. The benefit is that diversified ownership facilitates mergers and acquisitions, as government organizations can exchange shares after negotiations. Also, the SOEs can raise capital on privileged terms. But the downside is that so many organizations holding shares, and with competing interests, can make for a very messy corporate strategy. Not surprisingly, the market is volatile, regularly wracked by revelations of scams, and beset by dodgy accounting practices, as we shall see – not unlike capital markets elsewhere.

Enterprises in highly competitive sectors

Our second group of enterprises is highly exposed to competition. In areas such as consumer electronics, household appliances, autos, steel, foods and textiles, where competition has become intense and barriers to entry are low, the 1990s witnessed the emergence of more market-oriented SOEs and collective enterprises. The key to their successful transformation as Professor Lu Feng (1999) of Qinghua University has argued, is endogenous change, involving the re-assertion of managerial authority over operations. Tougher competitive conditions, combined with "corporatization", have no doubt helped, but they are not necessarily sufficient conditions for success. Haier, the home appliances group, is a case in point: in 1984, a city government official, Zhang Ruimin, took over the presidency of a failing enterprise, the Qingdao Refrigerator Factory, and renamed it Haier. One of the first things he did was to forbid workers from urinating and defecating on the factory floor. Assembly lines were disorganized and filthy, the roof leaked, and quality was appalling. Zhang decided to go up-market and provide service to customers. The factory moved to profitability in 1991. Zhang then embarked on an acquisition strategy, taking over failing but well-equipped state or collective enterprises. In nearly twenty takeovers, he used the same tactics: change corporate culture by using Maoist indoctrination tactics involving public confession of failings, raise manufacturing products and processes to international standards, and cultivate alliances with foreign companies to licence and develop state-of-the-art technologies. By 2000, Haier employed over 20,000 people in its own industrial park in Qingdao, with an annual turnover of US$2.7 billion, or almost 6,000 times greater than in 1985. The company operated via 30,000 sales outlets in over 100 countries, and manufacturing facilities existed in the Philippines and in South Carolina, USA. By 1999, the *Financial Times* named Mr Zhang Ruimin as twenty-sixth in the list of the thirty most respected "global entre-preneurs". Despite all this, Haier was still miles away from achieving Zhang's ambition to enter the Fortune 500.

Many of the more successful Chinese companies to transform from socialist to more market-oriented enterprises, such as TCL (television sets) and Legend (computers), shared other characteristics as well. Their leaders, like Zhang, are strong personalities with good political networks, eager to introduce the best from Western management and interested in forging international alliances. In the 1980s as local enterprises, they benefited by local government financial backing, and once they had established their positions in the market – often against competition from government-supported champions who have since disappeared – they were able to get listings on the Shenzhen, Shanghai or Hong Kong stock markets. Because the prime objective of these markets is to raise capital, they are ensured of long-term financing; government participation protects them from hostile takeover. They also tend to have come from medium-sized towns, which have become highly dependent on them for revenue and jobs, further aug-menting managerial autonomy. Changhong, a television set manufacturer, by the late 1990s had reached over $2 billion turnover, generated mainly from its factories located in the city of Mianyang in Sichuan province. These are more than the city's income from taxation or the combined turnover of other companies operating there (Huchet and Richet, 2000).

Changhong had been one of the 156 key projects constructed in the first five-year plan under Soviet assistance. In the 1980s, Changhong bene- fited from not getting privileged access to bank financing, as was the case of its much larger rival, Huaiyou, which failed to control its costs and exploit its foreign technologies and went bankrupt in 1993. The company had to look inwards to its own human and technology resources. By decid- ing to move on to the consumer market, the firm broke away from both bureaucratic control and protection. Later, it raised capital on the stock market. These moves helped management introduce changes in personnel policy and build up a distribution and after-sales service in Sichuan province. Changhong was thus well set to launch a price war in the early 1990s which catapulted it into volume production for the broader national market. Helped by a buoyant China consumer market, the company liter- ally grew out of its old constraints.

A ragbag of local SOEs

Smaller state or collective enterprises, often attached to local governments, are a ragbag. Most fell in the 1990s into severe financial difficulties (OECD, 2000). The biggest problems were evident in China's rustbelt in the north- ern provinces of Liaoning, Heilongjiang and Jilin, which totaled over half of all SOEs. With a hard budget constraint in place following the serious infla- tionary binge of 1993, local governments could no longer afford to finance the old Communist corporate-based social security system. Coastal provinces, such as Guangdong and Fujian, had led the way in letting go up to half of their small and medium-sized enterprises by 1996. Vice-Premier Zhu Rongji put his finger on the problem at a Party meeting, where he accused SOEs of delivering low returns on capital.[1] China, he was saying, had to use scarce resources much more efficiently than in the past. Household savings could not be frittered away on sustaining loss-making enterprises. With so many new competitors entering China's markets, from

---

[1] The state "has to inject an increasing amount of working capital through the banking sector into state enterprises" for "very low returns", he told a meeting of the Eighth People's Congress. *Peoples' Daily*, overseas edition, March 11, 1996.

abroad or locally, relatively unsuccessful firms would have to exit. Zhu Rongji's message had a hidden text: enterprises must adapt or die.

China's process of divestiture is creating a mosaic of differentiated corporate arrangements across the length and breadth of the country. The implication is far-reaching: the process of transformation is making China a more, not less, complex place to operate in for the foreseeable future. There are two sets of reasons for this, related to policy competition and cooperation between governments, or sectoral differences, and the different incentives and motivations of stakeholders in the process. Let's look at each in turn.

> The process of transformation is making China a more complex place to operate in

A. policy competition and emulation across China has become the norm, as local governments have devised their own privatization programs in the light of local circumstances. Shunde county, situated on the west bank of the Pearl River estuary in Guangdong province, is a case in point (Cao *et al.*, 1999). Local authorities first chose employee shareholding to privatize companies, and then looked to list local champions, such as Kelong, which makes refrigerators, and MD, the world's largest electric-fan producer, on the Shanghai and Shenzhen markets. They used management buyouts, established asset-management companies to monitor the assets, and – in measures that foreshadowed the 1998 ministerial reforms in Beijing – Shunde slashed its line bureaux and reduced staff by 33%. The policy has enabled the authorities to focus more on local public goods provision. In rural Shandong province, conditions are different (Chen, 1998). There, Mao's village work brigades have been transformed into village conglomerates under the leadership of local Party bosses. These party-state village conglomerates help the development of rural-based industrial activities. But the downside is that the local Party secretaries gradually transform into local tyrants, impervious to outside authority. Yu Zuomin was one such local grandee: president and Party secretary of the Daqiuzhuang village conglomerate, he won the title of "national peasant entrepreneur" and "national model worker" in 1989, became a deputy in the NPC, and began to build his own private empire. Eventually, he was arrested, but only after Tianjin local government had sent in 400 armed police to overcome local resistance. He died in October 1999 after six years in prison. Maybe his sin was to have failed to understand that his private ambition had been built on a party-state platform. In any case, the depth of such corporate resources of loyalty to local leaders in rural China is clearly a factor to reckon with in the future.

B. Incentives differ among stakeholders in the process of corporate transformation in China. Consider the following illustrations:

◆ Swapping the security of lifetime employment for the market-dependent quest for wealth has encouraged asset stripping. At the end of 1996, Shanxi Cotton Textile Factory debts were 175% of the estimated worth of physical assets. Given that bankruptcy law (for SOEs) in China absolves the debtor, the local government formed a holding company to auction enterprises. The head of the holding company made an offer for the net worth of the factory. He won, unopposed. The factory reopened under a new name, Xinkai. All debts were eliminated, 3,500 of the 14,000 labor force were laid off, and local banks provided supporting finance. The new owners were up and running.

◆ Active industrial policy keeps the gravy train of patronage running. Shichuan province, traditionally outward looking like Guangdong, was first to allow establishment of fully private firms.[2] But as one official observed, "they closed one eye, but continued to watch with the other". The government promoted local specializations, and corporate champions – like the Wanxiang Group, which started as a bicycle-repair shop in rural Shejian and grew into an automobile manufacturer within less than twenty years – plunged into trade promotion, created a social services system for the province, and introduced incentive packages for outside investors.

◆ Companies have won greater autonomy, but they are expected to give a helping hand in transformation. New Hope, the food corporation based in Chengdu in Sichuan province, bought up thirteen SOEs in various provinces between 1993 and 1998. Zhang Ruimin, boss of Haier, took over fifteen companies during the same period. In 1997, he struck a deal with Chen Jun, Acting Mayor of Hefei City in Anhui province.

---

[2] Interview with Dr Dai Pei Qun, an economic analyst in Anhui provincial government.

Ownership of the local television factory would remain in the hands of the municipality, but Haier would have a free hand to manage it. The bankruptcy law was mobilized to reduce debt. Zhang pledged to invest several million dollars in the plant.

◆ Employees gain by working under new management. In general, employee shareholder schemes do not work. There are exceptions, like the Sida Insulation Material Company in Zhucheng city in Shandong, where stock price, corporate revenues, tax yield and worker incomes all rose. Nonetheless, the experience of the Shunde government must be widespread. The temptation to extract wage hikes and fat dividends is high. Employee shareholding does not strengthen management, nor does it bring adequate capital to the enterprise. The best solution for workers is for corporate assets to be bought by outside capital. That's good news for foreign investors.

The private sector's emergence

Finally, the private sector in China boomed in the 1990s. There were 90,000 private firms registered in 1990 and 1.76 million registered ten years later. A composite picture of the average private firm is of a small-scale operation run by an owner–manager, younger than the average chief executive, with sales that are 95% in the domestic market (Schönleber, 2000). Three-quarters of the capital for start-up comes out of the owner–manager's own pocket, and another 12% comes from family members. Owner-managers formal educational attainments are modest, as illustrated by Cao Dawang, the founder of the Fuyao Group, who went to school for about seven years. Since China's policy change, Dawang has built up his firm to be a world-class manufacturer of windscreen glass for automobiles. Fuyao has 50% of the domestic market, 13% of the North American market and 15% of the Australian market (*South China Post*, 2001). Such firms tend to hire family members into managerial positions. Ideologically, they are Adam Smith entrepreneurs, permanently on the lookout for opportunities, quite secretive about their affairs, and very much aware of their political environment. They spend generously on public relations, including entertainment of clients and political patrons. Their expenditure on research and develop-

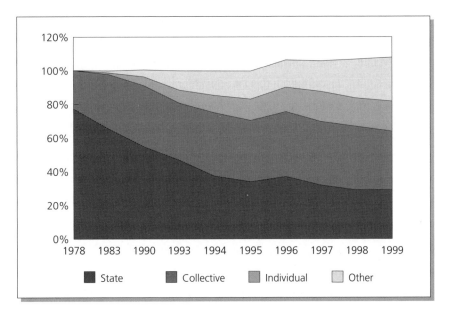

Figure 7.3 ◆ Percentage of ownership in industry output
Source: China Statistics Yearbook 2000

ment is minimal, but they are eager for partnerships and business opportunities. In short, they are ideal allies for foreign investors seeking to build up their own private networks to run their businesses in China.

Private business in China was outlawed for fifty years from 1949 to 1999, when the NPC voted an amendment to the constitution recognizing the contribution of private enterprise to the country's development. Before that, of course, conditions had been changing, private enterprises had been able to register, and local governments such as in Shunde launched their reform to "let go the small ones". When foreign investors rushed into China, they became concerned with protecting their property rights, not least on patents. Then came the successful bid for WTO membership. As an indication of the determination among the younger generation of economic planners to create the institutions for an economic society in China, the State Planning Commission announced that all inherited restrictions discriminating against private businesses would be lifted (*Asian Wall Street Journal*, 2000).

There were five major reasons for this shift in attitude, all of a piece with the Chinese regime's integration into the global system:

◆ The Chinese economy created twenty million jobs a year over the 1980s; the number fell below eight million new jobs a year in the 1990s. With fifteen million new entrants per annum through to 2020, plus restructuring in SOEs, TVEs and agriculture, unleashing private enterprise on China is the only way forward, short of an explosion of unemployment and violence in countryside and cities. Private enterprise created new jobs at the rate of +29% per annum from 1990 to 2000.

◆ Private enterprise managed well in a no-man's land of informal arrangements. But their very opacity also held a high cost. Hybrid forms of business registration, some with the Ministry of Agriculture and others with local authorities and townships, covered the range of activities from asset stripping through to value creation. Corruption, as we have seen, is a gangrene that can be dealt with in the medium term only by a clear recognition of property rights for Chinese people. In a well-functioning market society, contracts, whether verbal or written, have to be respected and ultimately enforced by law.

◆ There is an urgent need for China to use resources more efficiently as China enters the WTO. Private enterprises face hard budget constraints and use resources much more efficiently than others in China. As things are, Chinese enterprises face a host of incentives to diversify in order to reduce the risks they face from unpredictable shifts in government policies, to get around poorly functioning labor and capital markets, to preserve opacity so that they can move back into the shadows if political winds turn adverse and to expand downstream in order to ensure payments (International Finance Corporation). Where government policy is more predictable, as in Wenzhou, companies tend to be more focused.

◆ There is an obvious need for China to create a more level playing field for its own companies. That is one of the benefits to China of joining the WTO. As it is, bureaucratic structures are complex, responsibilities overlap, and there are abundant incentives for rent-seeking. Many markets are closed or have restricted access. Private enterprises, for instance, are not allowed into thirty sectors and up to seventeen further product lines in other industries. These include banking, railways, telecommunications and wholesaling – all sectors where SOEs and their ministries have privileged positions. Private businesses, especially, lack access to stable sources of outside finance, and they are very vulnerable to fees being imposed by bureaucracies hungry for funds.

◆ Above all, even the largest private enterprises such as Stone – the consumer electronics group created in 1984 by four scientists from the Chinese Academy of Sciences, quoted on the Hong Kong Stock Exchange, and with extensive employee shareholding – or New Hope – the animal food business based in Chengdu in Sichuan province – are minnows on the Chinese market. The five top SOEs have a turnover thirty-five times those of the five top private enterprises. In turn, the SOEs are minnows on the world business scene. Size, of course, is no predictor of future success. But China needs high-quality companies to develop their full potential. The best way to build national champions is not to subsidize them into dominant market positions but to encourage a context in which winners can emerge.

And there is the rub. Does the CCP want Chinese companies to emerge over the next few years, regardless of their ownership, or is the CCP only concerned with promoting the enterprises still under its patronage? In Taiwan in the 1980s, the Leninist Kuomintang, then the dominant party in Taipei, allowed private enterprises to emerge alongside the party-state-related firms. Their emergence as alternative polls of wealth and prestige was an integral part of Taiwan's move to democratization. In China, there are two trade associations for private enterprises, and both are under CCP surveillance. The Party faces a clear choice: promote China or defend its privileges. As the country continues to marketize, the two are no longer identical. This is evident when we look at the growth of the securities markets.

The new policy: financial market reforms

Let us swing back to November 1997 and the National Financial Conference held under the auspices of a Party financial working committee. There are about 180 top financial officials in China (Heimann, 2001). One result of their deliberations was to chivvy the China Securities Law through the NPC, where it had dallied for five years. The law was a truly Leninist creation: the finance committee of the Central Committee oversees the three regulators of banking, the securities markets and the insurance sector. The China Securities and Regulatory Commission (CSRC), set up in 1993, was elevated to ministerial level and placed directly under the responsibility of the State Council. The idea was to strengthen the CSRC's autonomy as responsible for nationwide supervision of securities markets. In similar vein, the PBoC's branches were reduced from forty-nine to nine interprovincial branches along the lines of the US Federal Reserve System. The credit plan, whereby banks were obliged to distribute credit quotas to SOEs, was wound down as a first step to introducing more commercial criteria into bank lending practices. The law gave the CSRC oversight of capital markets and powers over new issues. Insider trading was defined, and the CSRC was given powers to confiscate illegal profits and impose fines. But there are obvious limits to the legislation. Let's look at them one by one.

Regulators struggling for autonomy from the CCP

The law has not managed to reduce the *competition between regulators* inherent to an overlap of responsibilities between the three regulators, the State Planning Commission, the PBoC and the Finance Ministry. Who, for instance, has the final say in bailing out the banks: the bank regulator, the CSRC, the PBoC, the Finance Ministry as the source of funds, or the SPC? The problem is made more complicated by the fact that the Party committee has oversight of policy and key appointments. The regulators' mandates are defined and interpreted by Party officials. The CSRC, for instance, has to ensure that capital is raised for SOEs but at the same time maintain confidence in the market. It wants to keep the markets bullish by talking them up through positive editorials in the *People's Daily* and other media outlets. Not surprisingly, the market is highly politicized. But the government is also more than aware that creating a climate of "honesty and trust" (*chengxin*) is crucial to the success of China's marketization. Yet there is a glaring contradiction between the government's efforts to crack down on fraud in the financial markets and its use of the media to talk China's sixty million or so frequent share-buyers into buying dubious SOE stock. As its chief financial adviser has observed in public, continued administrative intervention in the securities markets is not the best way to promote them as a reliable, long-term source of capital.

The CCP choice between control of financial institutions and inflation

As we have seen, the banks are under party-state control and are the principal recipients of household savings. Up to the early 1990s, fiscal deficits, which began in 1979, were financed up to 50% by the simple device of having households hold government bonds, and the rest was financed by recourse to the printing press (Xu, 1998). The banks dished out funds to SOEs and TVEs as if there was no tomorrow. That led to the inflationary binges of the late 1980s and 1992–4, when inflation rates rose to over 24%. What to do? We can see clearly enough *ex post* that policy was decided by the party-state reaching a consensus between the growth-at-all-costs brigade and those favoring price stabilization. Two measures were adopted at an interval of four years. In both, the government took two steps forward and one step back:

◆ The 1995 Budget Law mandated a balanced budget on current account but allowed a deficit on capital account to be financed by the bond market. The result was a surge in debt issuance to finance mega-projects such as the Three Gorges Dam and the development of the Pudong business zone in Shanghai. Inflationary financing of the budget deficit was disallowed, and much stricter revenue sharing with the provinces was introduced. By the end of the decade, about two-thirds of revenue, half of which came from value-added tax, accrued to the central government. The government also clamped down as much as possible on tax evasion. The counterpart to this was an explosion in fees charged by local governments, desperate for revenue.

◆ In 1998, the credit plan was ended, and much tighter controls on banks were introduced. Basel standards were imposed, with banks having to adopt risk-based lending. A $30 billion treasury bond was issued to finance a strengthening of the banks' capital base, and the banks were converted into share-system organizations. As a result, their lending dried up. At the same time, the central authorities clamped down on regional banks, most dramatically closing down GITIC, the Guangdong-based investment bank. The investment banks accounted for only 3% of total financial assets, and GITIC in particular had raised capital from Korean and Japanese banks. This was one cockroach that it cost little for the authorities to crush in the Chinese kitchen (Story, 1999).

Some accounting problems among Chinese corporates

The most urgent task in the wake of the Asian crash was to wash SOE debts, equal to about 65% of SOE assets, or $144 billion in non-performing loans off bank balance sheets. The method chosen was debt–equity swaps, to be managed by asset-management companies and modeled on the Resolution Trust Corporation – a US financial institution set up to clean up the losses from the savings and loans debacle of the 1980s. The Cinda AMC was the first of four companies, one for each of the big banks, with the specific task of taking over the non-performing loans of the China Construction Bank – the sector where corrupt practices were apparently most widespread. Within a year, one trillion yuan of SOE debts were transferred to the companies, helping to clear up bank portfolios and sharply reduce SOE debt. But the source of the SOE-bank debt problem was systemic: the AMCs dealt only with the symptoms. The political channels were still in place for the SOEs to get privileged access to funds, and the habit of falsifying corporate accounts from the command-economy days was still deeply in place. In 1999, the National Audit Office reckoned that 68% of the country's top SOEs had falsified accounts.

Priming the pump of China's economy

Another urgent task in the wake of the Asian crash was to pump-prime China's economy. This meant accelerated development of China's securities markets. China's bond market in fact began in the countryside, where arbitrageurs spotted an opportunity to buy government bonds and sell them for a profit in urban areas. Local governments tapped into informal markets in rural areas to finance the expansion of the TVEs – a process referred to as "raising funds from society" (*shehui jizi*). The banks set up their own investment banks for similar purposes, so that by the early 1990s there were well over 1,000 investment banks operating around the country. Then, in 1991, the simple device of forcing bonds on households was replaced by the creation of a treasury bond market, with banks serving as underwriters. Debt issuance rose rapidly over the coming decade, reaching $50 billion (418 billion renminbi) in 2000, or 4.6% GDP (see Table 7.1). The deficit of 2.9% GDP was manageable, with public debt at no more than 10% GDP. China's foreign debt is double, and readily servicable through China's booming exports and huge foreign exchange reserves, valued at $168 billion in 2000.

But Table 7.1 also shows that government reliance on "borrowing" (new issues) has risen as a portion of revenue from 12.6% in 1990 to 31% in 2000. For the central government, revenues depend 60% on debt issuance, with 70% going on debt service (Gamble, 2000). Writing in 1997–8, before the burst in China's counter-cyclical spending, Nicholas Lardy (1998), from the Brookings Institution, considered the government to be heading to a debt/GDP ratio of 110% by 2010. This meant the government would have to raise interest rates to keep Chinese households investing in treasury bonds. Already in 1998, the stock of government debt was $100 billion. That was practically doubled by the end of 2000. Another $100 billion was issued to strengthen the banks' capital base and to help finance the policy banks. Lardy (1998) calculated that the AMC bailout is $300 billion, not $144 billion – others place the non-performing loan bill even higher. In other words, total liabilities of the government are about 50% of the GNP. Add to this the government's unfunded pension liabilities and the government's total liabilities are well over 100% GDP ten years ahead of Lardy's deadline.

Limits on capital liberalization

Given this growing dependence of the government on the capital market, Beijing clearly has an incentive to keep China's massive savings pool at home. The party-state can draw on the pool to keep itself in business and

Table 7.1 ◆ China's public finances (Rmb bn)

	1990	1991	1992	1993	1994	1995	1996	1997	1998	1999	2000
Revenue	293.8	314.9	384.3	434.8	521.8	624.2	740.8	865.1	987.6	1.144.4	1.339.5
Tax	282.1	299	329.6	425.5	512.6	603.8	690.9	823.4	926.2	1068.6	1.257.1
Net subsidies to enterprises	−57.8	−51	−44.9	−41.3	−36.6	−32.7	−33.7	−36.8	−33.4	−29	−28
Borrowing[1]	37.5	46.1	66.9	73.9	117.5	154.9	196.7	247.6	331	371.5	418
Expenditure	308.4	338.6	374.2	464.2	579.2	682.3	793.7	923.3	1079.8	1318.7	1557.6
Capital construction	136.8	142.8	161.3	183.5	239.4	285.5	323.3	364.7	417.9	506.1	
Debt service[2]	19	24.7	43.8	33.6	49.9	88.3	135.5	191.8	235.2	192.4	230
Deficit	−14.6	−23.7	−25.8	−29.3	−57.4	−58.1	−52.9	−58.2	−92.2	−174.4	−249
Market capitalization		10.9	104.8	353.1	369.1	347.4	984.2	1752.9	1950.6	2647	4809
Market cap (% GDP)		0.5	3.9	10.2	7.9	5.9	14.5	23.4	24.5	31.8	53.8

[1]Recorded on new issues in *China Statistical Yearbook*.
[2]Payment for principal and interest of debts.

Source: China Statistical Yearbook, 2001, China Securities and Futures Statistical Yearbook

the economy turning. After all, it controls the banks and capital markets. There is an exact parallel of China's present condition to those of France and Italy of the early 1960s, when Paris and Rome rejected the European Commission's proposal to liberalize capital movements; Paris and Rome wanted to use control over the capital market for their national purposes. Like Beijing in 1996, Paris and Rome were ready to allow convertibility of their currencies on current account – in other words, for business and travel. But they waited another thirty years before liberalizing capital movements and did so only by linking this to support for a new currency arrangement in the EU. Monetary union is the result. What Paris and Rome feared most was speculative waves of capital outflows to strong-currency countries. Let us use this analogy to highlight China's policy regarding liberalization of capital markets.

Before the depreciation of Asian currencies by 20–80% in 1997–8, there had been some discussion in Beijing about freeing capital movements. This was the mantra of the global financial institutions at the time. If you free up your capital markets, they were saying, you'll get access to the vast pool of global savings. Faster growth will be the result. Of course, global funds won't invest unless you get your domestic business system shipshape, i.e. balanced budgets, well-regulated financial markets, transparent corporate accounts, etc.

China's emergence as a pillar of financial stability

None of this was conclusive for the party-state. China, after all, had a vast pool of domestic savings. Rapid flows of footloose funds in and out of currencies, the Asia-Pacific crash showed only too clearly, destabilized whole societies. Then came the collapse of the Russian rouble in August 1998, when Moscow decided to renege on debts to foreign investors in government bonds. For Beijing, the lesson once again was to do things step by step. Better to keep capital controls and tolerate some evasion of regulations: indeed, from 1979 to 1997, $80–100 billion had leaked out of the country, mainly into Hong Kong and Macao (Guoqiang, 1999). Much of this was "round-tripping" by SOE managers, investing in Hong Kong stocks or recycling them back to the mainland. This trend rose sharply in 1998 when managers had some reason to hedge against devaluation.

Beijing decided against devaluation and duly received plaudits from the Clinton administration. Had China devalued the currency, then its Asia-Pacific trade competitors would have been squeezed on exports, and the US external deficit would have widened considerably. Enlightened self-interest also played a part. China's exports are still relatively low valued-added, while imports are primarily capital goods. China would therefore have been earning less per unit sold and paying more per unit bought – not a good business proposition. Foreign investors already in China would see their assets devalued in local currency. Not least, the Hong Kong dollar was fixed to the US dollar. A renminbi devaluation would have left Hong Kong massively overvalued relative to its mainland supplier. So China stuck to a dollar–renminbi rate of 8.27. It then went a step further and earmarked a billion dollars to the Japanese proposal for an Asian Monetary Fund (AMF) – a complete reversal in policy. The AMF is Asia's equivalent of the EU's 1979 proposal to stabilize foreign exchange rates of member states through a partial pooling of foreign exchange reserves. The idea was torpedoed by the Bundesbank, which preferred to run EU exchange rate policy in relation to the dollar, on its own. No doubt conflicting national interests will hobble the AMF, just as they undermined the EU's proposal. But China's support of the AMF proposal in principle marks the country's entry into global financial diplomacy. The message runs thus: China is a pillar of (financial) stability.

Keeping savings at home

The same message is all the more important for being heard at home. Keeping China's pool of savings at home means that the party-state has to win the public's confidence in the currency. One way of so doing is for the party-state to build up a firm reputation in favor of price stability – the consumer price index at the turn of the millennium hovered either side of zero. Another way of giving households a real rate of return is to provide alternative outlets to place their savings. Otherwise, Chinese savers may lose confidence, withdraw their savings from the banks, and stuff their mattresses with gold. Providing savers with alternative outlets gives them an opportunity to migrate across financial channels and between financial agents in search of higher returns. This is what awaits Chinese banks as the securities markets continue to develop: the more transparent securities markets become, the more savers will switch from low-yield deposits to bonds and equities. The banks have little interest in such a development. But the Chinese leadership is in a quandary: they want to fund their big projects and their SOEs, and the only way to do so is to rig the market. That is not compatible with keeping the public's confidence.

There can be little doubt that China's financial leaders know that they have much to learn from abroad. In June 1993, the PRC and the Hong Kong Authority signed a Memorandum of Regional Cooperation, authorizing the listing of mainland companies on Hong Kong's markets. Both Qingdao, a brewery, and MD were early examples of mainland companies ready to meet global reporting standards for the privilege of a listing in "H" shares. Then, in August 1994, the CSRC signed a Memorandum of Understanding with the New York Stock Exchange (NYSE) and the Securities and Exchange Commission (SEC). Mainland companies could now list in New York as "N" shares. This all took place at the height of the Western corporate China dream about China's overtaking the USA by 2003 (Studwell, 2002). Deflation followed elation as night follows day. One example is Brilliance, a Shenyang minibus company selling about 10,000 units in 1991, which listed on New York and on its first day trading was the most actively traded stock after Ford. By 1994, it was clear that sales had barely risen, and the Brilliance stock fell to under half of its listing price. When China's Finance Ministry tried initial public offerings in New York and Hong Kong in 2000 for its three major state oil companies, the mood was much more downbeat. The hope was to raise $15–20 billion, but humiliation was avoided only when the world oil majors and some Hong Kong conglomerates put up a tenth of the money. After years of disappointments in global markets, China's SOEs turned back to local markets.

Creating trust in financial markets is a long-term proposition

From the start, China's equity markets in Shanghai and Shenzhen have been a casino. Indeed, the CSRC was set up in response to a shareholder riot in Shenzhen in summer 1992, when one million people were sold shares in fourteen companies that had failed to disclose either balance sheet or prospectus (*The Economist*, 1992). What to do? Zhu Rongji and financial experts discussed different financial systems, but ended up focusing on Hong Kong, New York and London. Hong Kong's regulatory authority, with its parastatal status and high flexibility with respect to salaries and personnel, provided the model for the CSRC. Zhu Rongji rode roughshod over the Party's *nomenklatura* system to bring in top personnel to the CSRC from Hong Kong. The CSRC's powers were strengthened by the 1999 law.

There are over 100 securities firms operating in the two markets, which account for 1.2% of total financial assets in China by 2000. So the field is crowded, and the party-state has encouraged mergers to create about seven market leaders, which are hoped to be able to take on the world's leading investment banks. Foreign investors have been able to trade in "B" shares, which account for 5% of trades. "A" shares, mainly in SOEs, face much less demanding requirements to list. Not surprisingly, "A" shares – so called "red chips" – have traded at a steep discount to "B" shares. Listing is decided by a highly politicized quota process, where new issues are kept firmly in the Communist Party family: 99% of investment decisions on the Shanghai Stock Exchange, and decisions relating to key personnel and their remuneration, are taken by the Communist Party committee in the firm, in agreement with the local government (*Financial Times*, 2000). The CSRC and its Party supervisor are the ultimate arbiters. When these arrangements were modified in the course of 2000–2001, giving more space to market underwriters to decide on listing, and allowing domestic investors to buy "B" shares', the bottom fell out of the "A" share market.

Other factors played on "A" share performance, not least the puncturing of the world dot.com boom. It is all too clear that China's reforms cannot proceed unless there are deep reforms in the corporate governance of SOEs. This message was carried in no uncertain terms back into China by the humiliating failures of SOEs to make the grade on world stock markets. This retreat recalls the obvious fact that while there may be a firewall between the local capital markets and the global capital market, all national economies are interdependent. Technologies are transnational, and markets function in similar ways around the globe. China's is no exception. China's listed corporations may want to trade at multiples of earnings in a rigged market, but they will not attract investors.

The conclusion is clear enough: the Chinese economy is more than ever in the hands of consumers and savers. The production system, controlled by the CCP, has to adapt or die. So far, the CCP has preferred to adapt. If it is to cleave to this policy, as it has so far, the steps for the next decade are clear enough: resources must be allocated better than hitherto, regulators particularly in the financial markets have to be more effective, corporate management has to be further taken off the drug of bank subsidy or rigged equity valuations, the Party has to step back much further from corporate

> The Chinese economy is more than ever in the hands of consumers and savers

patronage, private enterprises have to be placed on a footing of equality with their competitors, and private property rights have to be inserted at the heart of China's political system. What the CCP has going for it is the stock of public lethargy on which it can continue to draw. But the stock is far from limitless. Let's trace what this means for foreign investors, whose experiences in China have, are and will be rhythmed by the heartbeats of the Chinese chimera.

References

Asian Development Bank, 1997, *Emerging Asia: Changes and Challenges*, Manila, The Philippines, Asian Development Bank.

Asian Wall Street Journal, 2000, January 20 "State power caused China's decline", *Wall Street Journal*, New York, 2000, January 6.

Yuanzheng Cao, Yingyi Qian and Barry Weingast, 1999, "From federalism Chinese style to privatisation, Chinese style", *Economics of Transition*, 7(1), pp. 103–31.

Weixing Chen, 1998, "Politics and paths of rural development in China: the village conglomerate in Shandong province", *Pacific Affairs*, 71(1), pp. 25–39.

X.L. Ding, 2001, "The quasi criminalisation of a business sector in China", *Crime, Law and Social Change*, 35, pp. 177–201.

Economic Daily, 1998, August 1.

The Economist, 1992, August 15 "China's stockmarkets: open outcry".

Lu Feng, 1999, *State, Market, and Enterprise: The Transformation of Chinese State Industry*, PhD dissertation, Columbia University.

Financial Times, 2000, November 5 Richard McGregor, "Market focus: Shanghai's excessive interference critics".

William Gamble, 2000, "The Middle Kingdom runs dry", *Foreign Affairs*, 79(6), pp. 16–20.

Long Guoqiang, 1999, "Outward FDI: a novel dimension of China's integration into the regional and global economy", *China Quarterly*, 160, pp. 856–80.

James Harding, 1999, "An uncomfortable reality", *Financial Times*, October 1.

Sebastian Heimann, 2001, "Der Aktienmarkt der VR China", *China Analysis*, 3, Vol 1: http://www.ahk-china.org/download/aktienmarkt1.pdf. Vol 2: http://www.ahk-china.org/download/aktienmarkt2.pdf.

Jean-François Huchet, 1999, "Concentration et emergence des groupes dans l'industrie chinoise", *Perspectives Chinoises*, 52, http://www.cefc.com.hk/cgi-bin/restricted2.cgi.

Jean-François Huchet and Xavier Richet, 2000, "Between bureaucracy and market: Chinese industrial groups in search of new forms of corporate governance", CEFC working paper no. 2, http://www.cefc.com.hk

International Finance Corporation, "China's emerging private enterprises: prospects for the new century", http://www.worldbank.org.cn/English/IFC/pssr.pdf

Ian Johnson, 1999, "Group suits let aggrieved in China appeal for justice – peasants take on local authorities over taxes", *Asian Wall Street Journal*, March 26.

Nicholas R. Lardy, 1998, *China's Unfinished Economic Revolution*, Washington, DC, Brookings Institution.

Moody's Investors Service, 1999, "Banking system outlook China, the start of a long march", http://www.moodys.com

OECD, 2000, *China in the Global Economy. Reforming China's Enterprises*, Paris, OECD.

Oxford Analytica, 1997, "President Jiang Zemin opens the 15th Party Congress", *Oxford Analytica*, September 15, http://www.oxan.com/

People's Daily, 1999, March 21, http://english.people.com.cn/

Reuters, 1994, "Tycoon Zhang sets personal aim of out-achieving Li-Ka-shing", December 4.

Helmut Schönleber, 2000, "China ACFIC partnership project", http://www.acfic.com.cn/dihtpage/e-pe2000.pdf

Tinjin Shi, 2001, "Cultural values and political trust", *Comparative Politics*, 33(4), pp. 401–19.

South China Post, 2001, November 8.

Jonathan Story, 1999, *The GITIC Crackdown (A) Killing Cockroaches in the Kitchen*, Fontainebleau, France, INSEAD.

Joe Studwell, 2001, *The China Dream: The Quest for the Last Great Untapped Market on Earth*, New York, Atlantic Monthly Press.

US State Department, 2002, "Country reports on human rights practices, 2001", March 4, http://www.state.gov/g/drl/rls/hrrpt/2001/

Richard Whitley, 1999, *Divergent Capitalisms: The Social Structuring and Change of Business Systems*, Oxford, Oxford University Press.

Xinhua News Agency, 1995, September 17, http://www.xinhuanet.org/

Xiaoping Xu, 1998, *China's Financial System under Transition*, London, Macmillan.

Minghua Zhao and Theo Nichols, 1996, "Management control of labour in state-owned enterprises: cases from the textile industry", *China Journal*, 36, pp. 1–21.

8

Getting China right: the multinational experience

FOR MANY WESTERN BUSINESSPEOPLE, China is a mystery wrapped in an enigma, to paraphrase Winston Churchill on Soviet Russia. Unlike Japan, say the China bulls, the Chinese leadership has embraced reform with a vengeance. Their policies are laying the foundations for a shareholder culture, where both foreigners and Chinese people can make money. Bears counter that investing in China is a sure way to lose money, as realistic as nineteenth-century textile manufacturers' dreams of unlimited wealth acquired by lengthening the coat tails of all Chinese males by one inch. To Chinese nationalists, by contrast, Western corporations are devouring Chinese enterprises, as China's industrial assets are absorbed into their global operations. Professor Lu Feng from Qinghua University begs to differ: Chinese enterprises, he says, are perfectly capable of developing their core competences and beating the multinationals at their own game. Zhang Ruimin, CEO of Haier, the Chinese conglomerate, puts it more bluntly: "Chinese enterprises must become wolves instead of sheep if they want to win in the competition for business after [China's] entry to the WTO ... To become wolves, Chinese enterprises must learn how the market works ... The key is meeting customer demands fast."

In this chapter, I argue that the multinationals are learning how to operate in China, and to incorporate local partners into sharing their wealth. Let's look first at some facts about foreign investment in China, ask why China is so popular, discuss how corporations are learning fast, and show through examples how China's transformation directly affects the details of doing business there.

China's El Dorado

At the very moment China began the open-doors policy in 1978, the world economy decided to change shape. For fifty years, national governments had claimed the commanding heights of their economies, pulling a panoply of levers to promote growth, redistribute income, develop public services, guide trade, control finance and manage foreign exchange. The results were evident in the growth of public deficits, high inflation, and turbulent foreign exchange markets, alongside the expansion of global capital markets and of foreign investment by large industrial corporations and banks. Over the following five years, the global foundations were laid for less government activism and more space for market forces. As national economies were opened wider, the market in corporate assets took off, leading to the creation of the mega-corporations that presently bestride the world. Foreign direct investment accelerated. As multinationals scoured the world for new markets and production platforms, they pulled their subcontractors and suppliers in their wake, thereby creating a worldwide network of competing but associated business activities. Subcontractors and suppliers in their turn merged and married to extend their scope and competences. Worldwide, corporations have entered bargains on a bilateral basis with states (Stopford and Strange, 1991).

Inevitably, China has been caught up in this new diplomacy, characterized by bargains between states and corporations, where control over outcomes can be negotiated. As can be seen in Figure 8.1, the trend flow for inward investment has been consistently upwards. FDI flows stayed at a modest trickle in the 1980s; contracted flows then surged in the early 1990s in response to Deng's statement that henceforth it was considered glorious

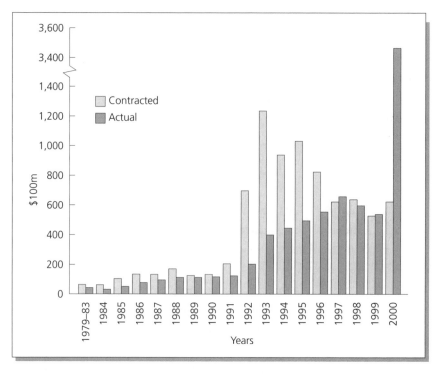

Figure 8.1 ◆ Annual inflows of FDI to China: contracted and utilized
amounts 1982–99 (US $100m)
Source: China Statistical Yearbook, 2001.

to be rich. In effect, the wave of FDI was also instigated by a combination
of factors at home and in the world economy. Slow growth in Japan,
Europe and the USA at the start of the decade sent chief executives scouring
the world for business opportunities, while Chinese SOEs responded to
greater competition on their domestic markets by seeking help from abroad.
By 1995–6, FDI accounted for 25% of domestic investment, 13% of industrial output, 31% of exports, 11% of tax revenues, and sixteen million jobs
(*Chinese Economic Review*, 1998). This placed China among the top three
recipients of FDI, alongside the USA and the UK, and by far the largest
recipient of FDI among developing countries, accounting in the mid-1990s
for 25–30% of the total to all developing countries. Actual inflows continued to rise until 1997 – the year of the east Asian financial crash – and then
tailed off. Clearly, one motivation behind China's bid to join the WTO was
to ensure that the multinationals kept coming.

Over time, the distribution of FDI has undergone significant evolution. On a sectoral basis, the bulk in the early 1980s went to geological exploration – reflecting the government's hopes for energy self-sufficiency – and to real estate and tourism. Following regulatory changes in 1986, FDI inflows shifted to export-oriented industries. Since the surge in 1993, the largest proportion has gone into manufacturing, with about half being directed to labor-intensive industries such as textiles and clothing, and the other half split equally between technology-intensive activities, such as pharmaceuticals – and capital-intensive operations, such as petroleum refining and chemicals materials. Services have been closed off by government fiat. Further market opening and China's entry to the WTO will surely prompt a new wave of investment, this time in financial services. Meanwhile, the world's leading investment banks keep a presence in Hong Kong and an ear to the floor in Beijing. In terms of geographic distribution, the FDI pattern reveals great disparities. The eastern region, for instance, holds nearly two-thirds of GDP and takes up to 88% of FDI. This, too, is largely policy driven, as the early open-door policies resulted in much FDI bunching along the eastern coast. Most inland provinces are still closed economies. WTO entry is likely to benefit the coast much more than these inland provinces.

The main impact of FDI has been on stimulating the domestic economy and accelerating China's insertion in the global division of labor. Such large injections of resources have stimulated growth, especially in those provinces that have received most. With output of foreign enterprises growing in the mid-1990s at four times the rate of local enterprises, it was not surprising that they acted as locomotives on local economies, attracting subcontractors and stimulating suppliers. Domestic enterprises benefited by transfer of technology and managerial know-how. Not least, FDI has built a highly competitive and dynamic manufacturing export sector. Between 1978 and 2000, China's trade grew four and half times faster than global trade – an achievement unrivaled by any other country. Foreign enterprises played a key part: between the mid-1980s and 2000, their share in China's exports grew from 1% to 45%. The growth of this export sector is a central factor in China's future transformation:

◆ China runs large trade surpluses with the USA and the EU, and runs trade deficits with Asia. The foreign-invested enterprise trade with Japan is in balance. This indicates that China has become an assembly base for Asian subsidiaries exporting on to western markets and an operations center for US and EU corporations that have shifted activities to the mainland.

◆ The competitiveness of China's manufacturing exports has helped create the yuan as a hard currency. As a whole, the country has thus been able to digest the cost of a higher yen, but Chinese-owned corporations have suffered. In other words, Chinese companies have been penalized by policies that have favored multinationals at the expense of local companies. Entry to the WTO should reduce the present advantages enjoyed by foreign corporations over local competitors in China.

◆ FDI has been a major source of external financing, by contrast to many developing countries that became overdependent on short-term capital flows. From 1992 to 1998, FDI provided 70% of total external resources injected into the economy. This has enabled China to develop a manageable foreign debt and vast foreign exchange reserves. It has also helped develop China's profile as *the* key developing country partner, leagues ahead of Russia, India and Indonesia and at least on a par with Brazil.

If China is such a major target for inward investment, then its own corporate outreach remains strictly limited. The importance of this statement lies in the following: China is first and foremost incorporated in the global business system. The development of the Chinese outreach lies in the future. Since 1989, China has begun to build up a considerable international portfolio, with a total stock by 1999 of $25 billion, twice as much as Brazil's (Cai, 1999). India has only $1 billion of outward invested assets. In that year, Chinese foreign affiliates numbered about 9,000, with a presence in over 180 countries. Much of this expansion reflects the ending of the central government's trade monopoly, and the explosion in the number of trade companies set up by ministries and provincial and municipal governments. Not surprisingly, two-thirds of Chinese overseas investment is in trade-supporting activities – the very early stages of a country's corporate outreach. If we add Hong Kong's outward stock of FDI to the mainland figures, then China's total outward

> China is a pillar of the global economy and *the* prime target of investment for global corporations

stock reaches $200 billion. This places China well ahead of Italy. Add in Taiwan, and China is in a whisker of overtaking France as a source of FDI. Given the accelerated integration of Hong Kong's economy since 1997, and the lure of the mainland for Taiwan's corporations, China is unique among emerging markets: it is at once a pillar of the global economy and *the* prime target of investment for global corporations.

Why is China so popular?

Investing in Communist China is not the first idea that might occur to a budding capitalist. Yet over time, successive governments in Beijing and in the provinces have learnt how to improve the climate for investors. By 2002, Deloitte Touche Tomatsu, in collaboration with *CFO Magazine*, produced a report, "Foreign investment in China: fitness survey", providing compelling evidence that multinational corporations saw China as the key growth market in the world and that expansion there was a priority.

The initial mix of motives to help attract investors to China are shrouded in secrecy: the new leadership in 1978 was concerned about growing external deficits, the prospect of dependency on Mideastern oil supplies, the backwardness of Chinese technology as demonstrated during the short war with Vietnam, consolidation of the alliance with the USA against the Soviet Union, and the demonstration effect of Asia-Pacific's remarkable economic transformation. What is less in doubt is that from the start, the party-state sought to attract FDI into China as a means of introducing new technologies, transferring management skills and capital, and strengthening the external sector. Two mechanisms in particular have been applied consistently: foreign investors have been granted tax incentives, and the special economic zones have been opened up outside of state plans. Tax concessions have come in the form of tax holidays, import rebates and reduced enterprise tax for technology- and/or export-oriented companies operating on the mainland. The same privileges are available to all companies, domestic and foreign, operating in the special economic zones. There, firms benefit by a high level of managerial autonomy, minimal controls on the flows of goods and services, and flexible labor markets. The benefit for the zones' authorities is that they can build up infrastructure financed largely from their own resources. With so many winning, it is not surprising that FDI boomed.

China's opening door

From the start, there has been considerable ideological resistance to the open-door policy. Initially, laws and regulations were restrictive, but over time policies have adapted as China has marketized. Whether the party-state learnt how to respond to investor preferences or changed government policies to better achieve their changing objectives, legislation became more accommodating with regard to foreign investors. Initially, joint venture was the party-state's preferred vehicle to attract foreign investors and tap into Western technologies. (See Box 8.1.) The July 1979 law stipulated that foreign capital must account for at least 25% of the total capital of the joint ventures. Further adaptations came with experience, notably the 1986 law allowing wholly owned foreign enterprises, and the 1988 law, which provided a more complete legal framework for foreign corporations, protection against expropriations, access to local markets, and a distribution of profits no longer dependable on partners' stakes. This cooperative form of joint venture became particularly popular among Hong Kong investors in the 1990s, accounting on average for about 20% of inward investment. The major change in the past decade has been the popularity among Western corporations for wholly owned operations, which have come to represent about half of the total of actual commitments. This shift to wholly owned operations signals the replacement of overseas Chinese by Western corporations as the prime foreign investors on the mainland. Wholly owned foreign enterprises are the natural allies of Chinese private firms to strengthen property rights there.

The overseas diaspora

One determinant of China's success in attracting FDI is the large Chinese diaspora, with Hong Kong, Singapore and Taiwan as the prime traditional sources and accounting for about 50% of all new commitments in 1999. Another way of arranging this figure is to say that overseas Chinese investors hold about 80% of the stock of FDI on the mainland, but that Western corporations have increased their commitments, often with investments registered as originating from Hong Kong. Hong Kong is thus the prime source, with Taiwan the second biggest investor. This is the heart of the formula for China's reunification: rich, overseas Chinese businessperson meets powerful, mainland Chinese politico. A deal is done.

Why rich overseas Chinese are bullish about China deserves some explanation. One reason for this is the straight-forward economic incentive to shift labor-intensive operations to cheap-labor locations on the mainland. But the fact that rich, overseas Chinese investors have been drawn to put their money into territories subject to Communist rule, from which many of them fled in the 1940s, clearly goes beyond economics. For instance, Li Ka-shing, a Hong Kong-based tycoon, began as a poor immigrant from China selling plastic flowers and combs. He now owns Hong Kong Telecom, a third of the Hong Kong Stock Exchange, and is heavily committed to the mainland, where *inter alia* he plans to create a world-class, privately funded business school. A canny operator like Li Ka-shing would not risk his fortune unless he considered the party-state to be solidly in power, capable of managing the giant country's transformation and pro-business in orientation. Such confidence in China's fundamental stability is strengthened by overseas Chinese ties of blood and kinship often to invest back in the provinces from which they came originally, notably Guangdong and Fujian. Not least, they have grown rich on account of their ability to operate in political markets throughout Asia where *guanxi* – relationships – are at a premium. Evidently, Chinese overseas investors consider that they can put these skills to good use on the mainland.

Western investors' rationale

Why Western investors are drawn to China is much more about economics once differing views about political stability are discounted. They are attracted by the large domestic market, low wage costs, and investments in infrastructure. Let's look at each of these in turn:

◆ Despite the fact that China is far from being a unified market, Western corporations have been attracted by China's huge potential. As we shall see, this gap between corporate vision and local reality has generated much grief. Experience shows that getting the entry strategy right can save a lot of trouble: a China commitment is expensive in time. For overseas Chinese, these considerations are less important as their investments are geared more to global export markets. US and EU corporations, by contrast, direct about two-thirds of output to the domestic market (Tseng and Zebregs, 2002). That is where Chinese corporations still keep a dominant position – controlling 85% of domestic demand for industrial goods. Domestic corporations have less than 70% market share in only two sectors – instruments and electrical and electronic machinery, and below 80% in transport equipment and machinery. Foreign corporations are doing particularly well in highly protected sectors. This suggests that mainland Chinese producers may stand to benefit extensively by WTO entry, as they learn to drive costs down and keep productivity up.

Box 8.1 China's FDI regime has been progressively codified

1979: Law on joint ventures using Chinese and foreign investment.
1982: Revised constitution authorizes FDI in China.
1983: Regulations for implementation of the 1979 Law provided more details on operations and preferential policies for joint ventures. Also law to protect trademarks.
1984: Law on patents. China starts signing agreements to avoid double-taxation with trade partners. This leads to subscribing to international agreements on respect of intellectual property rights.
1985: Law on contracts with foreign enterprises.
1986: Law on enterprises operated exclusively with foreign capital permitted the establishment of wholly foreign-owned enterprises in special economic zones. State Council notice on incentives to foster FDI using advanced technologies and for exports. Later codified in the 1988 Cooperative Joint Venture Law.
1990: Amendments to the 1983 and 1986 Laws, notably that the chairperson of the board of a joint venture does not have to be appointed by Chinese investors. Protection provided from nationalization.

1993: Law on unfair competition on holding company formula.

1994: Tax provisions to unify gradually the treatment of domestic enterprises and foreign-funded enterprises. Standard 33% corporate income tax and in designated cities; 18% in SEZs and technology development zones. Chinese organizations able to list as joint stock companies.

1995: Interim provisions in guiding FDI (revised 1997 and 2002) classified FDI into four categories: projects are *encouraged* and *permitted* in designated industries that introduce new and advanced technologies, expand export capacity, raise product quality, and use local resources in central and western regions. *Restricted* and *prohibited* are projects in designated areas that make use of existing technologies, compete with domestic production or state monopolies, make extensive use of scarce resources, or are considered a danger to national safety and the environment (e.g. airports, nuclear power plants, oil and gas pipelines, subways and railways, water projects, aerospace, automobiles, defense, high-tech vaccines, mining, printing, shipping, satellite communications, and tourism).

2000: Regulation permitting individuals to sign franchise contracts with foreign corporations.

2001: WTO commitments include non-discriminatory treatment of foreign and domestic enterprises, rules on intellectual property rights, elimination of requirements on FDI such as foreign exchange, technology transfer, local content and export performance. Sectoral commitments include national treatment for foreign firms, ending geographic and other restrictions in automobiles, telecommunications, life insurance, banking, distribution and personnel, although the payoff comes in terms of proximity to the market, listening to customers and taking on the local competition.

◆ China's abundant supply of cheap labor is another source of attraction. Here, too, lies a source of much grief for foreign investors, as we shall argue. Labor costs, it is always worth remembering, are a component of operating costs. Nonetheless, labor costs can play a significant role in determining investment location decisions. This is especially the case for companies from Taiwan, Hong Kong and Singapore, and to a certain extent from Japan, which have been hit by rising wage costs. More open world trade enables companies to move part of their production capacities to low-labor-cost countries. In the case of China, the attraction is all the greater because of fiscal packages, tariff import reductions, the special economic zones, and the almost indefinite supply of cheap and low-productivity labor. Asia-Pacific investors have used China as a platform for labor-intensive manufacturing exports. This is evident in the more than 40% of exports accounted for by foreign enterprises in areas such as garments, leather products, toys and sports goods. But China also has potential to develop as a source of highly qualified labor. In 1999, there were 1.6 million students enrolled in engineering courses in institutions of higher learning, a very large number. Chinese universities churn out 20,000–40,000 computer science graduates every year. Still, China is far from enjoying a comparative advantage as a source of skilled labor: only 0.6 people out of 1,000 are recorded as having science and technology backgrounds, compared with 0.3 in India and 5.4 in France. Of course, if the skills are not available on the mainland, then it is always possible to recruit in Taiwan: about 150 mainland Chinese firms recruited several hundred high-tech and financial experts from Taiwan, paying up to double the salaries they got in Taiwan (Agence France Press, 2002).

◆ Like all emerging markets, China has huge requirements to develop infrastructure. Both central and local governments have been active in wooing foreign business: once a locality has started to attract investors, then others tend to come along. Such considerations have direct impact on corporate strategies. Consider Equant, a telecoms service provider corporation. At a meeting in September 1998, the board learnt that the top five provinces would account for more than 60% of Equant's potential customers, the next ten provinces for 30.8%, and the rest for 9.2%. Fifty per cent of total potential customers were estimated as concentrated in the top three cities in each province. Given such conditions, diminishing returns eventually set in as costs rise in high-concentration areas and cheaper, less well-endowed locations appear on investors' radar screens. This is where central government enters the picture. Fortified by the country's high savings and growing foreign exchange reserves, Beijing has gone in for a classical Keynesian deficit spending boom. The famous Three Gorges Dam project in

Hubei province, started in 1997, is probably the best known example: corporations from eleven countries are involved, including well-known players such as Alstom, Siemens, Mitsubishi, ABB, Caterpillar, C.S. Johnson, and not to forget the US Army Corps of Engineers. As Premier Zhu Rongji kept reiterating, capital expenditure builds up wealth-creating assets for the future. It also keeps the wheels of Western business turning.

◆ Following the shift of much global manufacturing to China, the next wave of investment by foreign multinationals is research and development (R&D). China has long been a recipient of telecom technology. Corporations such as Intel, Motorola, General Electric and Microsoft set up small research laboratories in the 1990s. Over time, these research activities are upgraded. In Shanghai alone, over forty multinationals, including IBM, Microsoft, Alcatel and Bayer have set up regional or global R&D centers. Alcatel has teamed up with a Chinese venture capital fund, New Margin, to invest $18 million to support innovation and telecoms engineering facilities. To advertise China as innovation and technology friendly, Shanghai is bidding to win a World Expo in 2010, in competition against Moscow, Buenos Aires, Qheretaro in Mexico, Yosyu in South Korea and Wroclaw in Poland. The plans are to invest $25 billion in the bid, including $2.5 billion for construction on venues and further investment in infrastructure.

China's champions and the big beasts of the global jungle

Who benefits from all this FDI is not surprisingly a controversial matter. A pessimistic view holds that China's corporations are dwarfed by global giants: the average assets and sales of the country's top 500 companies are 0.9% and 1.7% of the top Fortune 500 corporations (*The Economist*, 2000). Only China Mobile and China Unicom, both of which benefit by monopoly positions, are included in the Financial Times 500, which ranks corporations by their market capitalization (*Financial Times*, 2001). Such figures have prompted Peter Nolan (2002), working at the Judge Institute, Cambridge, UK, to argue that while the party-state has tried painfully to build up national champions capable of taking on global competition, the world's top firms have undergone revolutionary changes. China's national champions are minnows, the message runs, about to be devoured by the big beasts of the global corporate jungle.

Matters are not quite so straightforward, as Whirlpool, the US home appliances giant, discovered when it entered the China market. Like many other rich-country corporations that thundered into China in the early 1990s when growth was low at home, Whirlpool expected the China market to equal that of the USA within a decade. By the winter of 1994–5, the US corporation had signed four joint ventures. Thereafter, almost everything that could possibly go wrong went wrong. Whirlpool discovered too late that the four Chinese joint ventures had separate, non-complementary and underdeveloped distribution networks. Bringing their production standards up to scratch cost heavily in terms of ex-pat salaries and the absorption of scarce managerial resources. Above all, Whirlpool senior management gravely underestimated the local competition. In 1997, it pulled out of its refrigerator and air-conditioner operations, citing overcapacity. The top ten producers' market share had reached 90% of the market, with foreign brands accounting for only 5%. Two years later, Whirlpool signed a deal whereby Kelon, along with Haier, one of the prime domestic competitors, would sell Whirlpool washing machines under its own brand name. By 2001, Haier had fifteen design centers and forty-six manufacturing plants worldwide, plus 25% of the US refrigerator market. Kelon, which had started out as a TVE in the 1980s, became the first non-state firm to float shares on the Hong Kong Stock Exchange; it went on to carve out a quarter of China's refrigerator market, based on a China-wide distribution network. Other global brand names, such as Procter & Gamble, Unilever and Nestlé, strode into China only to see their markets eaten up by local brands and pirates.

Nor has the merger craze of the 1990s been an unmitigated blessing for Western corporations. Take the experience of AT&T, the former US telecoms monopolist for the domestic market. Its highly experienced China team had managed to recover from the decision in 1989, following the Tiananmen affair, to withdraw from China. As punishment, the State

Council issued a directive, no. 56, excluding AT&T from participation in joint ventures to produce switches. Meanwhile, the likes of Alcatel, Siemens and Ericsson nestled more or less comfortably into the local market. To catch up, AT&T in February 1993 signed a memorandum of understanding with the State Planning Commission, spelling out a "long-term partnership" in ten potential areas of business. With government relationships back on track, the next step was to ensure a coherent strategy for China by creating a regional unit to coordinate the activities of the corporation's twenty-one separate business units. Successful completion of that arduous task was complemented by vigorous championing in Beijing and in Washington, DC to reverse the first Clinton administration's policy linking the human rights agenda to US-Chinese trade relations. Thus, by 1995, AT&T was in a position to exploit its advantage of being seen by the Chinese government both as a major source of technology and as a prime political player. That was the moment that headquarters announced the decision to split AT&T into three in pursuit of shareholder value. In short, AT&T's board clearly considered that AT&T's size was a problem, not a blessing.

By 1997, the initial gloss was off the China boom. There were plenty of foreign investors with tales of woe. Chinese bureaucracy is a maze, the story ran. We had no idea how long it would take to negotiate a joint venture. Once we more or less owned the place, we discovered that our partner had a huge hidden agenda, which he revealed to us bit by bit. Trying to bring standards up to match our brand name has proven inordinately expensive. We thought we were buying into China, but we discovered that we could not sell outside the city walls. The plant has been regularly inactive for lack of power. The distribution system is a nightmare, and we are not allowed to set up our own. We failed to calculate demand correctly. As Wilfried Vanhonacker, Dean of the China European Business School in Shanghai (CEIBs) has said: "Most companies that previously thought it would take three to five years to get out of the loss-making phase now think it will take nine to ten years to break even" (Yatsko, 1997). The motto? Operating costs in China relative to the rest of the world are much higher than are labor costs.

Corporate capabilities and market entry

A global corporation's strategy is shaped by the special features of the industry and the top team's view of what constitutes right policy (Prahalad and Doz, 1987). Take Nike, the US sportswear group. Learning about China proved an unknown quantity. Michael Knight, CEO and founder, saw the China of the early 1980s as an ideal platform from which to source manufacture and exports of shoes. The vision was of China as a low-labor-cost base, from which production could be geared up to produce a million units a month by the middle of the decade. As it turned out, Nike reached only 150,000 a month by the end of 1984, prompting Knight to sigh that China had to be one of the toughest places to do business in the world. Interpreted into the bottom line, what this meant is that the non-labor costs of operating there were nearly a third higher than in Korea. In addition to labor costs at 10% of Korea's came the import of ex-pats to train, the problems of finding local suppliers, the difficulty of getting the staff to appreciate international quality standards, the discovery that the workforce in SOEs had no incentive to improve, and unanticipated transport costs, to name just some. No wonder that Nike became interested in shifting its operations to an SEZ (special economic zone), where free market conditions prevailed.

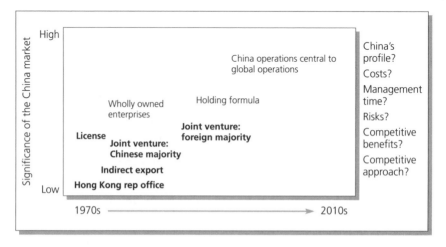

Figure 8.2 ◆ Evolution of entry mode to China's markets

In the early 1980s, multinationals treated China much like other developing countries as places to sell old products or as locations for the manufacture and distribution of old technologies. Because they knew little about the country, they often proceeded tentatively. The party-state behaved no differently. Public ownership was to be protected, but sufficient incentives provided for a successful absorption by local firms of Western technologies and know-how. The interaction of evolving public policy, as depicted above, and a collective corporate learning process about how to operate in China is illustrated in Figure 8.2. The horizontal axis traces the widening of options available to foreign investors as public policy changed, while the vertical axis traces the prospective significance of the China market to the corporation's top management team. On the right hand horizontal planes are the basic questions that the top management team would have to be considering. What is the risk of doing business in China? they would be asking. We don't know much about the country, so perhaps we should find out first. Definitely, we don't know ahead of time what the costs of operating there will be. All we can do is to make a guestimate of the expected benefits. Those are going to hinge very much on how we enter the country. So what approach should we adopt?

In the 1980s, before Beijing, like other emerging market governments, had opened up to welcome FDI, corporations tended to consider market-entry strategy as best explored sequentially (Root, 1987): by the turn of the millennium, with more options available, corporations could choose across a range of options from opening up a wholly owned operation to licensing their technology to locals or just dipping their collective toe in Chinese waters to test the temperature. So the first step could involve establishing a rep office in Hong Kong, possibly manned by an overseas Chinese person with local savvy, or at least by a tried and tested manager with knowledge of the Asia-Pacific. A Hong Kong base could be used, of course, to service global markets while exploring opportunities on the mainland. As soon as the corporation began to find domestic customers and start importing through an import agent, officials would start to push for local production, either through a licensing arrangement with a state enterprise or by a joint venture. Realizing that corporations would start to transfer technologies to China only if they could be assured of some control over operations, Beijing

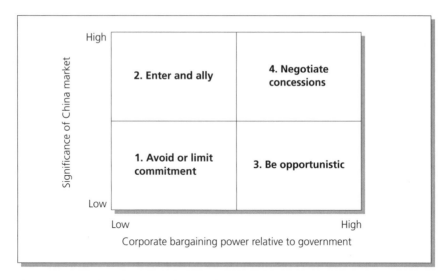

Figure 8.3 ◆ The China market and corporate–government bargaining

widened the entry option in 1986 to full foreign ownership. In 1993, the holding company formula received official sanction, allowing corporations to start using it as a mechanism for integrating their activities China-wide. That would be a necessary condition for them to fit China activities into their global business.

The entry mode is one question that top management must weigh. Their answer, which depends on two other considerations, yields a simple matrix (see Figure 8.3) (Björkman and Osland, 1998): the expected significance of the China market to our global operations is measured on the vertical plane as ranging between low and high, and the corporation's expected bargaining power with the government is portrayed vertically as ranging from low to high. The matrix produces four broad predicaments:

1 If the significance of the market and the bargaining power of the corporation are both low, one approach is *to avoid trouble* by not going in, or *to limit commitments* while keeping options open for the future. Many corporations have taken this line. Take for instance Japanese investors (Harwit, 1996). Japanese investors only became moderately bullish about China in the early 1990s, with the possible exception of electronic firms such as Hitachi concerned with reducing production

costs as a priority. By the mid-1990s, Hitachi had twenty-eight joint
ventures operating across China. But in general, Japanese investors
looked at China and saw trouble, preferring to invest in other Asia-Pacific
markets or in the USA and the EU. Toyota, the global auto giant with an
annual output of about five million units, decided in 2000 to produce
30,000 units a year in a joint venture with Tianjin Automobile Xiali. A
year before, Honda began producing the Accord model in China.
Another example of limited commitment is General Electric's Jack Welch,
who got all fired up about China's huge potential after his visit in 1992.
GE duly bought into a joint venture with China's biggest lightbulb
manufacturer, Shanghai Jiabao, but spent too much time bringing the
production side up to scratch while ignoring the market. Welch drew the
lesson and axed projects that he considered to be heading for trouble, while
leaving GE business. Units experiment on a limited basis. Examples of
modest GE success are scanning equipment for hospitals, plastics and aircraft
leasing – not a portfolio with much synergy between the component parts.

2 If the expected significance of the China market is high, and the bargaining
power of the corporation is low, then one option is *to agree/go along/ally*
with local government demands. Here, the corporation's top management
considers that what counts most is to get a toehold in the China market.
In this frame of mind, the corporation is prepared to go a long way in
accepting the government's requirements, such as agreeing to a minority
share in a joint venture, to transfer technology as soon as possible, and to
be satisfied at least early on with government demands. Nike more or less
accepted the government's terms, but paid an economic price, and was
lured to the special economic zones. OTIS, a US elevator manufacturer,
had a similar experience. Powerful competitors were entering the
fast-growth market, and negotiations with the Tianjin authorities for a
joint venture were dragging out. So OTIS accepted a minority share, gave
the joint venture an exclusive right to distribute OTIS products, and agreed
to employ the local workforce, maintain the existing pricing system, and
accept an export clause – all with tongue in cheek. Not surprisingly, the
joint venture got off to a spanking start and then drifted into trouble as the
two partners' different agendas came to the fore. The deal was eventually

renegotiated at the turn of the 1990s by incorporating the Tianjin operations into a broader China strategy. By then, corporate bargaining power was given a big fillip in both Beijing and Washington, DC, by organizations such as AMCHAM (the US Chamber of Commerce) or the US–China Business Council.

3   If the corporation's expected bargaining power is considered high and the expected significance of the China market is rather low, then *an opportunistic* approach may pay dividends. Top management's attitude is: let's see what turns up in China, as long as we don't get sucked into some never-ending project that detracts our scarce managerial resources from their main markets. This was very much the approach of Jan Froeshaug, the CEO since 1987 of Danish children's entertainment company, Egmont. By the early 1990s, Egmont, as a Disney licensor, was responsible for 50% of Disney's stories. Froeshaug had been quick to spot the opportunities opening up in central Eastern Europe, and here was a new opportunity in China. China had about 200 million children aged 5–14, with a print size in the five major regions equivalent to the market size of the whole of German-speaking Europe. The problem was that publishing was out of bounds for foreign investors, and the powerful Ministry of Post and Telecommunications (MPT) had control over printing and magazine distribution through China's 53,000 post offices. Disney agreed to have Egmont explore the prospect, and Froeshaug was duly introduced to an agent, Shoul Eisenberg – multibillionaire, an Israeli national, escapee from Hitler's Europe, one of Mao's contacts with the Western world, and part responsible for the Nixon–Kissinger diplomacy with Beijing in 1971–2. Froeshaug relates how Eisenberg flew into Frankfurt on a Chinese military plane. With this outsize character as partner, Froeshaug stitched up a workable deal, just in time for the government to announce a ban on other foreign publishers undertaking joint ventures in China. Meanwhile, Children's Fun joint venture, Egmont's China baby, had to learn the hard way that Mickey Mouse and Goofy in the Stone Age was not a hit with Chinese parents and children. Egmont's China operations have done fine but, like many other investors, less well than might have been hoped for.

4 If both the corporation's bargaining power and the market's significance are high, then the corporation can challenge local demands and *negotiate favorable concessions* with public officials. Take the case of distribution networks, which the state began to marketize in the early 1990s. The sector was opened up to joint ventures, and rules about advertising were eased. Carrefour, the French retail giant, seized the opportunity to build up China's second biggest retail chain in the short space of five years. By 2000, Carrefour could boast twenty-eight outlets in fifteen cities and nearly a $1 billion turnover – all the while ignoring Beijing's required say-so to open retail joint ventures. A key to its success is to provide a simple, large store space, offering a large variety of products and low prices. The stores move goods fast, cut tough deals with suppliers, carry minimal stocks and cater to local tastes.

There are other reasons, though, for Carrefour's success. An intangible Carrefour asset is the managerial savvy acquired in its home market in France, and then across Europe. Europe is, in many ways, like China, composed of quite separate provinces, governed loosely by a distant emperor. Knowing the local barons and winning their support is essential to success. Thus, while Wal-Mart, its arch rival, stuck to Beijing's rules and to the Guangdong markets, Carrefour's managers raced around China cutting deals with city governments, promising local jobs and tax revenues. They had done much the same in expanding around Europe. An additional advantage for Carrefour is that China is a huge France: both countries pride themselves on their cuisine, both are convinced that they are the center of the world, both love mandarinates, and both know that rules are there to be bent. When, in 2001, Beijing opened an investigation into the lack of central approval for Carrefour outlets, Carrefour had already built up an extensive constituency across the country. It also put the opening of ten new stores on hold, just to hint at the cost of a negative decision. Given that there were 270 other foreign-financed retail outlets watching, Carrefour was given the nod.

Avon, a US direct-selling corporation, had a rather different experience. Like Carrefour managers, Avon found lobbying in Beijing unrewarding, and so headed for the provinces. Guangdong authorities were receptive, and the company began to roll out its plans for door-to-door sales. Others soon followed Avon's example, so that by 1997 there were about 2,300 direct-selling firms in China, employing up to twenty million people and generating a sales volume of $2 billion (Chan, 1999). But the State Council in April 1998 issued a blanket ban. All door-to-door sales operations were ordered to convert to standard retail distribution or go out of business. One reason for the crackdown was to flush out the get-rich-quick artists. But the main reason to stop door-to-door sales operations was political: officials did not like the rituals used to arouse enthusiasm at marketing meetings. They were too much like religious revivalist movements. Avon had to concede, and it swiftly altered its business model to turn its supply stores into retail outlets. The motto is that foreign investors must know when Beijing is in earnest, and when it is less so. Beijing is definitely in earnest about stamping out opposition movements, before they can organize.

The takeaway for businesses entering China is that there has been a learning process about how to enter the China market. This holds for both corporations and public officials. There are plenty of examples, of course, where firms that are fresh to China, and public officials with limited experience about dealing with foreigners, have to learn the hard way all over again. But it is equally true that the Nike and OTIS stories recounted here are more typical of the 1980s, and Egmont's is typical of the early 1990s. Shoul Eisenberg's skills as a go-between were rooted in the old planning system, still being vigorously championed by the MPT at the time of Egmont's entry. Since then, Eisenberg has passed on, and the MPT has transmogrified into the Ministry of Electronics and Informatics (MEI). Carrefour's and Avon's stories could occur at the turn of the century, because that is when the party-state was learning how to sort out its policies regarding the marketization of the wholesale and retail sectors. In the future, foreign corporations can choose from a range of options on how to enter the China market, whereas twenty years ago they would have had to proceed sequentially and slowly.

Even so, a few rules of thumb still hold for the future: be clear about your own objectives and those of your Chinese partners; don't tailor your strategy to government demands; control is best exercised by a majority stake (Child and Yan, 1999), but failing that considerable influence can be exerted by exploiting the leverage derived from the provision of know-how, technology, etc; being in there for the long term does not mean running a loss-making operation indefinitely; develop good antennae to help you learn about China's changing environment; remember that the government in China is not a monolith, and relations have to be cultivated at all levels of the state. Not least, remember that the best partner, as the Chinese saying goes, is one who shares the same dreams but not the same bed.

China's business system and corporate transformation

How to enter China is one part of the story. How China's changing business system affects corporate operations in China is another. Let's backtrack to our previous discussions on China's economic and political transition. We concluded that China was still in a pretransitional phase in terms of political evolution, and that the regime could be reasonably described as "mature post-totalitarian". China, we concluded, had experienced change short of redefining its key political norms. The regime, we went on, fashions policy through mutual tradeoffs between two broad and constantly changing coalitions of conservatives and reformers. It cannot stand put, even if it wanted to. In terms of the economic transition, we also concluded that there has been a very successful transformation out of a command economy. But the present degree of economic society achieved under a party dictatorship is clearly restricted, in terms of civil society, of the rule of law, of political legitimacy, or of bureaucratic viability. China's party-state, we concluded, has to continue to move towards laying the institutional foundations of a constitutional order if a market economy is to be consolidated.

> China has to continue to move towards laying the institutional foundations of a constitutional order if a market economy is to be consolidated

The implication for corporate operations in China is straight-forward: a central task of corporate strategy is to read the transition right, particularly as it affects the business system whose elements penetrate to the heart of corporate operations in China. This is illustrated in Figure 8.4. On the outer vertical are listed some of the larger questions that our top managerial team should be asking themselves: what is happening worldwide in terms of the ongoing redistribution of capabilities? How is this affecting the global structure? How is China incorporated in the global, interdependent economy? Not least, how is the transition proceeding in China? The vertical axis traces the political transition, and locates our present position as mature post-totalitarian. The horizontal axis depicts the key features of the business system, which we presented in Chapter 7. The base of the cube traces different features of corporate activities, such as the entry path to the China market, and management of human resources, of production, etc. The vertical also draws a time path, starting in 1978, heading to an as yet unknown or desired destination at some time in the future. Let's start on the horizontal axis, starting with the party-state's control over the financial system, and the discretionary powers it exercises. We can run through the elements of China's changing business system as they affect the detailed work of Western corporations. We'll then move up the vertical: we can skip market entry, which we have covered already, and discuss human resource management and production. We'll look at marketing in China later under a broader and related subject of corporate integration and corporate alliances. In the final chapter, we'll review the book in the form of a scenario for China's proximate future – that is the next couple of decades – and what this means for corporations operating in China.

Party-state discretionary powers

Party-state institutions remain recognizably the same, but their content in terms of financial and legal instruments has changed considerably. Nonetheless, managers in foreign corporations cannot take for granted the institutions that sustain business in non-Communist countries: private firms have only recently received constitutional recognition as contributing to the country's development, and the legal system is still in the early stages. With no history of rule of law in China, the absence of commercial ground rules gives public officials extensive discretionary powers. They can stop a firm

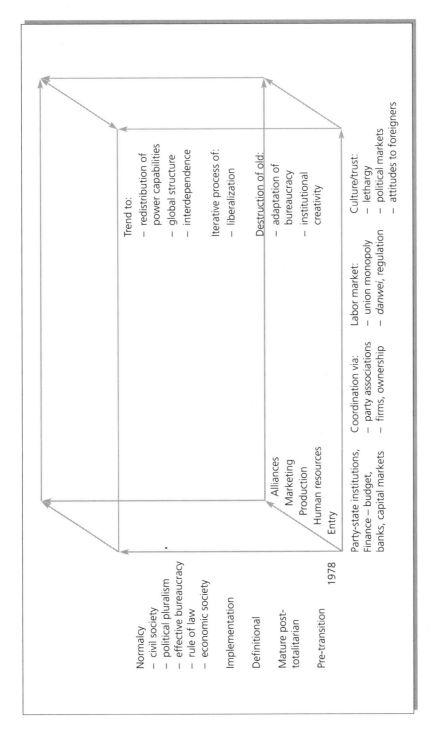

Figure 8.4 ◆ FDI and the transformation of China's business system

selling its products, close it off to procurement, and issue a decree against it – as we saw in the case of AT&T. They are quite capable of springing surprises – such as the famous decision of 1995 to phase out tax exemption on imports of capital equipment. Ending the exemption threatened to raise foreign corporate manufacturing costs in China by as much as 20%. Foreign companies lobbied successfully to have the exemption reinstated, but meanwhile they had to accept payment of the import tax. In a similar case, foreign pharmaceutical players piled into China in the go–go years of 1993–6, on the assumption of a boom in China demand. But then the government introduced healthcare reforms designed to curb public spending on drugs. The lesson is clear: on China's way to the market, the mixture of unclear rules and official discretion gives plenty of incentives for public officials and their private counterparts to indulge in opportunistic behavior. How to acquire and use *guanxi* will remain a key skill for a long time yet.

Coordinating *guanxi*

As long as the party-state is China's main coordinating mechanism, managers will have to deal with it. Take, for instance, the private ownership of land, which became legal in 1986. Government officials continue to manage access. Government approval of exemptions or licenses is another asset, which Patrick McGovern, the head of International Data Group (IDG), has turned to his own benefit. By carefully fostering *guanxi* in Beijing and elsewhere, he has built up a stable of twenty-two technology periodicals and thirty websites, despite the ban on foreign publishing. Of course, policy has opened the personal computer market to tough competition to the benefit of home producers, such as Legend, and the detriment of foreign producers, such as IBM, Hewlett-Packard and Compaq. Hewlett-Packard and Compaq, who have merged since. But non-policy on investor protection has created a situation where 90% of business software used in China is pirated. In the case of building retail outlets around China, companies have had to offer shares to officials or hire local leaders for protection. At the top of the pile are the princelings, such as Larry Yung, head of CITIC Pacific. Despite his family's old ties with the Swire Group – the family-owned British trading company with over 150 years in China – Yung bullied Swire's into decreasing its stake in the Cathay Pacific airline. Swire's did not grumble, but promptly entered other lucrative ventures. *Guanxi* is an acquired art.

Foreign investors and the Federation of Trade Unions

One prime resource, tied to its legitimacy, is the party-state's monopoly over labor representation through the All China Federation of Trade Unions (ACFTU). As long as the ACFTU operated in SOEs, where Party officials dominated all significant functions, it could not seriously claim to represent employees' interests. This changes when an SOE enters a joint venture with a foreign corporation, giving notably greater influence over corporate policy to union officials. Consider, for instance, the case of Lafarge, the French cement maker and multinational. It made a joint venture with an SOE mining company, located at Huaibei, one hour's drive north of Beijing. Lafarge inherited a demoralized workforce. SOE management had been top-down, overmanning was rife, discipline was absent, and severance promises had been broken. Yet within four years, Lafarge management managed to turn the situation around, boost productivity many fold, and receive the ACFTU's coveted "dual love" award, distributed that year to eighty-eight other firms out of 50,000 candidates. Among other contributing factors to this success had been Lafarge's upgrading of health and security measures, the introduction of a severe but fair discipline, and a clear commitment to employee development and training. Above all, management successfully enlisted the support of the trade union, which could act more autonomously now that it was not subordinate to management and Party, as in the bad old SOE days. The motto is that ACFTU members have an incentive to promote joint ventures, and wholly owned foreign enterprises.

Corporate culture and corporate turnarounds

Turning joint ventures around inevitably brings corporate culture center stage as a key consideration for foreign firms. The past twenty years have been littered with stories of joint ventures that have become unstuck due to the problems of turning around organizations whose workforces have developed attitudes appropriate to a planned economy but now have to survive on their own selling goods at a profit to satisfied customers. As corporate transformation gurus remind us, there are three tasks that have to be performed:

◆ *First, ask about the organizational design:* who does what tasks, how is control exerted, what are the integration mechanisms deployed, and who gets paid what? In other words, learn first about how the organization goes about its daily round of activities as a prelude to action. If you start off by action first, you are likely to have to learn later: try introducing pay differentials into an organization designed under a socialist system, and you'll soon learn that there is a misfit between original design and new intent.

◆ *Then ask: who has the power in the organization?* The formal design chart records one distribution of power resources; the informal reality of an organization is likely to throw up quite another. Knowing who holds the power knots that have to be negotiated may save much managerial heartburn. In any turnaround, old power brokers will see their resources taken away from them, and new power brokers will emerge. They know that ahead of time, so they will be prepared. Change agents who see turning organizations around as one frontal attack on entrenched positions after another are not likely to survive long. Even less likely are those who try to disarm opponents by being cuddly. They will be served up as meat pie.

◆ *Finally, think about the key to changing behavior:* The clue to corporate as for any organizational turnaround was defined by Antonio Gramsci (1971), leader of the Italian Communist Party and imprisoned by Mussolini in the 1930s. Writing in his *Prison Notebooks*, he argued: "A social group can, and indeed must, already exercise 'leadership' before winning governmental power." In other words, change agents have to win the ideological battle for the high ground in order to create a shared corporate culture, as a prelude to changing behavior. Turning around a joint venture is a mini-example of how China is being transformed.

Management of human resources

Management of human resources is a key to success in China. A starting point is to recognize that China is not a cheap-labor country. Foreign firms operating joint ventures generally pay 20–50% more than local firms, while non-wage costs vary widely across regions. Many other features of the labor market conspire to drive up total labor costs. Western firms have to select employees with an ability to anticipate problems, and who are ready to speak out and to act (Weldon and Vanhonacker, 1999). This does not come easily to Chinese people, although younger generations are reported to be more used to challenging authority at home or in school. Then, once hired, companies have to invest in training and to develop attractive retention packages to keep the people in whom they've invested on board. In addition, workplace relationships are on the radar screens of Western social auditors, as Nike and Reebok discovered when conditions among their sub-contractors in China, Indonesia and Vietnam became headline news in the USA. Behind all this overt interest in human resources in China lies politics and Western attitudes about the party-state. Many corporations have insti-tuted their own voluntary standards programs designed to record their own performance and satisfy shareholders. Party-state labor laws have similar motivations. China is a prime topic of the world's own debate about itself.

Management of production

Once a viable operation has been set up, how to run the day-to-day business takes over. In essence, this entails managing the technology-transfer process, where the Chinese partners want the best fast but the foreign investor prefers a gradual build-up of local capabilities. In the early 1980s, foreign investors, such as Nike and American Motor, breezed into China expecting a low-labor-cost platform and learnt the hard way (see Box 8.2). The differ-ence since then is that foreign investors have acquired a body of practical experience about the many aspects related to raising productivity that any prospective investor would be wise to tap into. Questions may be classified under four broad headings: one, which we have dealt with in part, is how to go about the task of developing a skilled and motivated labor force, increas-ingly capable of taking on complex tasks.

A second cluster relates to the process of setting up a local supply chain, where the investor's prime concern is to ensure quality and to protect the

Box 8.2 Beijing Jeep

Beijing Jeep became the bellwether joint venture of the 1980s. In May 1983, W. Paul Tippett, American Motor's chairman and CEO, asserted that the joint venture gave the company a "low-cost manufacturing base" to compete against the Japanese in Southeast Asia. He was wrong. Beijing Jeep's foreign managers had annual production quotas set by state planners. Chinese factory managers were less concerned with efficiency than with welfare considerations. The real power, it turned out, lay with cadres in the municipalities, in government ministries, or in the Party leadership. "The foreign companies that set up operations in China did not obtain the massive sales or the low-cost production of which they had dreamed" (James Mann, 1989). If ever there was to be a large, unified China market, wrote Mann, it was likely to be captured first of all by the Chinese themselves.

brand name. Massive foreign investment in the 1990s in a full complement of supporting industries greatly altered the situation for companies relying on fast delivery. The build-up from importing assembled kits through to as near as 100% local content entails patience – it took Shanghai Volkswagen about a decade – establishing standards, bringing in home-country suppliers, choosing appropriate locations, and keeping a close eye on transport problems. President Sam Lo of Tai Sun Plastic Novelties, which makes toys for J.C. Penney and Carrefour in Guandong, was quoted in *Business Week* (2001): "You make a call, and tomorrow the parts are in your factory."

A third cluster is protecting intellectual property rights, in a country that is one of the world's champion infringers. Acer, the personal computer corporation originating in Taiwan, has moved an increasing amount of its production, and some of its research functions to the mainland, in particular to Shanghai. Its software codes, however, are sourced in Taiwan. Not least, there is the perennial problem of anticipating demand. A rule of thumb may be of value here: if you have to choose between volume sales and profits, go for profits.

Corporate integration in China and into the global business system

As China becomes better known to foreign companies, so the country's specializations have become increasingly shaped by the operations of firms. Chinese SOEs, TVEs and other corporate forms have kept their specializations in textiles, shoes and toys, and have won new positions in high-tech sectors, such as electronics and household equipment. Foreign companies are, by contrast, responsible for most of the gains and export growth in the higher-technology sectors. The prime manifestation of this is China's huge trade surplus with the USA and the EU, indicative of the massive multinational presence there in assembly operations and the country's inclusion in the global value-added chain. The trade figures show that foreign affiliates use China as a platform for the more labor-intensive processing activities that have been relocated there. China has thus become tied into the global production system. This is the heart of China's transformation story, rather than the incontrovertible fact that Chinese companies are dwarfed by the global giants that have emerged over the past two decades. As Peter Nolan, from the Judge Institute of Management, University of Cambridge, UK points out, in sector after sector, China's champion corporations at best challenge the world's leaders on their chosen ground, or more usually become integrated as dependent units in their operations. The domestic airlines buy from Boeing and Airbus, while AVIC has diversified into the non-aerospace business; in oil and petrochemicals, CNPC and Sinopec are bound ever closer into the networks of the global giants; the seven lead automobile manufacturers with two-thirds of the world market have only put a toe into the China market through small joint ventures. Many of China's smaller auto brethren have already exited, or will be exiting, from the business as the market continues to expand.

A common problem for multinationals in China is integration of the business units that have been negotiated across the length and breadth of the country at different times. Over time, the ways in which deals have been structured have grown more diverse, as the party-state has become less concerned about the legal form and more interested in what foreign investors transfer in terms of know-how and technology. In the 1990s, foreign investors followed the example set by Johnson & Johnson, the US pharmaceutical corporation, which decided to launch its oral care, baby hygiene and female hygiene products under the wholly owned foreign enterprise formula (Vanhonacker, 1997). The formula allowed for greater control over operations, quicker expansion, less time spent on arduous negotiations with public officials and managers, and more protection over patents. Motorola, along with Nokia and Ericsson, a major force in China's huge mobile phone market, went even further and created a hybrid wholly owned and joint venture operation: Motorola ran the integrated circuits and cell phone operation itself but entered joint ventures for marketing and sales. It thereby gave local partners a stake in the business and managed to develop country-wide. The risk for a wholly owned operation in China is to be a self-sufficient island, cut off from *guanxi* and therefore at risk of not winning contracts and placing orders.

Another way to consolidate is through the holding-company formula, opened up by government measures to allow companies to register as joint-stock companies. Foreign companies have been able to convert joint ventures and wholly owned operations into holding companies on the say-so of MOFTEC, and after demonstrating three years of profitable activities. Over 100 Western corporations, including Coca-Cola, Henkel, Siemens and Unilever, took advantage of the opportunity. In fact, the formula served both Western corporations and Beijing's top brass: the multinationals could overcome local particularisms in which their joint ventures were embedded by giving them a minority stake in the success of a country-wide and more efficiently run group. It served Beijing's top brass by accelerating the diffusion of technologies and management know-how around the country (Björkman and Lu, 1999). Helping the multinationals to achieve greater integration in China also helped Beijing achieve more of its industrial policy objectives. This was the theme of the State Development Planning Commission's report supporting the "Kodak model" (Vanhonacker, 2000). Kodak's management anticipated that China would be the world's largest film market by 2005–10. How to move fast, get products to market, and keep brand and quality were some of the major problems to overcome. The government's problem was how to avoid pouring more money into national champions that failed to fly, while developing a national capability in the industry. Eventually, government and Kodak negotiated a holding company formula that gave Kodak more centralized control over its joint venture partners and opened the prospect of making China the photo-film manufacturing hub for the world market in a decade. China is learning to hitch multinational corporate strategies to its own industrial purposes.

There are many other sectors where similar deals have been struck. Take the example of Cisco, which provides the hardware that powers the Internet. Cisco is helping to integrate the platforms of the Civil Aviation Administration of China, and in 1999 supplied the switches to the third phase of China's National Financial network, linking eight of China's financial institutions. The corporation's practice is to form strategic relationships with the leading US technology firms as a way into winning business in China's extensive para-public sector. Another is BASF, the German petrochemical giant. Petrochemicals are, *par excellence*, government regulated. Once BASF had established a joint venture with Sinopec, it began lobbying for an integrated petrochemicals site. The joint venture took five years to negotiate, allowing BASF to begin construction in 2001 on eight downstream units and a central naphtha cracker. Production is planned to start in 2005. BASF also has a $1 billion stake in a Shanghai operation to produce the raw materials for polyurethanes. In other words, BASF is on the way to creating a comprehensive basic industry empire in China, with the government as partner.

Franchising is another formula that is helping companies to expand their market reach. Franchise owners grant rights to franchisees to use their trademarks. In China, the appeal of this formula is to small, family businesses. It was used by Beijing's Quanjude, a well-known roast duck restaurant, to establish over sixty restaurants across China, and Legend has used franchising to build up its sales network. KFC, a US fast-food chain, used a special franchising formula to develop nearly 450 outlets, first on the east coast and then in the poorer, inland provinces, where families liked to go for weekend quality lunches at affordable prices. Affordable prices were helped by centralization of KFC's supply system. One of the secrets of Ericsson in taking the lead from Motorola and Nokia in the mobile phone business was to build up a franchising network among provincial telecom authorities. This enabled the Swedish giant to fasten its hold on China's richest regions, including Guangdong. The motto is that countrywide reach is achieved best by giving the locals a major stake in success.

The takeaway for business is that, barring a massive breakdown, we are in the very early stages of China's incorporation into the global business system. That brings us to the edge of the next chapter, where we look forward to China in the twenty-first century.

References

Agence France Press, 2002, May 24, "Mainland firms to hire high-tech, financial experts from Taiwan".

Ingmar Björkman and Yuan Lu, 1999, "A corporate perspective on the management of HR in China", *Journal of World Business*, 34(1), pp. 16–25.

Ingmar Björkman and Gregory O. Osland, 1998, "Multinational corporations in China: responding to government pressures", *Long Range Planning*, 31(3), pp. 436–45.

Business Week, 2001, October 22, "China and the WTO: will its entry unleash new prosperity or further destabilize the world economy?".

Kevin G. Cai, 1999, "Outward FDI: a novel dimension of China's integration into the regional and global economy", *China Quarterly*, 160, pp. 856–80.

Ricky Y.K. Chan, 1999, "At the crossroads of distribution reform: China's recent ban on direct selling", *Business Horizons*, September/October, pp. 41–5.

John Child and Yanni Yan, 1999, "Investment and control on international JVs: the case of China", *Journal of World Business*, 34(1), pp. 3–15.

Chinese Economic Review, 1998, 8(10), p. 29.

The Economist, 2000, April 6, "Wealth and power".

Financial Times, 2001, May 11, Survey: FT 500.

Antonio Gramsci (ed. Quentin Hoare, Geoffrey Nowell Smith) 1971, *Selections from the Prison Notebooks of Antonio Gramsci*, London, Lawrence & Wishart, pp. 57–8.

Eric Harwit, 1996, "Japanese investment in China", *Asian Survey*, 10, pp. 978–94.

Françoise Lemoine, 2000, "FDI and the opening up of China's economy", CEPII Working Paper No. 11, http://www.cepii.fr/anglaisgraph/workpap/summaries.2000/wp00-11.htm

James Mann, 1989, *Beijing Jeep*, New York, Simon & Schuster.

Peter Nolan, 2002, "China and the global business revolution", *Cambridge Journal of Economics*, 26, pp. 119–37.

C.K. Prahalad and Yves L. Doz, 1987, *The Multi-National Mission: Balancing Local Demands and Global Vision*, New York, Free Press.

Franklin Root, 1987, *Entry Strategies for International Markets*, Lexington, D.C. Heath.

John Stopford and Susan Strange, 1991, *Rival States, Rival Firms: Competition For World Market Shares*, Cambridge, Cambridge University Press.

Wanda Tseng and Harm Zebregs, 2002, "Foreign direct investment in China: some lessons for other countries", IMF discussion paper PDP/02/3, http://www.imf.org/external/pubs/ft/pdp/2002/pdp03.pdf

Wilfried Vanhonacker, 1997, "Entering China: an unconventional approach", *Harvard Business Review*, March–April.

Wilfried Vanhonacker, 2000, "A better way to crack China", *Harvard Business Review*, March–April, pp. 20–2.

Elizabeth Weldon and Wilfried Vanhonacker, 1999, "Operating a foreign-invested enterprise in China: challenges for managers and management researchers", *Journal of World Business*, 34(1), pp. 94–107.

Pamela Yatsko, 1997, "Rethinking China", *Far Eastern Economic Review*, 160, pp. 52–4.

9

China in the twenty-first century

WHERE SHALL WE SITUATE OURSELVES? In 2003, when this book was published, or in 2060, when the author's heirs decided to have it reprinted for the last time? If we were to place ourselves in the early years of the twenty-first century, the chapter that follows is written in the form of a scenario. Scenarios are not predictions. They are imaginative and credible creations of a future. They have to explain how things came about. In this case, placing ourselves in 2060 and enjoying the armchair comfort of hindsight – the general who never loses his battles – it is easy to see that at the turn of the millennium, China's deeper preferences were to evolution rather than to revolution. Revolution was all too present as a prospect. Indeed, it was the Communist party-state's nightmare. The leadership thought day and night how to avoid it. That's why the Party, we can see in retrospect, was sleepwalking to democratization – "China-style". Looking back from our vantage point in the winter of 2060, it is indeed the more serene judgments made at the turn of the millennium about China's chances over the longer term that have won out.

China is indeed the biggest dragon of them all. The many dangers facing it during its long transformation out of poverty and dictatorship have been surmounted or avoided. Far from being poised at the edge of another century of political disorder, China was a couple of decades short of a golden age of political stability, unprecedented prosperity and cultural achievement. The horrendous vision of the regime's sudden death at the hands of a peasants' revolt proved to be more of a residual nightmare from a vivid and recent past than a reasoned prediction of what happened. Paradoxically, it was this nightmarish vision of a turn of the historical wheel back towards civil war and chaos that helped the Communist dynasty to escape its own shadow. Nothing focused the CCP's attention more than the prospect of sudden death at the hands of an angry peasantry waging class war against rulers so eager to forget where they came from. In fact, the CCP faded away without committing suicide by changing its inner nature while discarding its outer skin. The feat is one of the more remarkable in the annals of the past century. Here, after all, in 1978 were Mao's political heirs putting class war on the backburner and bringing development to the front. Thirty years later, when the Beijing Olympic Games were opened in 2008, China was embarked on the path to becoming a market democracy in a federal state. The key to success was the leadership's ability to learn fast from the unintended consequences of its own actions. No blueprints for us, they entoned. We learn from facts. We are Chinese Tories. We walk backwards in our tentative exploration of an uncertain future.

China is a leading pillar of global society, along with the USA and the European Confederation. It co-writes the rules of the world, and it dominates its own region, much like the emperors used to before the advent of the Europeans in the eighteenth century. It holds about a fifth of the world population of nine billion; the population is highly educated and long lived, and the economy is one-third of the world's. The China mainland is the prime market for the countries of the Asia-Pacific region, Siberia, the central Asian republics, and also for India. Mandarin is studied widely around the world, and Chinese fashions, films, design and arts flourish.

The moment when the leadership launched the country on regime change came in 2006, two years before Beijing's hosting of the Olympic Games. This came as a major surprise to China watchers, who, not without reason, had thought of the Chinese Communists as "the anaconda in the chandelier" (Professor Perry Link quoted in Mirsky, 2002). The giant snake does little, but leaves it up to others to decide what to do. Rather than waiting for others to act, the Chinese Communists decided for a complex of reasons, which we shall recall, to take decisive action. The effect was to deepen China's political interdependence with the USA, Japan and the EU, and to open the doors of all of the world's most exclusive clubs.

China has long been a full member of "the international community", a key power in the UN Security Council, and an active and supportive participant in the WTO. In other words, China eagerly embraced the dull round of discussion on market-opening and standard-setting as the royal way to win respect in world counsels. Active participation in the politics of the global village has paralleled a domestic strategy of modernization. Initially, this amounted to little more than embracing the Western world's formulas for good governance and adapting them to local conditions. Now, China is a standard-setter precisely because the country's successful transformation has propelled it into the very front rank of the world's great powers. Much is written about the return of the Middle Kingdom to its old splendor; more to the point in a wired world without a center, it is truer to say that China is the prime Asian power.

Looking back over the past eighty years, it is surprising to observe how long it was before China's political arrangements ceased to be considered as anything other than interim. Some were fooled by the rhetoric that the Communists would never drop their monopoly hold on power. But what the party-state said and what it did were two separate things. It talked monopoly and played craps. It praised virtue and all too often practiced vice. The one thin line that stretched from Deng to the present has been the determination somehow to create and to sustain a strong state – not a centralized state, but strong precisely because of two factors: central control over a list of candidates eligible to senior positions, and a formal recognition of a division of powers in a federal structure. The key to this transformation was the state's regaining a degree of autonomy from the morass of obligations into which Communist doctrine and action had sunk it, enabling the leadership to focus on selection of qualified personnel in a Singapore-type "elitist democracy". This achievement was the result not of policy so much as necessity. Public and corporate liabilities grew so rapidly that the leadership had to sell off everything it owned. This brought forward the moment when private property rights and duties were given pride of place in the pantheon of the new China's code of practice and law. And because the details of market arrangements on the road away from Communist practice were many and varied, federalism, China-style was the reality on to which later economic and political reforms were grafted. Top-quality personnel has proven the key to success.

By the second decade of the twenty-first century, the Chinese state's functions were strictly limited to law and order, external security, and provision of public goods. Meanwhile, a vibrant civil society was in place, under a much more relaxed regulatory touch of the state. Political competition for office through open election among a list of selected candidates came to be entrenched across the political system. China's *de facto* federalism received constitutional sanction, as did the separation of powers. With fewer tasks to perform, the bureaucracy gained efficiency, prestige and pay. Major progress has been made in establishing an independent judiciary and a functioning legal system. But there is still a long way to go before rule by law becomes engrained in the habits of the Chinese people. Not the least of achievements has been the creation of an economic society, where economic activities flow along well-established paths, and where wealthy people are respected for the contributions they have made to the general welfare. In short, China has worked its way through to "democracy, China-style" – the phrase so much in use by the leadership of the period who seemed to doubt that democracy in China could be anything else but China-style.

Their concern, of course, was that the Western powers would acknowledge China as a great power only once it had imitated Western procedures rather than explored its own way to a legitimate and constitutional order. Curiously, the CCP leadership was much less inhibited about importing Western business system practices, as it were, off the shelf. China's business system has been very much shaped by membership of the WTO and the influence of its judicial proceedings and diplomatic practice on the evolution of China's market practice. Private property rights, as we have pointed out, are established. Banks, insurance and capital markets are subject to different regulators, accountable to the CSRC as super-regulator, much on the model of its counterparts in New York and London. Tough anti-insider trading regulations are in place, drawn up by successive governments only too aware of the importance of maintaining confidence of savers in the financial system. Business, farm and labor associations flourish at all levels of the state. Beijing remains as always the political capital, having won the dramatic battle of the early decade or two of this century against the encroachment of the Gobi Desert and the fall in the level of the water table. Shanghai has long since recovered the glory of its past, when it was one of the cosmopolitan wonders of the world before darkness descended in the form of war and revolution. The "whore of Asia' was the unkind description of André Malraux, a French novelist.

China is a prime location for investment. Investors go there because it is a key location from which to serve other markets, because of the size and depth of China's own many and varied provincial markets, and not least because of the political stability that China's successful transformation has achieved. It is not so much that China has joined the dynamic economies of the Asia-Pacific – the choice that Deng made in 1978 when he ditched class war for economic development as a priority. Rather, the economies of the Asia-Pacific, notably Taiwan, have become absorbed in the vortex of China's massive markets. As one mainland official had prophesied in 2002, "Our economy is our weapon. We won't attack them. We will buy them" (quoted in Tucker, 2002).The turning point, significantly enough, came in the 1990s. The first sign that America's cold-war economy of the Asia-Pacific was history came with the realization that Japan was sick as a dog. Then came the Asian crash of 1997–8, when one currency after another devalued. The experience sounded the knell of the Asian development state. Because China managed to avoid contagion, foreign investors switched to the mainland. In the case of Taiwan, investors caught "mainland fever": by the turn of the millennium, three-quarters of Taiwan's companies had an investment on the mainland, amounting to some $60 billion in more than 50,000 ventures. The mainland never looked back. Indeed, by 2020, twenty-seven of the Fortune 500 had switched their headquarters to China – a powerful statement of their commitment to their own and China's future. China became the prime world manufacturing location.

China's markets, politics and business cultures are much better known than they used to be. As a result, foreign and Chinese businesses operate in close intimacy with each other. This was not the case when the country first opened: the first twenty years in effect were spent by investors exploring the entrails of the business system, itself in transformation in a regime that said it was the same but kept changing while it talked. Even so, by the early 2000s, investors had a widening range of legal vehicles to manage their operations, and could look forward to gradual improvements in business conditions. Central and provincial governments were more than aware of the value of attracting foreign capital, and speeded up bureaucratic procedures to consolidate China's reputation as ever more open to foreign business. A well-developed pool of human resources provided an abundant supply of graduates and skilled labor. English-language schools boomed, as did demand for management training. A key to success in China, now as then, is the development of nationwide marketing networks with regional sensitivities, while a strong position in China is now a must for corporate positioning on world markets. Given the complexity of products and processes, alliances between Chinese and foreign-owned firms are the norm, and this in turn ensures that global anticartel authorities have permanent headaches. Mandarin is taught widely around the world.

Features of China's transition

The first question that businesspeople asked of China was quite simple: what direction, they asked, is China's development taking? We can now answer that with a confidence born of the knowledge of what happened. To observers who did not benefit from such hindsight, the answer to the question was much less clear. What happened, though, shaped the second question that people used to ask: when will China emerge as a great power? Then there was the third question: what do we need to know in order to widely do business with/invest in China? Let's look at the last question as the way in to considering the preceding two questions about the direction and timing of China's transformation.

What did businesspeople need to know about China?

Given what has happened, global corporations and investors who read the China transition right were able to develop long-term strategies that served them well. What they kept their eyes on was the permanent struggle in the regime on how to avoid doomsday. We know *ex post* what happened: the regime developed the rhetoric to embrace Western formulas for good governance within Chinese traditions – law, property, accountable institutions, economic society, and freedom of religion and speech. Property rights were no more absolute than was the freedom to worship, and the state reserved itself the discretion to judge the rights and wrongs thereof. But the leap to redefine governing norms was made after a prolonged internal struggle between conservatives and reformers. The inside story of this struggle is only now being unearthed by historians as the archives become available. What is clear is that the coalitions of conservatives and reformers were much more fluid than was conceived by contemporaries, and for the simple reason that the regime had to juggle so many balls at once: extending civil rights while keeping old powers; dismantling its own privileges while extending the catch of beneficiaries from China's transformation; establishing an independent judiciary in a country with no experience in the rule of law; and building an economic society, predicated on property rights, the abolition of which had lain at the heart of Mao's destructive revolution. This struggle over norms furthermore was not won and lost on a single day in 2006, but is shown in retrospect to have been a drawn-out affair precisely because the sharp end of reform was in economic policy and the business system. The battle of norms had to be re-won in all the discrete but linked policy domains that were drawn ineluctably into the reform process, from the setting of industrial standards to the elaboration of a labor code, and the development of a Chinese regulatory style over capital markets. Democracy in China flowed from the pork barrel of common marketization.

It is also surprising to learn how close to the wind the regime was sailing. In fact, it had no option, its prime motivation being to avoid doomsday. Paradoxically, this meant courting danger rather than trying to avoid it on four key accounts:

◆ The regime rejected mindless protection of an indefensible status quo on the grounds that "China is different". Confident in the knowledge of the country's specificity, the leadership encouraged learning from abroad. They asked: what can we learn from abroad, adapt to Chinese conditions, and apply here? About US federal politics; the EU's laborious common-marketization process; why Japan and Korea were such interesting models to follow in the late 1980s and early 1990s; how Israel managed venture capital as part of its military-industrial nexus; how Ireland became a Celtic tiger; what China could learn from financial market regulations in Hong Kong or Singapore, and so on. Then there were the lessons to be learnt on how not to do things: from the Soviet Union; from the Indonesian transition of 1998; from the advice of market Leninists, with their promises of Big Leaps predicated on cultural revolutions.

◆ China's accession to the WTO signaled clearly the regime's determination to accept the constraints and opportunities of economic and political interdependence. Playing the game of interdependence not only meant China's assuring its status as a power to reckon with in all manner of negotiations about the world's future, but it also helped to tilt the balance of domestic debates and battles in favor of regime reformers, and in favor of a confident China open to the rest of the world. This meant that the transition process entailed a permanent struggle over the sequencing of reforms, given the interrelatedness of policy domains. That translated into a permanent struggle to control discrete policy agendas and their content. This is where accession to the WTO weighed so heavily: the overall agenda was preset by the fact of membership, and its content was laid down in the terms of China's accession.

◆ China learnt the hard way from Mao's failures and disasters to avoid the politics of clean slates and big leaps. True, the leadership was reluctant to learn not to treat Chinese like mushrooms – kept in the dark and covered with ideological manure. But they were savvy enough to reject proposals of Western Maoists, who suggested that China had to undergo a cultural revolution to rid itself of its nostalgia for a past that was no longer relevant to the new post-modern world. Their achievement was to work through, by mistake as much as by foresight, to a conservative marriage of old and new that proved to be essential for China's confidence to take root. Occasional outbreaks of hubris and paranoia had occurred – under Mao, after the June 1989 massacre, during the March 1996 confrontation over Taiwan, in response to NATO's bombing of the Chinese embassy in Belgrade, and in early 2001 over the Hainan incident, when a US spy plane flying off the China coast collided with a Chinese fighter aircraft and had a forced landing on the island without Chinese authorization. For a moment, it seemed that China's relations with the USA would be hijacked by the hotheads in the regime. But the leadership soon returned to their established policy as an essentially status quo power. A confident China could see others as partners, not as enemies. An early sign of this confidence came in the form of Chinese officials' statements in the course of 2002 that China respected US interests in the east Asian region. Indeed, the aftermath of September 11 saw China begin to cooperate much more closely with the USA on non-proliferation issues. Allowing the leakage of dangerous technologies to such an unstable state as Pakistan, or standing by while North Korea built up nuclear capabilities, was simply not compatible with China's own security interests. Joining the lead powers of the world in creating a more secure environment for the twenty-first century required China to go all the way in taking leave for good from the remaining strands of Mao's radical foreign policies.

◆ Chinese leadership chose a wise foreign policy, predicated on prior alliance with the USA as a key partner in seeking to sustain a benign environment in which China could focus on its urgent agenda of economic development. This Sino-US alliance was regularly subject to tensions but just as regularly renewed and strengthened. In particular, Beijing decided to take the initiative to cement relations with the USA by proposing to freeze its missile deployments opposite Taiwan, in exchange for an agreement by Washington not to transfer missile defense capabilities and to restrict arms sales to Taiwan. This strengthened the US administration's determination to resist US Congressional demands for joint force planning with Taipei, built confidence in Taiwan about China's peaceful intent, and opened avenues to more constructive relations with the USA over theater and national missile defense issues. The Chinese leadership also toned down their continued concerns about the US presence in central Asia and strengthened relations with Russia and India. The prize was to resume its pre-1949 status as the US prime partner in Asia, and this required persistence in managing the complicated transition out of radical Communism. One reason for the successful transition was the prolonged period of pedagogy in the practice of markets and more open politics. The lessons that had to be unlearnt were all Marxist-Leninist, whereby business was a synonym for rip-off and employing someone was an opportunity to exploit and extract "surplus value". The lessons that had to be learnt were the importance of honesty and trust and the exercise of debate. Creation is so much more difficult than destruction, and the exercise of empathy so much more demanding than the practice of hatred.

The last thing that China's leaders wanted was a return to the political turmoil of the past. But they also wanted to preserve as many as possible of the privileges they had acquired. Mindless protection of the status quo was not viable politics, in view of the immediacy of the challenges confronting China on a daily basis over the whole period from 1990 to 2020. Here are the main rules of thumb that served to guide the regime:

1 *Number-one priority was jobs.* This derived from the demographic nightmare of the sudden-regime-death theorists. This held, as we recall, that hundreds of millions who lived off the land would flood into the cities in desperate search for work. At the turn of the millennium, a back-of-envelope calculation anticipated that the economy would have to find work for anywhere from 400 to 700 million people by the years 2015–20. How did the regime begin to approximate this exigency, one of the greatest successes of a sound labor market policy anywhere in the world? There were three key ingredients for success: one was to keep the labor market maximally flexible, often at the expense of the rights of workers; a second was to devolve much more responsibility to elected officials in medium-sized townships, in order to make the best possible use of scarce resources to build infrastructure; the third was to measure all related policies to the overriding consideration of using scarce resources efficiently. Most visibly, labor-intensive sectors, such as construction, in which capital had long been substituted for labor in developed-country markets, retained old methods well into the third and fourth decades of the century. Bamboo

scaffoldings at vertiginous heights were still visible in Shanghai into the early 2050s.

2 *Priority number two was growth.* At little more than 3% of world income and product at the turn of the millennium, China was still a very low-income country. Over 600 million people lived on less than $2 a day in 2000, compared with over one billion in south Asia. Two decades later, this figure in China was down to fewer than 200 million people living on less than $2 a day, out of a population of about 1.6 billion. The contrast with south Asia was striking: there, people living on $2 a day still numbered one billion. What differentiated China from India was the determination to use resources more efficiently. One force driving China's super-growth was the abundant supply of labor coupled with a rapid growth in labor productivity. This helped to fund pensions in the longer term as the population aged, while reflecting solid improvements in education at primary and secondary levels. A key problem for China remained the inadequate public funding for education, with the burden of financing borne largely by households. On average, the poor struggled to educate their children, but the upside was a very direct parental concern with school, which they financed by their own work.

3 *Priority number three was sustaining China's high savings rate.* As soon as they could, families resorted to saving for future generations in honor of their ancestors. They put their money in the banks, then in government bonds, and some in corporate equities. The implication for the party-state's policies was overwhelming: to keep faith in China's growing financial markets, the regime had to accelerate structural change, develop private enterprise, implement and develop a bankruptcy law more favorable to creditors, create transparency of financial markets, and crack down visibly and dramatically on crooks – including those from its own ranks. In other words, the party-state had no option but to withdraw from business and to end the policy of keeping the goodies in the Communist family. The effect was to drive up total factor productivity significantly, as management benefited greatly by the withdrawal of party-state politics from business calculations. But it also forced the Party to unravel its socialist pact with urban-based industrial workers. This was

done in the early years of the century's first decade, as urban unemployment edged up into double figures, along with crime and the spread of gang warfare.

4 *Priority number four was "push ahead with reforms".* The mindless Party members chanted: "Stick to the status quo." Reformers urged a slew of reforms, predicated on widening the application of President Jiang Zemin's "three representatives" theory, *san ge dai biao*. This concept declared that the CCP represented the most advanced mode of productive force, the most advanced culture, and the interests of the majority of the population. What this theory indicated was the Party's efforts to open membership to new social forces and classes. Undoubtedly, this was a significant step to pluralism within the Party structures. This fed through to a series of measures, which included widening the base of selection and recruitment to key posts, changing the name of the Communist Party, allowing for elections at all levels within the Party, extending the principle to competition between an accepted list of parties in open elections, and introducing a separation of powers in the party-state. Reformers urged reform from above to pre-empt revolution from below, to use the resources of the party-state to channel the process of reform, and to appeal to political forces in China outside the regime only too eager to avoid a disastrous return to great chaos, *da luan*. Initially, when the Asian developmental state was still enjoying world acclaim, China's common-marketization could be seen as a pragmatic managerial strategy to lead the country to prosperity. Its watchword was: we'll deal with that problem when the time is ripe. Democracy's time lies at the end of the rainbow, after economic policy has delivered prosperity. Let's deal with today's agenda and leave tomorrow's problems for later.

The problem of this gradualism was that it had the tendency to not address urgent problems, such as retaining the confidence of the saving public, dealing with the banks' non-performing loans, non-payment of wage and pension commitments, etc. It also begged the question whether a mature post-totalitarian regime could go far in pressing for necessary reforms in economic policy and in the business system. Yet the regime had become dependent for popularity on performance. This inevitably brought forward the question: is the party-state the prime barrier to the more efficient use of resources? Would any alternative regime do better? If so, how to get from here to there? If an alternative to the present regime is not on the cards, and there is no going back, but there is an obligation to go forwards along a stony road of detailed changes in the economic and business arenas, then does that not point towards laying the institutional foundations of a constitutional order? As long as economic society was not consolidated, there was always another game in town – more dictatorship or more democracy. China's Communist regime was at best on temporary lease from the Chinese people.

The dilemma of China – how to preserve but also reform – was nothing new. It had all been discussed more than two centuries earlier by Adam Smith and Edmund Burke. Adam Smith's description of the Whig state in his great book, *The Wealth of Nations*, described vividly the problem of reform: the beneficiaries of Old Corruption, as the British state was appropriately named, were not likely to abandon privileges lightly. Yet the only way to better governance was through winning over the beneficiaries by convincing them that there were ways they could do even better, short of revolution. The crucial battle was for the ears of political insiders in a battle of ideas, the outer manifestation of which was the evolution of public discourse. Burke, in his *Reflections on the French Revolution*, warned against clean slates, and the bloody tyrants who preached them to "lay down metaphysic propositions which infer universal consequences, and then ... attempt to limit logic by despotism". Constitutions were tangible arrangements that served people living in civil society, and derived from and modified by the conventions that governed it. They did not spring from the brows of enthusiasts. Lasting arrangements, both Smith and Burke say, arise from the conventions of human intercourse. Their rules of thumb: authority is necessary, but avoid monopoly. Patrimonial states centralize all abuse. Allow power to be dispersed, especially through the protection of property rights, and you gain it.

China's reform process, like similar precedents elsewhere, was schizophrenic: try to disentangle the totalitarian state from the ties that bind it to everything else, yet seek to conserve the benefits for the incumbents on the way to the market. In China, the process of disentanglement from the 1990s to the second decade of the new century created a mixture of unclear rules and official discretion that gave more than enough incentive to public officials and their networks of accomplices to indulge in opportunistic behavior. Take, for instance, the phenomenon of princelings. Jiang Mianheng, president Jiang Zemin's son, was the president's chosen instrument to turn China into a high-tech giant. Former Premier Li Peng's son was president and chairman of Huaneng Power International, the nation's largest independent electricity producer. Levin Zhu Yunlai, Premier Zhu Rongji's son, worked for US investment bank Morgan Stanley, which was active in selling off the state's crown jewels, dealing with the banks' non-performing loans, and disposing of the state sector in general. In all these cases, the defense could argue that the rapid evolution of markets in China's transition only made public policy more difficult to achieve. Trust in the no-man's land between state and market was a scarce commodity. So the leaders chose family members. The prosecution would not fail to make the point that family members were paid handsomely for their public spirit.

This is the point where distributional justice and procedural justice reared their heads. The families of unemployed urban workers bitterly resented the royal treatment of princelings. They felt betrayed by the CCP leadership. At best, the Party's monopoly over labor representation continued to be exercised in the plants of foreign corporations, as the official trade union seriously claimed there to defend and promote workers' interests. But these proved minor benefits for Chinese workers compared with those raked in by managers, associated with foreign capital in the fire sale that went by the name of marketization. The sole legitimacy left for the Party, it was already obvious at the turn of the millennium, lay in its claim as guide to chart China's road to prosperity. That is why the Party was prisoner of the Chinese public both as consumers and as savers. The Chinese people were already sovereign before the leadership decided in 2006 to take the plunge, embark on regime change, and modify the norms of government.

By that time, foreign corporations operating in China enjoyed a panoply of market-entry instruments and were well advanced in integrating their corporate activities in China into their worldwide operations. Chinese industrial policies were as often as not made with the intimate participation of foreign corporations. In short, foreign business became restless at the thought that their necessary close relationship with the government of China might spell their demise in the event of the transition spinning out of the party-state's control. They were not alone in appreciating that the future evolution of China's business system lay outside their specific competences, and in the realm of China's politics.

What direction did China's development take?

China's accession to the WTO signaled clearly the regime's determination to accept the constraints and opportunities of economic and political interdependence. When China joined, the USA was still at the epicenter of world affairs. This state of affairs changed gradually over the coming decades, as first the European Confederation emerged to challenge US pre-eminence, followed by China. Even at the pinnacle of its power in the 1990s, the USA had great difficulty in getting its own way in international affairs. The world was too diverse and complex for its peoples to fall into line behind one leader. But all were affected by the ongoing evolution in world (in)security, production, finance and information flows – none more so than China:

◆ Successive Chinese leaders stuck to the prior relationship with the USA as the main partner in shaping a benign environment for the country to focus on development. This policy endured through to the 2040s, when it had to be modified significantly in the light of China's emergence as a world power of the first ranking. Meanwhile, everything had been done to place US-Chinese relations on a sound footing, including an ever greater alignment of the norms of governance on US preferences. The difference in internal regime norms had been the main sticking point in relations between the two countries. The decision of China's leadership to launch the country on regime change in 2006 was informed by their ambition to draw the maximum favorable publicity to China during the Beijing Olympic Games. One component of this crucial decision was domestic. It was evident that keeping the existing norms of the party-state was not compatible with the introduction of an economic society. That meant democratization, not at one go but as a process that greatly widened the scope of representation in public affairs.

◆ The move to launch China on regime change in 2006 was preceded by the country's accession to the WTO in 2002. Accession really signaled the end of Asia-Pacific's cold-war economy, built around the US policy to contain Communism and elaborated in 1950 at the time of the outbreak of the Korean war. The policy had entailed the build-up of pro-business states across Asia-Pacific, and under US protection. It began to unravel as Japan's trade surpluses widened, sharpening US and EU concerns that perhaps China could become a new Japan if it were not incorporated rapidly into the WTO. Hence, the two trading giants' support for Beijing's accession, and Beijing's interest in joining the world trade club as a lead member. Greater China had four seats there, while Russia and Saudi Arabia were absent for the first decade after China's joining. Furthermore, China valued its reputation as a reliable business partner. It needed to maintain access to crucial Western markets, as well as to ensure the continued flood of foreign investment to the mainland. Increasingly, China's deep integration into the global production system came to differentiate it from India and Russia as leader of the poor countries. Membership of the WTO enabled China to better defend its position in textile manufacturing against protectionism in the rich world. Not least, China became the undisputed hub of the Asian and the Pacific economies.

◆ By the 2020s, China's financial system held peculiarities, as did all others around the world, rooted in their different histories and evolution. But what was particularly notable is how many similarities there were to those of the USA and the UK. This was not surprising, as China's world-class financial markets were originally located in Hong Kong. For all the problems associated with the domestic markets of Shenzhen and Shanghai, China's financial elite drew heavily on regulatory experience of financial markets in the USA, the UK, Singapore and Taipei. As in all other dimensions of China's evolution, there was no standing still for the government. Maintaining confidence of Chinese savers was a paramount concern. This meant that the government had to mount a long-term effort to ensure that the very best personnel choices were made, based not on Party affiliation but on competence. It meant pursuing a consistent line against fraud. It meant developing a culture of trust. Because none of this could be accomplished overnight, the Finance Ministry officials in Beijing resisted calls for an early liberalization of capital movements. Linking China's still young and underdeveloped local capital market with the world capital market, dominated by the large Western investment banks and institutions, was recognized as opening China unnecessarily to the whims of Western investors. These were likely as not to take fright at the daily fare of news in China about corrupt officials, battles between peasants and Party bosses, the deficiencies of the legal system or the natural disasters. When China eventually got round to liberalizing capital movements in 2015, enough progress had been made to create confidence in local markets to limit the outflow of domestic savings to market-based calculations of Chinese investors and institutions to diversify their holdings around the world. The fears of those who argued against a great leap forward into the world financial markets proved unfounded.

◆ The relation of authorities to markets was influenced above all by the world's ongoing information revolution. The abundance of technologies providing citizens with access to news, data and associates effectively undermined the party-state's monopoly over information. Even in the 1980s, the Soviet Union had more or less successfully outlawed the use of faxes. In the 1990s, Beijing actively promoted mobile phones, thereby creating the conditions for extra-party groups to organize. This meant that local dissidents could enter into contact with sympathizers abroad and that information available to the rest of the world was available quickly to Chinese citizens. In the face of such competition, party-state news media had to increase the quality and credibility of their reporting. This entailed them taking a more critical and objective look at events in China, which in turn increased the information available about China to the rest of the world. The full pluralism of China's vast society came into view much more clearly: businesspeople, Party officials, bandits, sects, city gangs, peasant leaders. It was obvious, indeed reported on in the party-state press and media, that people were organizing their lives more and more outside of the Party – often with Party members as active participants. All of this shaped China's brand as a location to do business, as a reliable partner, as a country worthy of trust among the world's leaders. Here lay one of the main motives prompting the leadership in 2006 to launch regime change: in two years, the eyes of the world would be on Beijing, just as they had been on Tokyo in 1964 and on Seoul in 1988. Better, the clinching argument ran, to be seen as a successful Korea, entering the comity of advanced nations, than to be seen as a Communist relic like Moscow in the 1980 Olympic Games heading to decline, and then on to humiliation and collapse.

China's inclusion in the global economy provided a permanent goad for China to emulate, adapt or protect its own arrangements. Inevitably, once the regime came to accept the challenges of interdependence, the direction of policy and performance away from autarky tilted the balance heavily in favor of emulation and adaptation, leaving protection as a partial strategy to ensure support from threatened constituencies – located especially in the rustbelt provinces of northern China, and in central and Western China where state enterprises remained the prime employers well into the second decade of the century. In this, China proved no different from the other major member states, with the notable difference that once it climbed aboard the WTO process, the regime came to realize that it was on an express train if not to democracy in the immediate future then at least to fundamental changes in its norms and procedures. Resistance to change often took the form of nationalist rhetoric, but it also came at visible cost to China's standing in world counsels. As status was a prize that the leadership cherished, and the developed coastal regions depended heavily on international business, the balance of forces in the regime always tended to swing back in favor of moderation and compromise. Over time, China became an ever more unavoidable partner in the Asia-Pacific region, and by the second and third decades of the century it was a great power on the world stage. An ever wider range of global concerns demanded that China participate as a key player in any settlement, or as a central participant in the world's many partial accords. Ever fewer matters could be dealt with in exclusion of China.

By 2010, China had imported $300 billion of capital goods. Fifty per cent came from suppliers in Japan, the USA and the EU, with the rest coming through Hong Kong as well as from Taiwan, Singapore and South Korea. The weaker state enterprises crumbled under the sharpened competition. Given the high percentage of workers employed in SOEs, urban riots were frequent. Workers took to the streets to vent their anger in the face of unpaid wages, their exasperation at management incompetence or corruption, and their despair over the prospect of unpaid pensions. What made the political situation in China seem particularly threatening was the simultaneous challenge to the agricultural sector. China also experienced a big increase in food imports, particularly to the more prosperous cities along the eastern coastline. This reduced outlets for the more vulnerable of the peasantry. Already in the 1990s, up to 100 million had entered the cities, looking for work. In the subsequent decade, a further 120 million followed in their footsteps. Throughout the decade and beyond, China resounded to the sound and fury of rural unrest and urban riots. Social meltdown was avoided by a hair's breadth: one solvent was the extraordinary capacity of the Chinese economy to absorb labor. Simply, the regime turned a blind eye to labor market regulation and handed China's workforce to the tender care of employers. The other solvent was a relatively successful program across China to build up medium-sized towns, keeping people in the broader rural economy while allowing for a better provision of infrastructure. Improvements in infrastructure in turn underpinned the growth of local business and attracted foreign investors to inland locations.

China was a major beneficiary of the more competitive business environment. Whatever public officials may want to have done when faced with desperate demands for continued subsidies, they were permanently confronted by tight budget constraints. The result was visible: managers and workforces in SOEs and TVEs realized that they had either to sink or swim together. Many learnt, along with private enterprises, to stand on their own feet. Adaptation proved more difficult for foreign enterprises that had invested in China in the highly protected sectors, or that had accumulated a jumble of joint ventures without rhyme or reason other than to build up a presence there. Chinese producers were the major beneficiaries of WTO entry. Overall, much more competitive markets across China served Beijing well enough in its two-level games with foreign partners and domestic interests: to the extent that China became a quilt of local settlements on the road to the exit from socialism, Beijing could plead credibly that it needed time to iron out anomalies. Would foreign partners be patient, please? On the other hand, when local interests dug their heels in to defend the status quo, they could be overruled by broader appeals to the national interest in maintaining open world markets. Not least, there were plenty of occasions when Beijing could opt in favor of non-action: buying time was required to allow the old to wither away while nurturing the new.

There was no disguising the trend to pluralist politics in China. The pressure for the state to disentangle from the economy proved relentless. For a moment in the 1990s, there had been some hope for China to learn from Japan and Korea. But Japan's lost decade, and the won's collapse in January 1998, blew a hole in any expectation the regime may have entertained to morph the CCP into an Asian developmental state. In any case, the Asian developmental state was centralized, while the reality in mainland China, as we have seen, was to decentralization. Furthermore, the Asian crash of 1997–8 revealed how financially precarious the Asian development state had become. The surge in China's non-performing bank loans in the subsequent years served only to underline the dangers of state involvement in the capital-allocation process. Meanwhile, the institutional pluralism inherent to mature post-totalitarian regimes was accentuated, as companies owned by ministries from central, provincial or city governments competed and cooperated with each other across political and sectoral boundaries. Selling off businesses became an urgent requirement to pre-empt competition from markets filtering up political hierarchies and aggravating interbureaucratic rivalries. This was a prime motivation in the regime's moves to accelerate the process of separating business and politics as fast as possible. At the same time, efforts to shift government functions more in a regulatory direction encouraged business interests and government departments to form lobbies. Foreign corporations were already organized as official lobbies in Beijing. Chinese corporations followed suit, while local governments plied the Party networks for influence as hard as they could. Here was another source of policy debates in the Party, leading to the momentous decision of 2006 to embark the country on an explicit path to regime change and to constitutional innovation. China was *de facto* pluralist: the party-state could no longer operate as if it were a monopolist. Ever in the background lurked the negative example of the Soviet Union's collapse into Russia's mafia state.

Taking the plunge

It was a well-known truism by the late 1990s that the genie of market reforms was out of the China bottle, and that the genie of reform from above or revolution from below was struggling to escape. Originally a revolutionary party, the CCP leadership was only too aware of how carefully it had to tread in order to preserve its position as the sole political force in such a vast country as China. As far as possible, pre-emptive steps were taken to avoid implosion. It steered clear of war, a crucible of revolution – as Communist doctrine taught. Deng's reforms ensured rejuvenation of the CCP leadership, compared with Brezhnev's approach that all his cronies age with him. It offered the people prosperity, and it wielded a big stick. It wheeled and dealed among the swirl of changing coalitions within its own ranks in order to spread out pains and gains from economic and social transformation. Party ideology was used flexibly, and Western market-Leninist proposals for big bang policies were ignored in favor of careful exploration of alternative avenues for action. Incontrovertibly, though, the Party's monopoly on power was shrinking fast, just as the regime faced an ever-widening list of problems. This became even more evident in the key years from 1998 through to 2006:

◆ An ever-widening gulf was opening between official ideology and Chinese realities. For China's proletariat, Marx was alive and well. Rural incomes were stagnant, the floating population was on the rise, and peasants were drifting into the cities, only to be swept out again by the police. Lawlessness was on the rise. In the countryside, angry peasant mobs regularly burnt Party officials' houses. In the cities, jobless workers drifted into criminal gangs, with access to ever-more sophisticated weaponry. In late spring, 2001, the Chinese Communist Party organization published an open report on popular unrest entitled "China investigation report 2000–2001: studies of contradictions among the

people under new conditions" (see Tanner, 2001). The report drew
attention in particular to the tendency of dissidents to link up, and to
appeal to the apolitical majority concerned about crime, corruption or
simply the harshness of living conditions for many. The regime faced a
crisis of legitimacy: over fifty years in power, no election, and its core
constituencies of workers and peasants alienated or at best indifferent.

◆ The Party's ability to mobilize enthusiasm had atrophied as the Party left
its revolutionary past and credentials behind it to become a party of
managers. Their happy hunting ground was the extensive political
markets that grew out of the bureaucratic maze, characteristic of China's
mature post-totalitarian state. Only very fine distinctions could be drawn
between politics and business. It was almost as if a central function of
the CCP was to ensure the prosperity of *nomenklatura capitalism*.
Corporatization and divestment, cynics argued, merely redistributed
public assets from some Party members and constituencies to others.
This was known as keeping the assets in the Communist family.
Unfortunately, the proceedings were accompanied by an explosion of
corruption, asset-stripping, and high living. Kickback and scam ratios,
summing to about 10% of a transaction's value, crept upwards, rather
like Western CEOs' remuneration packages at the height of the great
Clinton boom. Visible greed stimulated visible envy, causing rifts within
the Communist emperor's household between winners and losers, and
even more so between incorruptibles and the rest.

◆ As the gravy train gathered speed, the distance between insiders and
outsiders opened up. The argument that the CCP was holding the fort
of privilege for the greater good of China sounded less and less
reassuring. No doubt the benefits of relatively incompetent government
in China were not negligible. Prosperity was on the rise; personal
freedoms were greater; careers were open to talents, particularly in
business; above all, the party-state was not overburdened by high public
expectations with regard to performance, and it was true that the party-
state was at least a known entity. But it was equally clear to those with
eyes to see that the ranks of the discontented were on the rise, that the
means to organize collectively were expanding, and that the space

between activists and the passive, non-political majority was narrowing fast. It was also clear that the capacity of the party-state's coercive apparatus to deal with the mounting discontents was inadequate to the task. Strong-arm tactics showed diminishing returns. And the old recipe of keeping the engines of growth purring served only to accelerate the transformation in society.

◆ There were recurrent temptations for frightened Party cadres to use foreigners as scapegoats. The foreign bigs were eating up the Chinese smalls in the global battle for corporate supremacy, they said. The USA and other Western imperialists were set against China's resurgence as a force to reckon with in international affairs and were out to undermine the regime. There was no better recipe for that than exporting to China the Western ideologies of political pluralism and free elections. If ever they were implemented in China, the country would tear itself apart. The night of great chaos, *da luan*, would descend, and China would slide into the abyss of civil war. On the other hand, there was the realization in the regime that seeking to form national cohesion around a common enemy in the form of the USA was a dead-end. Once again, the Soviet Union served as a reminder of the risks involved in a developing country adopting a posture of permanent defiance. There was no need for China to suffer from exacerbated nationalism, when the future stretched out ahead, promising prosperity, status, and – who knows? – democracy China-style.

To many foreign observers at the time, it was clear that the political status quo in China was not sustainable. Outside the citadel of the party-state, the signs of imminent collapse were incontrovertible. Inside the Party citadel, the muffled sounds of excited debate drifted outwards to the ears of bystanders. This is what they heard. Prosperity is a must, but so are stability and patriotism. The CCP is the sole guarantor of law and order, but there is less and less of it. We cannot afford one-man-one-vote politics on the Western model. If we move to multiparty politics, who knows what parties will emerge from the backwoods of China. We can have freer media, but no free media. Nor can the party-state lay down the mandate from heaven, not least for reasons of material interest. Nor, as Philip II sings in Verdi's opera, can rulers legislate for the hearts of men. The party-state can neither defend an indefensible status quo nor proceed with gradualism as a formula for policy in a China that is changing ever faster. If the CCP were by oversight or plain stupidity to allow another disaster to occur, it would never be forgiven.

In came the reformers, riding on the coat-tails of the fourth-generation leadership installed in late 2002 to replace the outgoing older guard. The CCP, the voices whispered within the citadel, has to do more than defend the status quo: it has to introduce reforms in the Party in the name of China's political stability. Evolution, not revolution, is the recipe for success, and right now the evolution of things should be speeded up. The key is to build on President Jiang Zemin's theory of the three represents and to extend the Party's constituency beyond its traditional boundaries to embrace a much wider section of the population. In this way, the apolitical masses can be pulled away from being drawn to the activist opponents of the regime. So let the Party rebrand itself, thereby putting distance between itself and past errors. We are riding a tiger called China, and it is increasingly difficult to stay on. Why not change identity in case we do fall off? Allow for more competition through elections to posts within the Party. Give much greater freedom to the eight political parties that presently exist within the shadows of the CCP. Without competition, the Party wallows in stagnation. A change in party ideally, has to be accomplished by a clearer separation of powers within the state, and of Party from state. In particular, we have to invite in representatives of the masses to share our banquet. Did not someone say something to the effect that "the free development of each is the condition for the free development of all"?[1]

These were the ideas circulating within the confines of the Party before 2006. That was when the balance of forces tilted irrevocably in favor of the reform coalition. The decisive factor was the ever wider range of common ground between regime reformers and Western democratizers. Joining the world, both agreed, meant China's acceptance of growing economic and

---

[1] Modern anthropology now traces this to an obscure pamphlet written in 1848 by Karl Marx and Friedrich Engels, entitled "The Communist Manifesto".

political interdependence. This was not taken to mean that China should ape the Westminster model or clamp a US-style constitution on itself. Both regime reformers and Western democratizers were not Maoists, seeking to rip the soul of Confucius from the ancient body of China. Only Western extremists called for such radical treatment. Their assumption often was that Confucian patrimonial culture had to be ripped, Mao-like, from the soul of China for democratization to succeed, and for decentralization to take root. What they forgot is the many different forms that democracies can take, from monoparty and centralized states, to highly decentralized and participative states. By the time the party-state embarked on its grand experiment in 2006, China was well along towards the participative end of the spectrum, albeit participation for organized lobbies in a *de facto* pluralist polity. Democracy's norm may be equality of citizens rights, but as often as not it effectively buttresses privilege. China's Communist Tories understood this only too well.

Where regime reformers and Western democratizers agreed was on the goal, leaving the timetable to circumstances and experimentation. Where both agreed in particular was that China's masses had to be inducted to the practice of political liberties, and what held for the Chinese masses held even more for public and Party officials. Proclaiming the goal meant in effect altering the norms by which the party-state governed. It meant widening the permissible scope of debate, and amounted to official recognition that the Chinese people were not mushrooms. Such a step proclaimed, too, that the Party was now officially courting the multitude of apolitical Chinese people who preferred quiet improvements to heroics. And the reformers realized that the timing of the announcement, two years ahead of the Beijing Olympic Games, would give them maximum opportunity to press their case in the light of the world's media.

When will China emerge as a great power?

Another crucial consideration for the leadership in deciding to launch regime change in China was the much more turbulent world conditions of the early decades of the new century. The Communist regime was more than aware that China was a great power in name only, and was likely to remain so for years. Until such time as reality came more into line with ambition, the only viable set of external policies for China was to avoid strutting on the world stage, to focus on development, and to win status where possible. Because China was in any case nearly one-fifth of humanity, the rest of the world could not ignore it. There was maximum benefit, at minimum risk, for China to aspire to join the lead group, to co-write the rules, to learn from the rest of the world, to accept the constraints of inter-dependence, and to secure co-responsibility in the counsels of the world. As China developed, so prestige would move its way and power along with both. The key in the short and longer term was therefore to secure as benign an international environment as possible. That meant repeatedly opting to accommodate US preferences as far as possible, short of risking the regime's own domestic position. Problems arose when global conditions in the first decade of the millennium deteriorated to such an extent that Beijing could no longer count on the USA as guarantor of security for Asia. China had to offer the USA more than the longer-term threat to US leadership implicit in China's ambitions. If China's long-term security objectives were to be met, then the USA had to be given additional incentives to befriend China.

Looking back from the perspective of 2060, it is obvious that the shift back to a Sinocentric Asia-Pacific did not occur painlessly. There were some particularly tense moments following the events of September 11, 2001, and the accelerated recasting of US world strategy when the USA focused on homeland security complemented by a doctrine of pre-emptive strikes against unspecified threats arising anywhere. It was as if President George W. Bush had taken a leaf from Big John Wayne's lexicon to the effect that "out there, due process is a bullet". Facing a more trigger-happy USA, what should China's regime do to assure as far as possible continued US coopera-tion in sustaining a benign international environment for China to grow into regional, and then perhaps world, leadership? The debates on external policy orientation in China's regime swirled around three alternatives – to constrain the USA through countervailing alliances, by a posture of resist-ance, or by conditional cooperation:

1 Hotter heads proposed to redress the imbalance in favor of the USA by forging countervailing alliances with other powers. This had already

been tried in the 1990s, but without much success. Most importantly, both India and Russia valued relationships with the USA more highly than with China, and China continued to rely on US naval power for protection of the sea-fares to the Gulf. In line with the trend to give priority to efficiency considerations, Chinese oilmen opted for price over security of supply with the result that by the 2020s, as had been anticipated, 90% of oil imports came from the Gulf. Fortunately for China, the transformation in the correlation of forces in the Gulf following the events of September 11, 2001, took Chinese diplomacy off the hook of having to choose between supporting the USA in the region or keeping in with local interests hostile to US interests. Saudi Arabia and Iran felt their way to reconciliation, thereby making feasible a withdrawal of the USA offshore. This helped towards a peace settlement in the wider region, while representing a key factor in the redefinition of US geopolitics towards the Euro-Asian landmass. What this strategy heralded was US primacy in space and on the high seas, along with the selection of key allies, including Russia and India. This reinforced fears in Beijing that the USA was indeed seeking to encircle China in preparation for its emergence as a major power on the world scene. Russia was a key alternative to Saudi Arabia as a source of energy supplies, and India was a prime partner in containing radical Islam. Cooler heads in Beijing prevailed when it became all too obvious that none of these objectives was incompatible with China's interests: Siberia only became a viable supplementary source of energy supplies once the Russian-US alliance was consolidated. And China, like India, developed a distaste for proliferation of weapons of mass destruction (having themselves acquired them first). There was more for China to gain by adapting to than countering US policy.

2   Hotheads in Beijing also lost the policy battle in favor of a posture of resistance to US primacy. It was not difficult to demonstrate that saying no was little more than posturing, when saying yes is what China was most eager for in terms of alliances, prestige and market access. China's leadership was well aware of comparisons made in US debates about China comparing it to Wilhelminian Germany. And as they realized only too well, from the 1890s to 1945, a foreign policy of grievance got Germany nowhere. China had nothing to gain from being labeled a rogue state. Nurturing hubris and security paranoia was not readily compatible

with a steady-as-you-go development strategy. It played only too readily into the hands of hotheads, with their tendency to escalate rhetoric. At some unknown point, rhetoric could easily translate into rash action, with a deluge of unintended consequences and unanticipated costs to follow. Nor was a policy of angst very dignified for a potential great power, any more than casting the USA as a scapegoat could be credibly sold as a foreign policy. At best, it represented a domestic stance. Nor was anything much to be gained, and much was to be lost, for China to play the wrecker in the region. On the contrary, what China as a poor country with great potential craved most was prestige and status. This was won by reassuring populations in China's vicinity that it was not about to behave as an unruly 800-pound gorilla. It meant reducing the occasions when the leadership wrapped itself in the flag, appealed to Confucian paternalism, or talked of Asian rather than global values. In particular, it entailed bringing policy and practice more into line with discourse. This summed to three phrases: open markets, human rights and regime change. Cool heads prevailed in the inner citadels of the party-state, whereby it was understood that launching China on a process of democratization and regime change would kill two birds with one stone: it would greatly widen representation of Chinese people in public affairs, and it would greatly strengthen the pro-China lobby's influence in Washington DC and in the European Confederation. The pursuit of prestige required nothing less.

3 Cooperation was the obvious winner. Most importantly, regime change opening on a process leading to democratization helped to anchor China's alliance with the USA. With the USA moving to even more of a maritime-cum-commercial strategy as the world's offshore continental island, it was more necessary than ever to reassure the USA about China's reliability. Conversely, China was eager to ensure a predictable relationship with the USA stretching forwards over the coming decades when the country's energies would have to be developed to the prime task of development, both economic and political. What sparked Chinese concern about the evolution post-September 11, 2001, in US geopolicy was that the ambiguities in US maritime strategy prompted pressures within Japan to go nuclear, and to protect its own supply lines down to

Indonesia, and round to the Indian Ocean and the Gulf. Taiwan and
Korea, too, began to consider anticipatory steps to secure the oil routes
round from the Gulf, through the Malacca Straits, the South China Sea,
and up towards the Taiwan Straits and the Sea of Japan. The Chinese
leadership knew only too well that the USA was a vital partner in
constraining Japan and in managing the transition in Korea. The one
major barrier to close cooperation between Washington DC and Beijing
was their dispute over Taiwan, and at the heart of that dispute lay the
nature of the Communist party-state. It was not enough for the Chinese
leadership to simply buy Taiwan. An elitist democracy on Singapore
lines, it was realized, would be in a much more powerful position than a
Leninist dictatorship to negotiate with the USA the political form of
China's unity. Not least, there was a close fit between China cementing
the alliance with the USA in the Asia-Pacific, continuing to pull in
foreign investors, and playing to the global gallery for prestige and status.
The 2006 announcement of regime change, followed by the Beijing
Olympic Games, signaled the confirmation of the US-Chinese relationship
as the central axis of Asian-Pacific and continental Asian affairs.

In short, the first decade of the millennium laid the foundations for
China's transformation in the coming decades. China's economic
dynamism invigorated its magnetism. In fact, its strategy was really simple.
Let's just grow, and grow, and grow, and grow. As we develop weight in
world affairs, so our policies can be modified gently as we move forward.
That was the expectation. Looking back from our vantage point in 2060,
we can see that by about 2040, China's emergence began to convulse US
politics. Is China a challenger or is it an ally? If it is a challenger to US primacy, what can be done about it? And if it is an ally, does it matter that
China is a challenger for primacy? The debates are becoming ever more
strident. The one thing that is sure is that the master move was taken by
China's leadership in 2006, when it was announced that democratization
was not at the end of the rainbow but a fundamental norm that the
Chinese leadership was pledged to introduce in the coming years and
decades. Thereafter, there was no turning back. China became a great
power precisely because it managed the transition to democracy, Chinese-

style, successfully. Now that China's democratization is a reality, and China is a contender for world primacy, the structure of the world is more multipolar. Beyond that, the future is obscure. That has ever been the case.

References

Jonathan Mirsky, 2002, "China in the eye of the ostrich", *China Brief*, 2(14), http://china.jamestown.org/pubs/view/cwe_002_014_001.htm.

Murray Scot Tanner, 2001, "Cracks in the wall: China's eroding coercive state", *Current History*, 100(647), pp. 243–9.

Nancy Bernkopf Tucker, 2002, "If Taiwan chooses unification, should the United States care?", *Washington Quarterly*, 25(3), pp.15–28.

Index

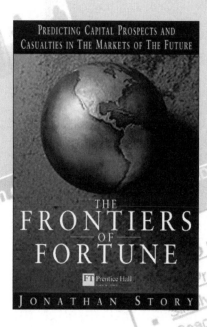